Gender and Politics series

Series editors: **Johanna Kantola**, University of Helsinki, Finland and
Judith Squires, University of Bristol, UK

This timely new series publishes leading monographs and edited collections
from scholars working in the disciplinary areas of politics, international
relations and public policy with specific reference to questions of gender.
The series showcases cutting-edge research in Gender and Politics,
publishing topical and innovative approaches to gender politics. It will
include exciting work from new authors and well-known academics and
will also publish high-impact writings by practitioners working in issues
relating to gender and politics.

The series covers politics, international relations and public policy, including
gendered engagement with mainstream political science issues, such as
political systems and policymaking, representation and participation,
citizenship and identity, equality, and women's movements; gender and
international relations, including feminist approaches to international
institutions, political economy and global politics; and interdisciplinary
and emergent areas of study, such as masculinities studies, gender and
multiculturalism, and intersectionality.

Potential contributors are encouraged to contact the series editors:
Johanna Kantola (johanna.kantola@helsinki.fi) and Judith Squires
(judith.squires@bristol.ac.uk)

Series Advisory Board:

Louise Chappell, University of Sydney, Australia
Joni Lovenduksi, Birkbeck College, University of London, UK
Amy Mazur, Washington State University, USA
Jacqui True, University of Auckland, New Zealand
Mieke Verloo, Radboud University Nijmegen, the Netherlands
Laurel Weldon, Purdue University, USA

Titles include:

Gabriele Abels and Joyce Marie Mushaben *(editors)*
GENDERING THE EUROPEAN UNION
New Approaches to Old Democratic Deficits

Sarah Childs and Paul Webb
SEX, GENDER AND THE CONSERVATIVE PARTY
From Iron Lady to Kitten Heels

Jonathan Dean
RETHINKING CONTEMPORARY FEMINIST POLITICS

Mona Lena Krook and Fiona Mackay *(editors)*
GENDER, POLITICS AND INSTITUTIONS
Towards a Feminist Institutionalism

Gender and Political Series
Series Standing Order ISBN 978–0–230–23917–3 (hardback) and
978–0–230–23918–0 (paperback)
(outside North America only)

You can receive future titles in this series as they are published by placing a standing order.
Please contact your bookseller or, in case of difficulty, write to us at the address below with your
name and address, the title of the series and the ISBN quoted above.

Customer Services Department, Macmillan Distribution Ltd, Houndmills, Basingstoke,
Hampshire RG21 6XS, England

Sex, Gender and the Conservative Party

From Iron Lady to Kitten Heels

Sarah Childs
Professor of Politics and Gender, School of Sociology, Politics and International Studies, University of Bristol, UK

Paul Webb
Professor of Politics, Department of Politics and Contemporary European Studies, University of Sussex, UK

First published 2012 by
PALGRAVE MACMILLAN

Palgrave Macmillan in the UK is an imprint of Macmillan Publishers Limited,
registered in England, company number 785998, of Houndmills, Basingstoke,
Hampshire RG21 6XS.

Palgrave Macmillan in the US is a division of St Martin's Press LLC,
175 Fifth Avenue, New York, NY 10010.

Palgrave Macmillan is the global academic imprint of the above companies
and has companies and representatives throughout the world.

Palgrave® and Macmillan® are registered trademarks in the United States,
the United Kingdom, Europe and other countries.

ISBN 978-1-349-32674-7   ISBN 978-0-230-35422-7 (eBook)
DOI 10.1057/9780230354227

This book is printed on paper suitable for recycling and made from fully
managed and sustained forest sources. Logging, pulping and manufacturing
processes are expected to conform to the environmental regulations of the
country of origin.

A catalogue record for this book is available from the British Library.

A catalogue record for this book is available from the Library of Congress.

Contents

List of Boxes, Figures and Tables

Boxes

Figures

Tables

Methods Appendix

List of Abbreviations

AML	Additional Maternity Leave
APL	Additional Paternity Leave
APPG	All Party Parliamentary Groups
AWS	All Women Shortlists
BME	Black and Minority Ethnic
CB	Crossbencher
CCHQ	Conservative Central Office/Head Quarters
CF	Conservative Future
Con	Conservative
CWCC	Conservative Women's Constituency Committees
CWF	Conservative Women's Forum
CWNC	Conservative Women's National Commission
CWO	Conservative Women's Organization
EC	Executive Committee
EPFW	Equal Pay and Flexible Working Bill, 2009
FGM	Female Genital Mutilation
GE	General Election
HFEA	Human Fertilization and Embryology Act, 2008
Lab	Labour
LD	Liberal Democrat
OPL	Ordinary Paternity Leave
PPC	Prospective Parliamentary Candidate
PMB	Private Members Bill
QWPA	Quasi Women's Policy Agency
SME	Small and Medium Enterprises
STC	Science and Technology Committee
WAG	Women's Advisory Group
WIWT	*Women in the World Today*, 2008 Report
WFA	Work and Families Act, 2006
WPA	Women's Policy Agency
WPG	Women's Policy Group

Acknowledgements

When we first worked up a proposal for research on gender and the contemporary Conservative party, we were confident that our project was timely: that a Conservative government was, for the first time in many years, a distinct possibility and that gender might turn out to be of great importance to the modernization of the Tory party, not least given the observable feminization of British party politics in the last decade or so. We were also sure that the gendered lacuna in the extant research on the contemporary Conservative party was self-evident. Even so, gaining external funding is about more than simply having a timely (and coherent) research project. So, we thank the Economic and Social Research Council (ESRC, RES-062-23-0647) for both accepting our contentions and funding the three year project upon which this book is based.

Without the formal cooperation of the Conservative party this book would have been very much harder, if not impossible, to write. At the very least, it would have been much more limited in its findings. Many of those with whom we have spoken or surveyed – MPs, Peers, party workers and members of the voluntary party – agreed on the basis of anonymity, and so we thank them collectively for their time and their insights. Others can be singled out: two previous Party Chairmen, in particular, demand significant thanks, Francis Maude for supporting the project even before it received funding from the ESRC and Caroline Spelman for maintaining that support, and facilitating our research in its key years. As Shadow Minister for Women, Theresa May also provided invaluable assistance, as did Fiona Hodgson and Pauline Lucas, the previous and current Chairmen of the Conservative Women's Organization, and Anne Jenkin, co-founder of Women2win. Again, without the selflessness of all the individuals who assisted us this project would have been much poorer. As has been said before, it is too easy for the media and public to criticize our party politicians – we have found them to be most generous.

Our thanks go to Ipsos-MORI for conducting our focus group analysis. At all times they acted most professionally. But, more than that, in their everyday interactions, overarching insights and wider interest in our work, they were first rate. In particular, we would like to acknowledge the contributions of Julia Clark, Graham Keilloh, and of course, and for his enviable political knowledge, Roger Mortimore. Our survey of party members was undertaken by the internet polling firm, YouGov. Again, they, and in particular Peter Kellner, were most professional, and enabled us to access the right people and, we are confident, to ask the right questions.

We would like to specifically thank at the University of Bristol: Louise Chambers for administrating the bid; Dr Rob Dover (now of Loughborough University) who was party to the conversation out of which the title of the book first emerged; Prof Anthony Forster (now of Durham University) for first encouraging the research proposal, and then providing detailed comments on drafts of the bid in its various iterations; and finally, Jean Pretlove for her administration of the project's early years, including, but by no means only, helping host the IPSOS-Mori focus groups. Our research officer for the project was Dr Sally Marthaler, at the University of Sussex. Sally provided us with invaluable assistance, not least her weekly updates of Conservative party news; the collation of party documentation; research papers on gender and centre/right political parties; undertaking some of the interviews with MPs and Peers; reviewing and editing research papers and articles; and facilitating other aspects of the project, not least in terms of liaising with MPs and Peers. In sum, she made the project doable on a day to day basis in its first 18 months.

Sex, Gender and the Conservative Party also benefits from insights garnered from our wider research networks – networks that provide us with friendship and intellectual stimulation. More specifically, and in alphabetical order, we would like to acknowledge individuals with whom we have worked on research that either feeds directly into the book or provides part of our intellectual knowledge that underpins our approach. Jeanette Ashe, for co-authoring a paper on the 2010 General Election (*British Politics* 2010); Rosie Campbell and Joni Lovenduski for the 2010 British Representation Study and for co-authoring works on the 2010 General Election (*Parliamentary Affairs* 2010 and *British Politics* 2010); Karen Celis, for co-authoring an article on conservatism and representation (*Political Studies* 2011); Philip Cowley, for sharing his data on the Human Fertilization and Embryology Act 2008 and for making Sarah think hard about gender and representation, as well as for co-authoring a piece with her on localism and representation (*Political Studies* 2011); Chrissi Eason for data on the House of Lords; Elizabeth Evans, for providing research data on candidates and elections and for co-authoring a paper on the 2010 General Election (*British Politics*, 2010); Nada Ghandour-Demiri and Mathew Hope, post graduate students at the University of Bristol, who undertook a variety of research assistant tasks, including bibliographic and data searches; Mona Lena Krook and Johanna Kantola for work also with Karen Celis and Sarah on the substantive representation of women; Rosa Malley, Sarah's PhD student at the University of Bristol for proof reading the manuscript and providing the index; and Kristi Winters for data input and analysis on the focus group questionnaire data. Many of the above also reviewed draft chapters, as did Adrian Flint, Richard Heffernan and Judith Squires. Of course, any limitations and, or errors are our responsibility.

Throughout the period of research we also presented, and received feedback, on 'work in progress papers' at various UK and International

Universities and academic conferences: Bath; Birkbeck College, University of London; Bristol; Carleton (Canada); Cork; LSE; Manchester; Newcastle; Nottingham; Ohio State (USA); Oxford (Women & Politics Society); Southampton; and Surrey. Conferences included: the American Political Science Association; Canadian Political Science Association; European Consortium for Political Research; European Conference on Politics and Gender; Elections, Public Opinion and Parties; Political Studies Association; and Women and Politics.

An earlier version of Chapter 7 appeared as, 'Wets and Dries Resurgent? Intra-party Alignments among Contemporary Conservative Party Members', *Parliamentary Affairs*, 2011.

We very much hope that *Sex, Gender and the Conservative Party* fulfils our ambition that working together would produce better research than that which would have been forthcoming had we individually undertaken it on our own. That bringing together a 'parties expert' and a 'gender expert' would produce more innovative insights and analysis. We were, indeed, at various times, enjoyably, and we would maintain productively, forced outside our respective academic comfort zones. Paul, for example, attended his first ever 'gender and politics' conference and Sarah her first 'mainstream' parties workshop. As new collaborators we also learnt lots about each other's ways of working – that Paul would routinely order chocolate cake 'to share' and that Sarah…shared it.

Finally, and as ever, we have been supported in our research by partners, family and friends. Especial thanks must go to Sarah's 'big' and 'little' brothers, the latter, living under the same roof as her for the last year of the project, had to put up with more of the stresses and strains than he might have wished to. Paul is just grateful that his family continues to tolerate him.

Introduction

The sound of modern Britain is a complex harmony, not a male voice choir.[1]

On becoming leader of the Conservative party in 2005, David Cameron inherited a multi-faceted problem with women. His party had few women MPs – they numbered just 17 compared with the Labour party's 98. Women party members and their party organizations were, if not openly revolting, clearly unhappy with what they considered to have been their marginalization in the previous few years at the 2005 general election. The party's election manifesto had trailed in third place in terms of policies 'for women' and women voters, long associated with the party, appeared as yet unwilling to walk away from New Labour and return to the Conservative fold. Jump forward five years. Ahead of the 2010 general election the Conservative leadership was confident that it would make good on Cameron's commitment to redress the 'scandalous' under-representation of women in the parliamentary party. There was talk of the likely election of more than 60 women MPs. The party's women's organizations also looked healthier, with sell-out annual conferences and new formats and, most high profile at least around Westminster, the establishment of an independent, but associated, ginger group, Women2win. New women's policies had been developed too, not least on employment and the work/life balance, which the party believed would be well received by the women of the country. On May 6th 2010, Election Day, this confidence looked to have been mostly well placed. The Conservatives more than doubled the number of their women MPs, to an unprecedented 48, rising to 49 three weeks later, following a delayed vote in one constituency. The Tories' general election manifesto was more competitive on the women's terrain this time around too. And early, if by no means definitive, analysis of voting (Campbell and Childs 2010) suggested that the party might have done well amongst middle class women voters, the so-called 'Mumsnetters'.

Should one conclude that the contemporary Conservative party has, then, successfully experienced a process of feminization? If feminization is defined as the integration of women and their concerns into our political parties and political institutions, the criteria for any evaluation of the

1

Conservative party should be straightforward (Lovenduski 2005a): more women in the party and more 'women's policies' than before. Yet, both dimensions are more complex than they first appear. Take the first dimension, the integration of women. In terms of party members, the Conservatives have long been renowned for being a party *of* women, even whilst questions have been raised about women's role in the higher echelons of the party. At the Parliamentary level, the party has a poor record, notwithstanding some notable firsts: Nancy Astor, the first woman to take up her seat in the House of Commons (1919) and, of course, Margaret Thatcher, the first, and to date only, woman British Prime Minister (1979–1990). In historical context, the 2010 Conservative parliamentary party has many more Conservative women MPs than hitherto. But relative to their male colleagues they fall far short of parity and remain way below Labour's record 101 women MPs returned more than a decade ago in 1997, as well as the 81 Labour women MPs elected in 2010. And this Conservative tally is true at a general election which, thanks to the parliamentary expenses scandal of 2009, had many more openings for new MPs – more than a third of all MPs were newly elected in 2010. In this context the Conservative party's 2010 top line figure of women MPs is less than sufficient, welcome though the increase is. In any case, counting women's bodies neither provides, in itself, information about why women's presence is at its current level, either in the parliamentary or voluntary party. Nor does it account for change over time, or explain why it is better in one political party relative to another. It also tells us very little about women's *integration*, as distinct from their simple, numerical, inclusion. There may be more women Conservative MPs in 2010 than ever before, and more active women's organizations than for some time, but does this change anything, beyond the physical make up of the party?

Assessing the second dimension of feminization, the integration of women's concerns, and its relationship to the first, has its own attendant problem: the difficulty of operationalizing *that* which is to be integrated. What constitutes women's 'interests', 'issues', 'concerns' and 'perspectives', is widely contested. Different women (from varying socio-economic, cultural, or political backgrounds and experiences) might well hold different views about what counts as a 'women's issue'. Different women are, moreover, likely to hold varied and sometimes conflicting or incompatible views of these issues. Hence, feminist, less- or non-feminist women, and left and right wing women, will likely have different views of what constitutes women's interests even if they agree on what constitutes women's issues (Celis et al 2010). Thus, whilst it might be easy enough to agree in the UK that, say, policies on women's employment or violence against women constitute 'women's issues' the cause of, and appropriate response to these – the specific policies one might advance to address them – are likely to generate contestation rather than consensus. Take the gender pay gap. Are mandatory pay audits for companies found guilty of sex discrimination a better way to reduce the pay gap between men and women, as the 2010 Conservative party manifesto suggested? Are such measures more efficient than voluntary codes or the compulsory auditing of *all* companies, policies the two other main parties advocated? In any case, how well a government 'acts for' women is more than just simply evaluating implementation of explicit policies 'for' women. Many, if not all, of a government's agenda is likely to differentially impact on women and men, given what we know about men and women's familial, social and economic roles. Questions must, then, be asked about the 'fit' between specific policies 'for' women and a government or political party's larger project and associated policies. In the contemporary period government policies will be implemented within a wider economic and political context characterized by the late 2000s global economic crisis. This would likely heavily constrain all governments, and might particularly be so when, like the current Conservative-Liberal Democratic coalition, it avowedly seeks to sharply and swiftly, some would contend preemptively, cut the UK budget deficit.

To date, the gender and politics research mapping the process of feminization of British party politics has almost all focused on the Labour party (Perrigo 1996, 1995, 1986; Russell, M. 2005). Existing gendered accounts of the Conservatives are not only few in number but also, and often, historical in their approach (Maguire 1998) or limited to the Thatcher era (Campbell 1987; Nunn 2002). We lack, then, analysis of the 1990s Conservative party, with which to compare the contemporary one (Campbell et al 2006). Nonetheless, two observations, already made, are likely to be relatively uncontentious and provide some useful context. The first relates to the historic levels of women's participation in the voluntary side of the party, and the second to the extensive support for the Conservatives amongst women voters. In respect of the former, it has been said that, for large parts of the 20th century, the Conservatives were the political party most hospitable to women (Maguire 1998; Lovenduski 2005a). Not only did they mobilize women prior to women's enfranchisement, women members are widely recognized as having been critical to the party's functioning for much of the 20th century. In respect of women voters, Conservative support from women is long recognized as significant for Conservative electoral success. According to the first mass surveys of British public opinion women were more likely to say that they voted for the Conservative party than men (Goot and Reid 1975) and, at its peak in the 1950s, the pro-Conservative gap in vote choice between women and men was about 14 percent (Campbell 2006).

Both of these observations are now, however, under challenge or, at least, subject to qualification. In brief, under New Labour the Conservative party lost its hold on women voters (Campbell 2006). The pro-Conservative gender gap in the post-1979 era fell to around 3 percent and thereafter there was some evidence of a gender generation gap emerging, with young women more likely to favour Labour than either older women or younger men

(Norris 1999b: 156).[2] Turning to women's participation as party members it has been said that by the 1990s Conservative women were of two distinct, and arguably, conflicting types (Maguire 1998): (1) the traditional woman member infamous for making sandwiches and stuffing envelopes, and (2) the 'career' Conservative woman who was seeking political office. If the former were now fewer in number than before as working women found themselves with little time or inclination for hosting Conservative tea parties, the latter represented a challenge to traditional Conservative conceptions of women's appropriate gender (and political) roles. Moreover, the second type was herself few in number as those seeking selection found it difficult to be selected for the party's vacant held and winnable seats, the most efficient route into Parliament.[3] These contrasting types of Conservative woman revealed, at best a latent tension amongst the party's women. In addition, the Conservative woman candidate and MP's disinclination to see herself as a representative of women, or even as a gendered being, was in sharp relief with Labour's women MPs who confidently asserted their gender identity, and had feminized the agenda and legislative output of the 1997–2010 New Labour governments (Childs 2004, 2008; Lovenduski 2005a; Annesley et al 2007; Annesley 2010). Against this backdrop the Conservative party leadership's apparent failure to keep women voters and women members in its line of sight, pre-2005, made the contrast between the two main political parties look stark. Behind the scenes, women in the Conservative party were, to be sure, organizing to both increase the number of women in Parliament (and other elected party offices) and to ensure that the party paid more attention to women's issues, but they did so mostly out of the public eye and mostly unsuccessfully in both respects (Childs 2008).

Recent accounts of Cameron's tenure of the Conservative party place only a limited emphasis on feminization as central to his 'modernization' of the party.[4] Adopting more mainstream analysis, for example by emphasizing ideology, and to a lesser extent organization, as if gender was not relevant to both of these, they seek mostly to determine whether the party is an embodiment of 'compassionate Conservatism', a return to 'One Nation' Conservatism, or some other form of post-Thatcherite Conservative party. What many of the accounts published in the run up to the 2010 general election agree on is that Cameron's efforts at 'decontamination' – of making his party one that non-Conservative voters will, at least and at last, listen to – have been largely successful (Bale 2010; Snowden 2010; Kenny 2009). In so doing, Bale writes, Cameron has 'done as little as he can get away with and as much as he can afford' (2010: 20). There was little evidence to support claims that voters enthusiastically desired a Conservative government in the spring of 2010, and quite a lot, not least the smaller opinion poll leads in the period before the election, to suggest that the country was less than positively enamoured. This interpretation remained true at the general election when the party, whilst winning the most seats in Parliament (305) and the highest vote share (36 percent), fell short of an overall majority (326 seats were needed for that). This left the Commons hung for the first time since 1974 and with the first peace-time coalition Government since the 1930s.[5]

At the minimum, Cameron's modernization meant the Conservatives appeared no longer to be perceived as the 'nasty' party that Theresa May so infamously brought to the attention of her party Conference back in 2002, even if the electorate were not totally convinced by the Tories' ability 'to perform in office' (Denver 2010: 23). In these accounts, and amongst wider public consciousness, Cameron appeared to embody a more modern party leader (Bale 2010) – a nice young man, with a well-dressed working wife. The political terrain upon which Cameron sought to situate the Conservative party in advance of the 2010 general election also looked different from that under the previous three party leaders, William Hague, Iain Duncan Smith and Michael Howard (Green 2010). Issues, which for the post-1997 elections were seen to dominate – most notably Europe and immigration – were replaced in 2010 with an emphasis on the NHS, education, the family, a 'sound' economy, and in the manifesto and campaign itself, talk of the 'big society', at least until the leadership debates addressed immigration head on. Tackling the budget deficit – and the balance between cuts and tax increases – was largely left to the aftermath of the election.[6]

To underplay the importance of feminization to the Cameron project is, in our view, to limit one's understanding of Conservative party change over the last five years (Campbell and Childs 2010; Childs et al 2008).[7] Cameron himself made it central, not least in his regular statements about the need for the Conservative parliamentary party to be more descriptively representative, as well as in the regular statements he made on women's issues.[8] He was, moreover, not shy in suggesting a link between the greater presence of women in his party and in Parliament, and the content of his party's policies. In a speech in December 2005 he stated:

[The recruitment of women] has got nothing to do with crude political calculation, or crazed political correctness, It's about political effectiveness…If you put eight Conservative men round a table and ask them to discuss what should be done about pensions, you'd get some good answers…but *what you are less likely to get is a powerful insight into the massive unfairness relating to women's pensions.* We need people from diverse backgrounds to inform everything we do (emphasis added).

Or, take a speech the following spring (March 2006):

Ask ten men and ten women what they think are the big issues of the day and you might get the same answers. I doubt it…*rank those issues in order of priority, or...raise issues of particular concern to them, and some fundamental differences will start to appear.* (emphasis added)

Cameron's commitment to women's greater descriptive and substantive representation was not just rhetorical. His reforms of the parliamentary selection processes, whilst in our view ultimately limited, were hardly hidden under a bushel. On the policy front the 2010 election manifesto included explicit pledges in respect of flexible working, gender pay audits, parental leave, maternity ward closure, mixed-sex hospital wards, and rape and sexual violence.[9] There was also, and much more high profile in media terms,[10] his personal commitment to the recognition of marriage in the tax system – as he told listeners to BBC radio 4's 'Woman's Hour' in February 2010.[11]

Establishing that a party, like Cameron's Conservatives, is experiencing a process of feminization is one thing. That can be achieved by counting more women MPs than previously and observing more policies that address women's concerns, with the aforementioned qualifications momentarily put to one side. But this is not the same as deducing that a particular party has become more *feminist* as a result (Childs 2008).[12] A feminist party requires (L. Young 2000): sex parity amongst elected representatives or, in the interim at least, sex parity amongst its newly elected representatives. This might be secured either because the party uses particular (s)election guarantees or because all informal barriers to being selected as a candidate have been eliminated. A feminist party is also open to electing a woman leader, and where this occurs, any failings by the woman leader would not be immediately attributed to her sex. Finally, a feminist party is one where feminist perspectives are central to policy development, and where feminist policies figure prominently in a party's electoral programme and are speedily and diligently enacted once the party achieves office (ibid). In contrast, a *feminized* party might similarly include women representatives, and senior party women, as well as addressing women's concerns, but would do so without the party signing up to a feminist project, of whatever feminist hue.

Drawing out this distinction between feminist and feminized political parties, Table 0.1 outlines a typology of ideal type feminized political parties. It distinguishes between parties on the basis of whether the party makes positive (feminist), neutral and, or negative (anti-feminist) responses along the twin dimensions of feminization. It reveals that, in the case of Responsive Party I, a party can be feminist in both dimensions, having high to moderate representation in the parliamentary party, integrated women's organizations, and feminist policies. The Non-responsive party, in contrast, fails to integrate either women or their concerns. However, the Anti-feminist party has low descriptive representation, either anti-feminist but integrated women's organizations or women's 'auxillary' organizations

Table 0.1 Feminization and Party Types

	1st dimension		2nd Dimension
	Integration of women parliamentary elites	**Integration of women party members**	**Integration of women's concerns**
Responsive Party I (Feminist both dimensions)	High/moderate representation; Well designed and fully implemented quotas; or absence of obstacles to women's representation	Parity of members; women's organizations are fully integrated into party policy making	Positive and in feminist direction
Responsive Party II (Feminist 2nd Dimension)	Low representation; absent or poorly designed/ implemented quotas	Fewer women members; integrated women's organizations	Positive and feminist
Co-optive Party (Feminist on 1st dimension, neutral 2nd)	High/moderate representation; may have quotas	Parity of members; auxillary women's organizations	Neutral or where positive, in a neutral direction
Anti-feminist Co-optive Party (Feminist on 1st dimension, anti-feminist on 2nd)	High/moderate representation; may have quotas	Parity of members; either anti-feminist women's organizations fully integrated into party policy making or 'auxillaries'	Positive but in anti feminist direction
Non-responsive	Low representation; absent quotas	Indifferent to representation of women; auxillary women's organizations rather than integrated ones	Negative
Anti-feminist Party	Low representation; rejects principle and practice of quotas	Indifferent to representation of women; either anti-feminist women's organizations fully integrated into party policy makin or auxillary women's organization	Positive in an anti-feminist direction

Source: Childs, 2008 amended from L. Young 2000.

together with anti-feminist policies. In short, it fails to integrate women but nonetheless addresses women's concerns, albeit in an anti-feminist fashion.

This new typology (admittedly of ideal types) suggests that gender and politics research on political parties – including this study of the British Conservative party – should seek to investigate the following: (1) the level of women's participation in party structures, including, but importantly not limited to, the parliamentary party. Such enquiries should explore whether the party employs specific mechanisms in both party structures and the parliamentary party to guarantee women's descriptive represent-ation; (2) whether women's participation is substantive across the party's various structures and activities or symbolic and limited to certain forms or places; (3) the nature of the role, remit and ideology of women's organ-izations and, in particular, whether these are integrated formally into the wider party structure and policy making bodies, and to whom they are accountable, both upwards and downwards (with bearings on notions of intra-party democracy); (4) whether a party regards women as a corporate entity capable of being represented (both descriptively and substantively) and if so, whether the party is susceptible to feminist arguments for this. This might include whether the party makes gender based and or feminist claims rather than non-gendered, neutral or anti-feminist claims; and finally (5) the extent to which party policies are gendered and in what ways.

In considering the feminized political party, and its development over time, it is worth noting that political parties and party politicians may have reasons other than the principled ones identified in the gender and politics literature (such as justice and fairness) for seeking parity amongst its par-liamentary representatives (see for example, Phillips 1995). Once there is a competition over women's descriptive representation other parties are likely to see electoral benefits from increasing their number of women rep-resentatives (Kittilson 2006). In such a scenario party leaders might intro-duce measures to enhance the diversity of their representatives despite, and not because of, themselves. Accounts of party change that derive from the study of the earlier feminization of the UK Labour party, and which iden-tify a convergence in the aims of feminist activists within the party with the goals of the party leadership, look instructive for understanding gen-dered party change under Cameron (Russell 2005; Kittilson 2006). His leader-ship may constitute an analogous fortuitous moment (Campbell et al 2006), with party members more favourably disposed to modernization (Snowdon 2010: 212). Not only had there been three successive general election defeats (1997, 2001 and 2005), the extra-parliamentary party was supportive of Cameron and his modernizing agenda, in fact more so than the parliamentary party, although he had considerable support from them too (Childs 2005). Accordingly, Cameron could claim, as he frequently did, a 'mandate' for reform. When the mobilization of senior women in the parliamentary, extra-parliamentary and professional party, working alongside women's equality advocates in civil society and the media, are factored in the likelihood of significant feminization of the party looked, at this time, greater than ever. Of course, no political party is entirely monolithic. Any analysis of party change must therefore take account of the various strata and components of the organization, drawing out the nuances and tensions between them. In the case of the British Conservative party, the parliamentary leadership has always been accorded a wide degree of autonomy in policy matters (McKenzie 1955). Yet, there remains a subtle sense in which it is constrained by the wider party in the country. Grassroots members may not have formal power over the party programme, but those who know the Conservative party best have been inclined to argue that they play a significant role in establishing a 'mood' to which the leadership should be sensitive in shaping its course of action. If anything, the importance of this seemingly intangible relationship between parliamentary leadership and the party in the country has only grown in significance with the introduction of members' right to elect leaders since 1998. In addition, the party has always operated a complex system of ancillary bodies, many of which have their own conferences and representatives within the wider party's organizational structure (Kelly 1989). And these include various expressions of women's representation. Thus, in seeking to understand the way in which Cameron's Conservatives might have feminized, it behoves us to examine the distribution of grassroots opinion on gender issues, especially in respect of both parliamentary representation and policy.

Moreover, and as the party typology outlined above indicates, a political party's response to women's demands for inclusion, both descriptive and substantive, can vary. Wider societal forces, as well as more specific inter-party relations at a particular moment in time, are likely to impact on, and affect, the precise manifestations of feminization. Some of these forces, importantly, might be perceived differentially by parties of the left and right of the political spectrum. UK-wide relevant factors might include a generic shift away from strongly bifurcated gender roles in the last quarter century or so, not least in respect of women's participation in paid employment, and evidence of an increasingly feminist orientation amongst younger women (Campbell 2006; Campbell et al 2010). These changes are likely to impact all or, more probably most, mainstream political parties in a similar fashion. Nonetheless, it might be expected that centre-right political parties' responses will be influenced in some way by their party ideology. Such parties, whether in the UK or elsewhere, might be expected to constitute women and men as different, albeit complementary, sexes, with accompanying sex specific gender roles rather than seek to, or be able to, adopt a strongly feminist position, however this might be defined. In other words, if party ideology cross cuts gender ideology (Duerst-Lahti 2008) it is likely that what the Conservative party considers to constitute women's interests will remain distinct, either qualitatively (of a different type) or quantitatively (of a different degree) from parties of the left.[13]

Sex, Gender and the Conservative Party: Structure

The book's subtitle, *From Iron Lady to Kitten Heels*, plays on the sobriquet that was given to Mrs Thatcher by the Soviet Union in 1976, and refers to the type of shoe favoured by Theresa May, MP for Maidenhead since 1997. The book has four main sections. The first comprises the opening chapter which outlines debates within the gender and politics scholarship relating to the concept of political representation. The second section considers women's descriptive representation within the contemporary Conservative party. Chapter 2 looks at women's participation in the 'women's' parts of the party, voluntary and professional, with particular focus on the Conservative Women's Organization. The subsequent two chapters examine women's legislative recruitment, outlining, in Chapter 3, the current representation of women in the parliamentary party, and, in Chapter 4, exploring the reforms to the parliamentary selection process undertaken since 2005 and, drawing on both qualitative and quantitative data, evaluating party support for women's descriptive representation. The third section of the book addresses women's substantive representation. Chapter 5 includes an account of the development of policy 'for women' under Cameron and examines the attitudes of party members and MPs towards these and other, more mainstream, policies and ideological positions. Chapter 6 provides a case study analysis of Conservative parliamentary behaviour on 'women's' legislation in the 2005 Parliament. The fourth section of the book addresses the question of how the feminization of the party plays out in terms of party cohesion and electoral politics. *Sex, Gender and the Conservative Party* closes with a reflection on how developments within the British Conservative party might be best understood and how they speak to both the gender and politics and mainstream party literatures and, in so doing, beg future research.

Chapter 1, *Conservatism, Representation and Feminization* explores the challenges posed to gender and politics scholars' understandings of representation when conservative claims to represent women are acknowledged. In particular, it explores the ways in which conservative representatives' gender and party ideologies mediate the already complicated relationship between women's descriptive and substantive representation (Dodson 2006; Reingold 2000). Our approach reflects earlier research (Childs and Krook 2006a,b,c, 2008) that rejects the use of 'critical mass theory' in favour of investigating 'how the substantive representation of women occurs', and which points to the important role of 'critical actors' – representatives with lower thresholds for action who initiate campaigns for women friendly policy. Who these representatives are is not prescribed in advance and they may not even be women. We contend, accordingly, that whilst counting the numbers of women present in our political institutions (for example, parties, legislatures, executives) may establish the level of women's descriptive representation it cannot tell us very much about how representatives act. Even when predisposed to do so, representatives may find themselves unable to act for women. (Gendered) institutions may very well constrain their behaviour. In any case, we should not presume that representatives seek to act for women in the same way. Conservative representatives are likely to perceive of the substantive representation of women in different ways to representatives of parties of the centre or the left. Chapter 1 also explores recent developments in political theory that conceptualize representation as a process of representative claims making. Judith Squires' (2008) conception of the constitutive representation of gender holds that the substantive representation of women involves particular claims to represent women. Not only do these constitute gender in particular ways (again suggesting that conservative representative claims to act for women may differ from those articulated by other kinds of representatives), but they act as part of a wider economy of representative claims about the substantive representation of women (Saward 2006). The final part of the chapter considers how these newer concepts and approaches might be applied in practice, foreshadowing the later empirical analysis in Section III.

Chapter 2, *Women Members and the Party's Women's Organizations,* focuses its attention on the Conservative Women's Organization (CWO). It outlines its major activities, noting in particular recent developments such as Conservative Women's Forums, Summits and the Muslim Group, which indicate its changing form and focus, not least in the development of policy and the attraction to the party of a 'third' type of Conservative woman. She is younger, more likely to be in paid employment, and is more engaged with 'big P' politics. For these and other reasons, there is acknowledgment that the CWO in the mid-2000s became something more than its historic classification as a 'ladies auxillary'. Relations between the CWO and other 'women's' parts of the party and the party proper are also considered. Here, tensions are revealed relating to intra-party territorial battles and which reveal the lack of institutionalization between different 'women's' parts of the party. Accordingly, personal relations come to the fore and questions of representation and accountability are left begging. Interview data with MPs and Peers, moreover, reveal less than wholehearted support for the CWO, perhaps surprisingly so, from women MPs and Peers who often seek to distance themselves from what they consider an anachronistic organization, even whilst some may acknowledge its efforts for the party. In all this, intra-party relations and democracy are implicit.

Chapter 3, *Conservative Legislative Recruitment,* examines the descriptive representation of women following the 2010 general election, detailing both the reforms to the Conservative party candidate selection process for that election, and their outcome for the number of Conservative women MPs returned on May 6th. It draws on comparative studies which highlight numerous obstacles to women's political recruitment and, employing Norris and Lovenduski's (1995) 'supply and demand' model, emphasizes the importance of party demand for women representatives. Thus strategies to increase women's (s)election – equality rhetoric, equality promotion and equality guarantees – are regarded as key to understanding inter-party differences in women's descriptive representation at Westminster (Lovenduski 2005a). In advance of the 2010 general election all of the three main UK political parties were publicly troubled by the lack of diversity amongst their parliamentary representatives. David Cameron, along with Gordon Brown (then Leader of the Labour Party and Prime Minister) and Nick Clegg, (then leader of the Liberal Democrats, and now Deputy Prime Minister in the coalition) were unambiguous in their depositions to the 'Speaker's Conference' on Parliamentary Representation in the autumn of 2009. There were 'mea culpas' all around.[14] For Cameron, parliamentary selection – or rather a *strategy* of seeking to diversify Conservative candidates – constituted one means by which to signal modernization. Reforms were introduced almost immediately following his election as party leader. These fell some way short of constituting equality guarantees, measures that ensure the election and not just the selection of women. Unsurprisingly such efforts were limited, even if the party managed to more than double the number of Conservative women MPs in 2010. Our reading of party change in respect of legislative recruitment suggests that Cameron stepped back from taking on his party and imposing women candidates in order to guarantee greater numbers of women MPs, when he might have done so – a contention addressed more fully in Chapter 4.

Chapter 4, *Reforming Parliamentary Selection: Party Change, Parliamentarian and Party Member Attitudes*, offers analysis of the introduction of, and support for, reforms to the Conservative party's parliamentary selection processes introduced under Cameron. Drawing on focus group discussion with, and a survey of party members, as well as interviews with MPs and Peers, a picture is painted of a party that is largely uncomfortable with strong measures that will enhance women's (s)election as parliamentary candidates, even as it is supportive of the principle of women's greater descriptive representation. Nevertheless, we suggest that Cameron might have gone further in *leading* his party on this issue. That he did not do so, we contend, is the party's missed opportunity in 2010. Not only is there evidence of some support amongst younger party members, especially women, women Parliamentarians and the 'women's' part of the party, this could have been better mobilized to bolster the introduction of more radical reform, not least because Cameron was, notwithstanding a few 'wobbles', predominant within his party (Heffernan 2010).

Chapter 5 *Party Member Attitudes and Women's Policy, (by and for women?)* This chapter is composed of two distinct halves. The first analyses the development and content of Conservative party women's policy in advance of the 2010 general election. The result was a general election manifesto that was much more competitive on this terrain than its 2005 version. The main policy pledges reflect the Women's Policy Group 2008 Report, *Women in the World Today,* in which there is clear gendered analysis and critique. Both it and the manifesto centre women's work/life balance and deploy the concept of choice to advance policies that might be considered counter to traditional conservative conceptions of gender and the family. In addition to analysis in terms of constitutive and substantive representation, this section of the chapter also charts the development of 'women's policy' during the Cameron era. What had been a more collegiate approach across the 'women's' parts of the party was, under Theresa May as Shadow Minister for Women, clearly brought more closely into the remit of the party in public office. David Cameron's emphasis on recognizing marriage in the tax system is, though, one high profile 'women's' policy that notably did not come out of the women's policy development process. The second half of the chapter reports the results of a survey of Conservative party members (the views and behaviour of Parliamentarians is examined in Chapter 6). Here, attitudes towards gender roles and relations generally, and in respect of specific policies for women, are examined. Some sex differences are found. Women party members are more likely to be at ease with policies that address women's life/work balance and are critical of, and seek the ending of the gender pay gap, for example. Accordingly, we surmise that Conservative policies for women advanced at the 2010 election would be more supported by women party members than male ones, and that women voters, especially those to the feminist side of Conservative women members, might very well find them amenable. The reliance on 'choice' also suggests that party members, male and female, who are less predisposed to more modern gender roles, might be able to accept these policies, given that they mostly do not prescribe particular behaviour.

Chapter 6 *Sex, Gender and Parliamentary Behaviour in the 2005 Parliament.* How the Conservative party would act on women's concerns in the 2010 Parliament was unknowable at the time of writing. Analysis of how they acted in opposition during the 2005–2010 Parliament was undertaken as instructive. Three pieces of 'women's' legislation' in the 2005 Parliament are considered: the Work and Families Act 2006; the Human Embryology and Fertilization Act 2008; and the Equal Pay and Flexible Working Bill 2009. In each case how the Conservative party in Parliament constitutively and substantively represented women is evaluated. We expected to find inter-party differences and intra-party sex differences, with Labour members and women within each party, adopting the more progressive position. Comparing the three cases in respect of constitutive representation, three broad observations are drawn. First, all *see* gender; secondly, women are represented as both *sharing experiences* and of constituting an *heterogeneous group*; thirdly, women are regarded as *lacking agency*. Turning to substantive representation, we find few differences in vote turnout between women and men Parliamentarians, with party overwhelmingly accounting for the direction of Members' votes, as is to be expected in a legislature marked by high party cohesion. However, sex plays a greater role in the contributions to parliamentary debates. Not only do women over-participate in these, they are also more likely to adopt the gender equality position. Participating women Parliamentarians are also more interested in women's concerns associated with the legislation than the men. Even so, party remains highly relevant: the active women in the Commons are most often Labour MPs, and in the Lords Labour, Cross bench and Liberal Democrat women.

Chapter 7, *Feminization and Party Cohesion: Conservative Ideological Tendencies and Gender Politics*, considers the ways in which feminization relates to broader patterns of ideological differences within the Conservative party. In particular, it explores the likely impact of reform to both candidate selection and policy on intra-party cohesion. Analysing data from our party member survey we establish three main ideological tendencies within the party: *Thatcherites, Liberal Conservatives* and *Traditional Tories*. If the former are the most hostile to gender equality positions, the third tendency, who are also the most working class and the most female, are, whilst less 'feminist' than the Liberal Conservatives at the general level, on a range of specific policy areas, more progressive. On this basis we suggest that Cameron's efforts to modernize his party – on gender and other fronts – would be reflected upon favourably by these two groups of party members, albeit to lesser and greater degrees. Moreover, with the sex and class of the member significant to understanding attitudes, a changed party membership (by recruiting more women members, for example) might well see the balance between the three tendencies shift. Finally, analysis of party member attitudes towards economic policy suggest that women may be more likely to be on the 'wet' side of the party, if such a wet/dry divide were once again to come to the fore.

Chapter 8 *Feminization Strategy and the Electorate* investigates the ways in which feminization has been deployed as a strategy by the party leadership in order to convince voters that the party is moving onto the centre ground of politics. It explores how voters responded to the party's position on women's concerns by drawing on both British Election Study survey data and our own focus group discussions with non-aligned voters. Feminization might have helped the Conservative party's appeal either directly, by successfully addressing women's issues, thereby attracting women voters, or, it may have had an indirect influence, as the party's policies for women contributed to the wider decontamination strategy of repositioning the party in the centre-ground of British politics. In this way it would challenge people's perceptions of the Tories as the 'nasty' party of the post-1997 period. Our analysis suggests that there is evidence to support the contention that the Conservative party under David Cameron's leadership was more attractive to women in 2010 than it had been for some years. Focus group discussions suggest that women's issues, whilst not the most salient issues at the election, fed into a changing perception of the party, whilst the electoral data shows a larger Conservative lead over Labour among women than among men.

The book's *Conclusion* reflects back on the findings of *Sex, Gender and the Conservative Party* and considers how they contribute to conceptions of feminization and add complexity to conceptions of women's political representation. It ponders the likelihood for the greater descriptive representation of women by the Conservatives at subsequent elections, and goes beyond counting the numbers of women in parliamentary parties as the only indicator of descriptive representation, by reconsidering party types in terms of women's participation as party members and the nature of parties' women's organizations. In respect of the latter, questions are raised for future research regarding the institutionalization and accountability of the women's part of the Conservative party. Shifting its attention to substantive representation, and the ways in which conservative representatives might act for women, the *Conclusion* emphasizes that the Conservatives in 2010 were more competitive on the women's terrain. In this the party's manifesto pledges, alongside its actions in the 2005 Parliament, suggest a liberally-feminist stance. However, *Sex, Gender and the Conservative Party* stops at the time of the 2010 general election. It is, therefore, unable to assess how Cameron's Conservative party in government – or more accurately how the Tories in coalition government with the Liberal-Democrats – substantively represents women in practice.

Sex, Gender and the Conservative Party offers new and initial data and analysis that begin to address a lacuna in mainstream parties and Conservative party literature, which says almost nothing about gender. And whilst this book is based upon a single case study, it is, nonetheless, a case study of a right-of-centre party, a party type which gender and politics scholars have only recently turned their attention to. As the US scholars Sue Carroll and Debra Leibowitz identified some years ago (2003: 2), we need to know more about (big and small c) conservative women's decision to seek election; how they see their gender influencing their political priorities and behaviour; and the nature the impact of Conservative representatives' presence on the substantive representation of women. This book seeks, then, to provide some initial answers to such questions.

Section I
Women's Political Representation

1
Conservatism, Representation and Feminization

'Feminine', 'Feminist' or 'Anti-feminist' Politics?[1]

Better representation for women in politics is often equated with the greater presence of women representatives in our political institutions. Underpinning this is an assumption, either implicit or explicit, that the first dimension of feminization begets the second; that the inclusion of women representatives engenders the inclusion of women's issues (Lovenduski 2005a). In every day terms, that women politicians 'make a difference' to our politics and that women will be better represented as a consequence. Yet the difficulty of operationalizing *that* which is to be included is widely contested. Too often there is an implicit conflation between 'women's' and 'feminist' issues and perspectives which implies that the difference that will occur will be a feminist one. In turn this might generate debate about what constitutes feminism, again something that is marked by disagreement. Nor can the nature or extent of the inclusion of women's issues (once it has been agreed on what this refers to) be easily read off from existing empirical studies of women's political presence. Researchers often adopt different measures and employ a variety of research methods and designs, thereby, limiting comparability (Celis et al 2008; Dovi 2008: 154; Dodson 2006). So, at this point gender and politics scholars are not sure what difference women's greater descriptive representation has made, even if we can be pretty confident that, on the basis of a number of studies, there is a link between women representatives and the addressing of women's concerns (Lovenduski 2005a: 180; Childs 2008).

If disputes over what counts, quantitatively and qualitatively, as 'making a difference' reveal its conceptual limitations, the basis upon which women representatives might seek to 'make' a difference has also been found to be rather problematic. The widely recognized concept of critical mass holds that when women constitute a 'critical mass', feminized change (once again, whatever that might mean) will, by definition, happen. However, the assumptions of 'critical mass theory' are increasingly rejected by some, even if not by all, gender and politics scholars. Rather attention is drawn to the impor-tance of contextualizing representatives' attitudes and actions in light of the particular gendered institutions within which it occurs – these may be to a greater or lesser extent constraining (Lovenduski 2005a; Childs 2004; Dodson 2006).[2] New frameworks (Celis et al 2008; Weldon 2002), more-over, contend that in any case, the substantive representation of women may be undertaken by multiple actors in multiple sites, rather than only by women representatives in legislatures, although this does not mean that legislatures and legislators might not be one such site and actor.

Developments such as these in the gender and politics literature mean that the empirical study of women's political representation, such as that undertaken for this book, is much harder than was once thought. Of course, representation was a much contested concept prior to feminists taking a serious interest in it. Besides descriptive and substantive representation, there are other dimensions, not least symbolic representation. These have received relatively little, and mostly belated, attention by gender and pol-itics scholars.[3] New conceptualizations – representation as representative claims (Saward 2006) and constitutive representation (Squires 2008) – offer distinct and additional challenges to our analytic frameworks and empirical study. At a minimum, evaluations of the adequacy or otherwise of women's representation must, then, be clear about what dimensions of represent-ation are being considered and what the criteria of assessment is.[4] 'Adding in' conservative representatives further complicate our analysis.[5] Conservative women representatives, by dint of being women, 'count' for the purposes of descriptive representation but when what is at issue is symbolic, sub-stantive and, or constitutive representation, their presence may destabilize rather than confirm some of the previously held certainties of the literature, not least the acclaimed positive relationship between descriptive and sub-stantive representation (Dodson 2006). Of course, this relationship is already routinely qualified as complicated, probabilistic, and contingent (Phillips 1995; Reingold 2000; Dodson 2006), but conservative women seem to constitute an extra layer of complexity. They appear to make the expected outcome either less likely and, or distinct. In other words, conservative women represent-atives seem to challenge oft-made assumptions about the kind of change that the presence of women representatives engenders. They also beg questions about whether conservative representatives can and do act for women in a feminist fashion, as well as the associated question of what to do with non- or anti-feminist claims and actions by conservative women representatives.

The complicated relationship between descriptive and substantive representation

The descriptive under-representation of women is today, in western demo-cracies, rarely considered natural or just. Hence, the belief that women's descriptive representation can and should be effected.[6] But it is no doubt the possibility of a positive relationship with substantive representation that underpins many activists' advocacy of women's descriptive representation. It is not that women's presence should *depend* on demonstrating that women representatives 'act for' women, or even that their presence should depend on them acting *differently* from men. Yet, there remains a resilient assumption, if not expectation, that women representatives will seek to 'act for' women because they share gendered experiences (Mansbridge 1999). For feminists the hope is likely to be for a feminist re-gendering of politics. The difficulty comes with conceptualizing a causal relationship between women's descriptive and substantive representation. Faith was placed, for some time, and remains so amongst many activists, in the concept of critical mass, noted above.[7] Borrowed from physics, critical mass posits a straightforward relationship, one that is dependent upon a particular proportion of women being present in a political institution. Despite its apparent simplicity, and optimism, 'critical mass theory' has been found wanting by a considerable number of gender and politics scholars (see Childs and Krook 2006a,b,c).

The expectations of 'critical mass theory' reflect in part a mistaken reading of its founding texts, those by Rosabeth Moss Kanter and Drude Dahlerup (Kanter 1977a,b; Daherlup 1988). Kanter, posited three claims about changes when the numbers of women in an institution form a 'tilted' group' (where the ratio of men to women is 65:35). Her first claim contends that an increase in 'relative numbers' means that minority members are 'potentially allies' who can form 'coalitions and affect the culture' of the group. Secondly, Kanter holds that an increase in relative numbers might see 'minority members begin to become individuals differentiated from each other' rather than coming together. Her final contention is that, despite a lack of change in relative numbers, transformation might occur due to the presence of feminist or 'women identified women'. Too much attention was, however, subsequently given to Kanter's first claim at the expense of the other two.[8] Drude Dahlerup (1988), who held that politics is not physics (not least because factors beyond numbers might go further in explaining change or lack of change), explicitly gendered her account of the impact of numbers. Ultimately, though, she preferred the concept of critical acts over critical mass. Critical acts are initiatives that 'change the position of the minority and lead to further changes'. Crucially, such acts depend on *'the willingness and ability of the minority to mobilize the resources of the organizations or institution* to improve the situation for themselves and the whole minority group' (Dahlerup 1988: 296, emphasis in the original; see also Lovenduski and Guadagnini 2010). Unfortunately, readings of Daherlup's work thereafter often neglect her concept of critical acts, and imply instead advocacy of critical mass defined as anywhere between 15–40 percent, but most usually, at 30 percent.

Having reviewed the empirical literature on women's substantive representation Childs and Krook (2006a,b,c) conclude that higher numbers of women representatives do not deliver, in any straightforward fashion, women's substantive representation, as critical mass theory purports. Some studies do, indeed, find that the greater presence of women in legislatures leads to gendered (and, or feminist) changes in discourses, proposals, debates, and outcomes. But others uncover little or no relationship.[9] And what was once (or rather looked like) a critical mass can, as Debra Dodson (2006: 148–9) observes of the US Congress, 'disintegrate...*without* a decline in numbers' (emphasis added). Mediating factors on representatives' actions abound, including but not limited to: the external political environment; extant institutional norms; the impact of party – affiliation, ideology and cohesion; differences amongst women representatives; representatives' newness; institutional position, including front- and back-bench, and government or opposition membership; committee appointment and leadership; women's caucus presence; the existence of a women's policy machinery; and the wider vagaries of policy making.[10] Even factoring in such variables is not sufficient. As indicated above, and drawing on state feminism and feminist comparative policy literature, contemporary gender and politics scholars frequently acknowledge explicitly the multiple, rather than single, sites and actors involved in women's substantive representation (Weldon 2002).[11] Together these newer approaches contend, then, that the substantive representation of women is likely to take place at many different and interacting levels of political institutions and in a variety of political and other fora (Celis et al 2008, 2010). This is, of course, not the same thing as arguing that women representatives should not be present in our legislatures (women's descriptive representation) nor that women's presence has no re-gendering effect (Lovenduski 2005a; Childs 2008). At the minimum, as Lovenduski and Guadagnini (2010) argue, women legislators' interventions cannot take place if they are not present.

Developments in the gender and politics literature have been captured in the following shift in research question: from 'when women make a difference' to 'how the substantive representation of women occurs' (Childs and Krook 2008). Central to this is the concept of critical actors (Childs and Krook 2006a,b,c).[12] Critical actors are those who put in motion individual and collective campaigns for women-friendly policy change: they initiate policy proposals on their own, even when women form a small minority; and embolden others to take steps to promote policies for women, regardless of the proportion of female representatives. Their common feature is their relatively low threshold for action. Although they may hold attitudes similar to those of other actors, they are much more motivated than others to initiate the substantive representation of women (ibid). Even so, whilst they may operate alone, they may stimulate others to act, setting in motion a momentum for policy change. Alternatively, they may provoke a backlash. As such, their effects are neither guaranteed nor uni-dimensional.

Exploring 'how the substantive representation of women occurs' begs further questions (Celis et al 2007, 2008), which in turn allows us to ask '*what is* the substantive representation of women?' The first is, '*who* acts for women?' Namely, who are the critical actors and with whom do they act? What conditions are most conducive to their emergence and success? Here the possibility of competing conceptions of what constitutes 'acting for' women are acknowledged, in addition to ideas of collaboration and mutual reinforcement between actors. The second question is, '*where* does the substantive representation of women occur?' These are not limited to legislatures, and might vary across countries and over time. It is also crucial to consider institutional opportunities and constraints. The third question is, '*why* is the substantive representation of women attempted?' If before the assumption was that women would act for women because of their shared gender, this is now considered less than straightforward. Not all women are feminists (an assumption already referred to as underpinning much of 'critical mass theory'), nor are they necessarily gender conscious, and in any case, women's interests/concerns/needs are not necessarily homogenous but rather context related, and subject to evolution (Celis 2005, 2008). The fourth question is, '*how* is the substantive representation of women expressed?' This refers to the importance of exploring interventions at various points in political processes to identify the claims made in support of the substantive representation of women, the actions taken to promote this, as well as the outcomes of these attempts. To these questions, Joni Lovenduski and Maria Guadagnini (2010) have added: *Which* women are represented? *When* does the representation take place? *What* are the processes through which claims are formulated, refined and advanced, and to *whom* are representatives accountable? Whilst Suzanne Dovi (2008: 161) asks, 'how well different groups of women influence and sanction their representatives?' Together, these amount to asking: (1) how is representation done, (2) who does it, (3) in relation to which women, (4) what policies, (5) where, (6) when, (7) why, (8) to whom is it accountable and (9) how effective is the representation (Lovenduski and Guadagnini 2010; Childs and Lovenduski 2012).

Representative claims and the constitutive representation of gender

At the same time as more empirically based critiques became evident in the gender and politics literature, political theorists began to speak about representation as 'claims making'. Michael Saward's notion of representational claims starts from a concern with Hanna Pitkin's conception of the represented as 'fixed', 'transparent', 'given', and 'knowable'; those whose interests can be 'read off' by the representative (Saward 2006: 301, 310). For Saward the represented – 'or that which needs to be represented' – are constructed, constituted, framed and created by representatives: 'at the heart of the act of representing is the depicting of a constituency *as* this or that, as requiring this or that, or having this or that set of interests' (ibid, emphasis in the original).[13] The language of representative claims foregrounds, then, the performative aspect of representation and reveals how representatives make claims to know what constitutes the interests of 'someone or something', here women (Saward 2006: 302, 305). In line with the more recent substantive representation of women literature, representatives are, importantly, not just elected political representatives. Nor are representative claims, in themselves, either good or bad. Rather, successful representatives are those whose claims are not contested, although in an 'economy of claims' all claims can be contested (Saward 2006: 304).

Developing these ideas, Judith Squires (2008) advances the concept of the constitutive representation of gender. This refers to the process whereby representatives articulate women's interest 'in ways that inevitably privilege' and constitute 'particular concepts of gender relations'. In other words, what is of interest here is the ways in which gender is constructed in the representative process (Celis et al 2010: 4). Squires contrasts the constitutive representation of gender with traditional conceptions of women's substantive representation, which she refers to as the process by which representatives aim to speak for women by voicing women's 'preferences and consciously held interest' (Squires 2008: 187–8):

> Explorations of the substantive representation of women have...traced a bottom up representative process, starting with women and their interests (though not necessarily in an essentialist way), and seeking to establish the extent to which these interests are articulated and reflected by representatives. Explorations of the constitutive representation of gender would, by contrast, entail explorations of more top-down representative processes, starting with claims-making of representatives, seeking to establish the ways in which identities are narrated by representative claims (Squires 2008: 190).[14]

In the constitutive representation of gender the concern is not, then, about the adequacy or otherwise of women's substantive representation but 'how gender relations are constituted through representative claims making processes' (Squires 2008: 188 cited in Celis et al 2010: 4). Analysing constitutive representation empirically should reveal the 'extent to which, when claiming to speak for women, representatives are actively engaged in making claims about women, participating in the construction of feminine subject-positions' (Squires 2008: 192). In these ways, this approach offers new insights in respect of 'understanding the process of political claims making' and in raising questions about the 'nature of power relations' that shape them (Squires 2008: 200). Both the substantive representation of women and the constitutive representation of gender are understood by Squires as archetypes, albeit likely intertwined in practice. For this reason, she considers the latter to complement rather than replace the substantive representation of women.[15] Accordingly both become central to the study of women's political representation.

Substantive representation and the 'problem' of conservatism and conservative women

Peppered within the gender and politics literature are admissions of a gap in scholarship in respect of conservatism and representation, as well as a call to arms.[16] There is, for example, acknowledgement that ideological differences between women matter; that feminism does not speak for, or to, all women and that not all women representatives are feminists; that conservative women care as much as feminists about women's concerns (Schreiber 2008); that gender and politics scholars have no 'theory' that might explain the relationship between the descriptive and substantive representation of women by conservative women – that conservative women may, in fact, be one reason for why the relationship has proven so contingent in practice (Dodson 2006; Reingold 2008a);[17] and that there is a need to theorize 'acting for' women that might be considered harmful to women, regressive, conservative, non-feminist or even anti-feminist (Cowell-Myers and Langbein 2009: 514; Schreiber 2008).

Extant empirical studies of conservative women representatives are limited, in part because much of the gender and politics literature has been skewed to the study of left parties. This is itself a reflection of the greater likelihood of leftist parties to advance women's descriptive representation, but no doubt also reflects the prejudices of gender and politics scholars themselves. However, studies have, for some time, remarked on behavioural party differences. Analysis, in particular of the 103rd and 104th US Congress, which saw a shift from Democratic to Republican control (Swers 2002; Dodson 2006; Reingold 2008a,b), reveals, *inter alia*, that (1) Republican women historically are more favourably disposed towards acting for women in a feminist direction than their male Peers (and Democrat men in some cases); (2) that conservative women are themselves heterogeneous, divided between moderate Republican women and (the, then, newly elected) socially conservative women Republicans; (3) that Republican party leaders like to 'use women as tokens' thereby giving moral authority to party positions on women's issues;[18] (4) that changed institutional contexts impact on Republican women's behaviour. For example, moderate Republican women had fewer opportunities to act as they might have desired in the 104th Congress because they were now members of the majority party in a more partisan Congress, with a more conservative Republican leadership employing new practices in the allocation of positional power, and with more significant costs associated with rebellion; (5) that Republican and Democrat women talk about different kinds of women;[19] (6) that Conservative women may 'talk the talk' better than 'walking the walk', with 'little evidence of their feelings affecting their actions at the final stage of the policy process' (Dodson 2006: 104); and finally, (7) that it not clear as yet, whether the US' more recently elected, socially conservative Republican women will ignore women's issues or act on them in an anti-feminist fashion.

Beyond legislatures – and recall that contemporary gender and politics research look to multiple sites and multiple possible actors – Ronnie Schreiber's (2008, 2009) study of two US Conservative groups reveals how both act as women's organizations and make claims for women, despite their own criticisms of feminists for mobilizing around identity politics.[20] Such conservative groups, moreover, implicitly and explicitly challenge feminist definitions of women's interests and feminist representative claims to act for women, and they criticize feminists for limiting women's choices (Schreiber 2008: 83). These groups are though, and at the same time, 'gender conscious'. Indeed, they contend, contra to what they see as feminisms narrow and skewed understandings of women's lives (and hence interests), that their representative claims better represent women (ibid: 71), not least in respect of mothers, and especially 'stay at home' mothers. Furthermore, and recalling the American legislative research noted above, the strategic use of conservative women representatives' claims to act for women gains legitimacy for conservative perspectives, and conservative organizations access, to platforms that men could neither themselves receive nor acquire (Schreiber 2008: 28).[21]

Reflecting on the research to-date on conservative women representatives and conservative women's groups suggests five key points for gender and politics scholars to consider. First, that the 'diversity in women's views about gender and gender roles' is likely to give rise to a 'cacophony of gendered claims of problems, solutions and actions, that may be diametrically opposed to one another' (Dodson 2006: 12; see also Duerst-Lahti 2008; Dovi 2008: 148). Thus, giving acknowledgement to conservative women representatives' claims to represent women, forces, perhaps finally, an admission that women's bodies can no longer be elided with feminist minds, nor the substantive representation of women with feminist substantive representation (Childs 2004). Secondly, differences amongst women representatives are likely to have the effect of dividing women in political debate and within political institutions, of 'pitting some women's interests and preferences against other women's interests and preferences' (Dovi 2008: 148, 163). This is an empirical question, but, one likely to add further criticisms to 'critical mass theory'. Third, if conservative women are judged to be 'acting for' women this might constitute evidence of women's substantive representation occurring where previously it might not have been so regarded (Dodson 2006: 216), again questioning critical mass theory. Fourth, and taking gendered institutionalism seriously, scholars might wish to ask, as Dodson (2006) does, whether it is 'possible (or even worthwhile) to distinguish between women representatives' motives: do some act for honourable reasons (that is, for gender conscious reasons) while others for dishonourable ones (because it is demanded of them, for example, as 'cover' for their male colleagues?),[22] And does it matter if the outcomes are the same? (Dodson 2006: 238) Fifth, and arguably most importantly, an admission that conservative women might act for women – even if they do so in a non- and, or anti-feminist fashion – begs the question, just as Saward's conceptualization of an 'economy' of representative claims does, of whether there is any objective basis upon which to distinguish between competing claims to act 'as' and 'for' women?[23] To what extent, and how should anti-feminist initiatives be incorporated into our analyses? As Beth Reingold (2008b: 137) puts it: does all that any woman representatives do constitute the 'substantive representation of women'?[24] Rather than take representative claims and actions by such representatives as read, that is, as constituting women's substantive representation, these must be subject to closer scrutiny. '[There is a]…fine line between recognizing real intra-gender diversity and embracing essentialist images of women that …distort reality by accepting *anything* women do as the substantive representation of women' (Dodson 2006: 31). At the same time, might conservative women *act for* and *as* women – seeing 'themselves as very pro-woman – even if they disagree with feminists about what is best for women'? (Schreiber 2008; Duerst-Lahti 2008: 173)[25]

Gendered conservatism, feminism and anti-feminism

If one can no longer decry women's conservatism as false consciousness or depict conservative women as 'Stepford' wives (Schreiber 2008: 11–12; Campbell 1987; Dillard 2005), it needs to be admitted that conservative forms of gendered politics are either attracting gender conscious women to conservatism or that conservative organizations are attracting women who then subsequently become gender conscious.[26] Capturing the content of this gendered conservative politics is not helped by the oft-made claim that conservatism is not an ideology, merely a disposition, the noted 'ship' that is to be steadied, rather than sailed to any particular port. However, such accounts of conservatism as non-ideological can easily be countered by demonstrating that conservatives have particular views on, for example, human nature, the role of the state, and the meaning of liberty and equality. Box 1.1 provides a summary of the main characteristics of traditional conservatism and conservatism influenced by liberalism.

Nevertheless, conservative thought in the abstract, and in political theory texts, is not the same as that advanced or implemented by particular conservative political parties and governments in particular locations and moments of time. The dominant form of conservatism in the UK from the late 20th century has been that of the New Right – an 'uneasy alliance' between neo-conservatism and neo-liberalism (Gamble 1994). One of the 'critical elements' of the New Right was its anti-feminism (Bashevkin 1998: 106).

Box 1.1   Traditional and Liberal Conservatism

Traditional Conservatism	Liberal Conservatism
Rejection of radical change	Individual rights
Limitation of human reason	Individual opportunities
Importance of natural hierarchy	Rational calculation and competitive pursuit of self interest in a free market economy
Sentiment and tradition as a basis for social cohesion	Importance of the principle of meritocracy
Critical of abstract principles of equal rights	Importance of reason
Complementary sex/gender roles	Importance of self-interest in the public sphere counters the belief that women are best fulfilled in the private sphere
Importance of women's nurturing and reproductive roles	Private sphere nurtures individuals and constrains behaviour (in a positive fashion)
Importance of family; threat to family is threat to social cohesion	Rejection of state intervention in private sphere or economy to promote gender equality
Rejection of state intervention in private sphere or economy to promote gender equality	Natural inequality between individuals' abilities
Natural inequality between individuals' abilities	

Source: Bryson and Heppell (2010)

Feminism was regarded as a threat to the traditional family (Jeffries 1996: 44) that the New Right celebrated. In the latter's depiction, the family is a natural, biological and undifferentiated unit that stands as a 'bulwark against degeneracy and dependency' and an 'economic barricade against the state' (Campbell 1987: 100, 159, 166, 168). Yet, the New Right's social conservatism was much less strident in the UK than in the US. There was no significant religious right this side of the pond. Moral crusades on, say abortion and contraception, were limited in their voice and, for that matter, their effect.[27] Neither did the British New Right seek the overturning of women's greater participation in the paid employment market. Such social changes were largely accepted (Campbell 1987).

Despite obvious points of difference between the two ideologies of conservatism and feminism, conservative thought has sometimes overlapped with some second wave western feminist concerns and perspectives, even if ultimately, this overlap comes from very different starting points and may be seeking very different ends.[28] Accordingly it is possible to contend that conservatism, or rather aspects of conservative thought and practice, might be compatible with some forms of feminist analyses. This is most obvious in respect of the valorization of the values and practices of women's traditional gender roles, especially within the family and in respect of mothering (Stacey 1983).[29] Both radical feminists and conservatives might see these as alternatives to the competitive, atomistic individual characteristic of the public sphere of the liberal, and, or capitalist world. Socialist feminist campaigns around wages for housework also offer a re-valuation of women's domestic work, even if conservatives are unlikely to see this as 'work' in a socialist sense (Campbell 1987: 151–2). 'Conservative feminism' becomes more concrete, then, when it is centred on a commitment to privileging the family (Maguire 1998: 204; Bryson and Heppell 2010; Campbell 1987: 151). It is also possible in respect of women's experiences in the family for conservatives to regard women as constituting a group, albeit not one that privileges women's group identity over another, and one that might experience some disadvantage relative to men (Dodson 2006: 141; Bryson and Heppell 2010). A conservative liberal feminist critique is perhaps even easier to envisage, with its commitment to equal opportunities. And there is 'free-market feminism'. This approach holds that the market will not discriminate against individuals of equal ability on the basis of their sex. Hence, if women are naturally differently endowed (in motivation and preferences, skills, education, or childcare responsibilities, for example) then the market is right to discriminate (Conway cited in Bryson and Heppell 2010: 42; see also Campbell 1987: 229; Jeffries 1996: 34).

Agreement over the compatibility between some forms of conservative thought and some forms of feminism is not, and is unlikely to become, settled. Important points of dissonance remain between the two ideologies (Lovenduski 2005a). Of course, feminism is itself a heterogeneous body of thought, but it is nonetheless the case that the most high-profile second wave western feminist demands – for sexual liberation, an end to patriarchy and critiques of the patriarchal family and the traditional sexual division of labour – appear particularly challenging to conservatism. Bryson and Heppell's (2010) recent consideration provide the following definition: an ideology or policy is compatible with feminism 'if it recognizes the collective, structural and socially produced nature of men's domination and women's disadvantage and treats the promotion of greater gender equality and justice as a political priority'. This is a modern rendering of Beatrix

Campbell's observation (1987: 200), written more than 20 years ago, that conservatives (like liberal feminists, in her view) simply do not have a conceptual framework to explain women's oppression as a social system – hence the absence of terms such as oppression, exploitation and discrimination from the conservative lexicon. As a consequence of this limitation, conservatism is considered unable to 'support direct efforts to confront the domination of women by men' (Stacey 1983: 570). Neither can conservatives seek 'special assistance specifically for women' as this would encourage men 'to continue to think of them as in some way inferior' (Maguire 1998: 205). Similarly for some feminists, free-market feminism will be felt to leave unproblematized women and men's different resources, and unable, for example, to see a role for the state in providing or funding childcare in order to equalize resources. At the more conceptual level (Jeffries 1996), the individual so important to conservatism might be considered incoherent by some feminists. The individual is unmasked as 'male', for *he* relies upon women's labour within the traditional family. Without this, the individual (man) cannot acquire the necessary characteristics to play their role in the conservative society. Finally, it is worth stating that certain feminist positions – not least radical feminist views of the family – are themselves open to contestation by other feminist perspectives. Hence, accepting uncritically particular feminist analyses and contending that these are compatible with particular conservative principles may, itself, be reliant upon a partial and uncritical reading of feminism.[30]

It might be useful, in light of these observations, if not necessary, for analyses of conservatism and representation to draw a distinction between conservative-feminism, which can be, at least in theory, liberally feminist, and conservative representative claims which are anti-feminism, which cannot be, by definition, feminist.[31] Conservatives of the first type might not identify as feminists but they will support some definition of 'gender equality' (Dovi 2008: 154); seek to undermine rather than promote gender hierarchies (Dovi 2008: 163); or denounce a situation that is disadvantageous for women, advocate a policy to improve the situation for women or claim a right for women (Celis 2004: 3). In short, feminist-conservative representative claims for women accept some of the observations and tenets of (most probably liberal) feminism; that women and men should be treated equally for reasons of equality and justice – universal human rights; that women experience some disadvantages based on their sex and, or gender roles, as Dillard (2005) puts it. In this way, conservative feminism will likely advocate slow and cautious societal reform; recognize that perfect justice and equality cannot be achieved because of human nature; and address issues of gendered crime, women's 'cultural degradation', the problem of 'sex without commitment' and the feminization of poverty (ibid). Such concerns might constitute an agenda that is 'easier' for Conservatives to address (see also Ruiz Jimenez 2009) for they leave other relations and established hierarchies and traditions untroubled or untouched.

Another means by which conservatives in practice, in the UK at least, have sought to reconcile conservatism and feminism is through the device of offering 'choice'. This is nicely illustrated by a speech made by David Cameron in March 2006:

> Society shouldn't try to direct women...we should support the choices that mothers make for themselves...let us stop trying to tell families how to live their lives...we must combine our traditional position of support for the family with our belief in choice for everyone.

Here, prescription is rejected in favour of the privacy of the family. What individual women and men choose to do is not for others, not least 'society' and by implication government or the state, to decide. Hence, if women prefer the traditional sexual division of labour, so be it. Now for some conservatives this choice might reflect 'natural' differences (and inequalities) between women and men (Crompton and Lyonette 2005), but it need not be based on biology. Either way, the logic is clear. It is up to women to choose how to live their lives, whether that it is according to more traditional norms or not.[32] In practice, as will be discussed in Chapters 5 and 6, deploying choice might permit the development of more avowedly (liberal) feminist policies for women by individual conservative actors or parties, because it limits conservative opponents' criticism that such policies threaten the sanctity of the family and the wider established and revered societal structures and norms. Of course, some feminists may still find 'choice' insufficient. If feminism is about fundamental social change, then the offer of 'choice' to women – to opt for the traditional – may not be adequate.[33] And there may well be issues at the aggregate level. What if most women choose to stay at home? Might this have wider implications for other women's choices (by limiting their choices) perhaps, and especially, the next generation of women's choices? Indeed, the apparent squaring of the circle represented by choice might also be subject to criticism from some feminists for failing to offer a critique of the family as a site of women's oppression (even if, at the same time, it may also be a site of all sorts of other and more favourable experiences), or of failing to critique how women's unpaid domestic work leaves them economically dependent, and unable to participate equally in the public sphere.

Celis and Childs (2011) identify two approaches that might be adopted when considering conservative representative claims to act for women, regarding them, first, as part of the feminist substantive representation of women and secondly, as part of a wider economy of gendered representation. The former follows the assumption that the substantive representation of women equals the feminist substantive representation of women. Thus, when conservative representatives' claims and actions are 'feminist', conservatives would be considered to be acting 'for women'. However, this approach is dependent upon agreed criteria for judging something as feminist. This is most likely to be based on either feminist theory or women's movement demands. However, both of these are not necessarily unproblematic, given debates amongst feminists over feminist theory and the leftist orientation of many feminist movements (Celis and Childs 2011). This approach also suffers from a failure to appreciate that some conservative representatives' claims and actions might well be either explicitly or implicitly anti-feminist. In sum, this approach remains a method for studying *feminist substantive representation*. In contrast, the second approach considers conservative representatives' claims, *a priori*, on a par with feminist ones in an economy of claims for women (following Saward 2006). It provides analytic space for claims and actions that might be considered harmful to women, regressive, conservative, non-feminist or anti-feminist. The preference for this latter approach lies in the assumption that claims to act for women by conservative representatives are, by definition, gender conscious, albeit differently so, and maybe even only minimally so, or only so for instrumental reasons.[34] Nevertheless, to avoid the reductionist position (identified by Dodson and cited above, 2006: 31) this approach invites comparison between claims made by different actors. As Celis and Childs (2011) suggest, empirical research should be undertaken to establish: (1) the strength of the relationship between the claim by conservative representatives and conservative women's concerns in society; (2) correspondence between a particular claim(s) and subsequent action; and (3) how a particular claim 'fits' with other claims made at the same time by the same actor.

Applying the substantive representation of women and the constitutive representation of gender to empirical study

If bringing conservatism and conservative representatives into our studies of women's political representation challenges in some ways extant conceptual frameworks, shifting to studying 'how the substantive representation of women occurs' necessitates revised methodological frameworks. No longer is it sufficient to establish sex differences in representatives' attitudes and behaviours. In brief, whilst the presence of sex differences may constitute evidence of feminization, their absence does not necessarily prove the opposite (Childs 2008: Chapter 5). Their absence can be for a number of reasons, including but not limited, to a convergence in men and women's behaviour; the nature of the research design which might capture only one point of the legislative process;[35] and, finally, that gendered institutional norms might seriously constrain the actions of representatives (Lovenduski 2005a; Lovenduski and Norris 2003; Dodson 2006).[36] Indeed, taking feminist institutionalism seriously means acknowledging that representatives act in particular gendered institutions which must themselves be subject to analysis (Lovenduski 2005a; Krook and Mackay 2011). Political institutions are likely to be far from neutral to attempts to act for women. Political spaces are likely to be differently conducive (or 'safe') for those seeking the substantive representation of women (Reingold 2008b: 132; Yoder 1991; Krook and Mackay 2011). Distinguishing between the transformation of the political agenda (where women's concerns and perspectives are articulated) and the transformation of legislation (where policy outcomes address women's concerns and perspectives) can prove useful (Childs 2006; Franceshet 2008). It enables the acknowledgement that in some places and at some times, representatives may seek to act for women, but fail. But perhaps often more profoundly, feminist institutionalism might qualify our conclusions about the about the 'amount' and 'adequacy' of women's substantive representation. What looks like not very much may in fact be quite considerable, given the effort needed to achieve any kind of feminized change (Dodson 2006: 29; cf Childs 2008: 170).

For these reasons, Celis et al (2007) suggest a shift in research design and method in favour of process-tracing and comparison, to identify the critical actors and events that engender women's substantive representation. Rather than focusing on investigations at the macro-level (looking at what 'women' do) studies should look at the micro-level (looking at what specific actors do) (ibid). In such studies, process tracing allows the researcher to 'follow the unfolding of a particular set of policy decisions over time', identifying the actors and events that explain the particular outcome (Mazur 2002: 33). This approach is likely to reveal, to a much greater extent than before, the contextual environments in which representatives act and the wider features of particular policy making processes. A full analysis would process-trace the whole policy making process to determine whether, how, and to what effect issues and interests are taken up (Celis et al 2010: 16). This would answer, in turn, the nine questions identified above (Celis et al 2008; Lovenduski and Guadagnini 2010; Dovi 2008).[37] To address issues of accountability (Lovenduski and Guardagnini 2010) studies should also consider the relations between actors and the women they claim to represent.[38]

The newer concepts of representation as claims making and the constitutive representation of gender to-date lack clear or extensive guidance as to how one might apply them empirically. But combining this with newer approaches to substantive representation, suggests an examination of (1) 'the claims-making of representatives' in order to establish the construction of feminine identities (Squires 2008: 188–9) and (2) examining how the representatives seek to 'act for' women. To examine the latter, at least in the first instance, data might include policy statements, documents, commitments, pledges and legislation, (as in Chapters 5 and 6). Analysis of the former can be undertaken through exploring the construction of 'feminine' and 'masculine' identities and the nature of gender relations in the representative claims. Questions to be asked of representative claims might include: What is the nature of the interests claimed to be 'women's' and 'men's'? How is 'what it means to be a woman and a man' constituted? What is the acclaimed nature of the relations between women and men? Are these premised upon notions of sex- and gender-sameness or difference? Are they co-operative or conflictual, and, or hierarchical or egalitarian? The ways in which women and their interests are constructed through claims making would benefit from a distinction between women's issues and women's interests (Celis et al 2010). Women's issues refer to the 'broad policy category' of concerns whereas women's interests refer to the specific concern given to this category by various actors – this content reflect[s] and shape[s] views on who 'women' are and should be' (Celis et al 2010: 2). For example, if the women's issue area is work/life balance, women's interest may be represented as the provision of maternity leave/pay (for the mother/women) or of parental leave/pay (shared between women and men).

Given Squires' (2008) assumption that the constitutive representation of gender and the substantive representation of women are likely intertwined in practice, even if analytically distinct, it is also likely to be fruitful to compare these two facets of representation. In research that looks at more than one type of political actor (for example, Parliamentarians, civil society representatives, actors or musicians), one could explore the 'evaluation, contestation and legitimacy' of multiple representative claims, as Saward (2006: 306) suggests. Looking at a single case one can look for internal consistency. Do, for example, a particular actor's 'actions for women' map onto their claims about women's issues and interests, concerns or needs? Congruency might imply that the actions are a logical and appropriate response to the constitutive representation of gender (description of X, gives rise to critique Y, which is resolved with policy pledge Z). In turn, this might legitimize the particular representative's claims and indicate a substantive commitment to act for women. Alternatively, dissonance might suggest tensions (policy pledge Z may be in conflict with, or fail to address, either X or Y). Consequently, this might undermine the robustness and legitimacy of the constitutive representation of gender and, or signal a rhetorical rather than substantive commitment to 'act for' women (for example, X or Y might be misperceived, although policy pledge Z may also purposefully avoid substantively addressing X or Y, for any number of reasons).

Conclusion

Whether the contemporary UK Conservative party is feminized and hence better represents women cannot be established in a single snapshot. Both feminization and representation are best thought of as processes. Moreover, both concepts are more complex than everyday assumptions suggest. Any evaluation of the representation of women by political parties must take account of representation's multiple dimensions, or at least be explicit about what conception(s) of representation is being assessed. Here, it is women's descriptive and substantive representation, the latter of which includes analysis of the constitutive representation of gender.[39] In the first instance, the level of women's descriptive representation is easy to determine. You simply count the numbers of women's bodies. Parity of descriptive representation at the legislative level appears, though, very much harder to achieve in practice, as Chapters 3 and 4 suggest. In any case, it is not just the inclusion of women but the *integration* of women within the party that likely matters for substantive representation. Turning to this dimension, recent developments in feminist conceptions of representation render any simplistic suggestion that the numbers of women present in our political parties or parliaments engenders the greater substantive representation of women problematic. There is no magic in numbers (Beckwith and Cowell-Myers 2007).[40] Nevertheless, and, indeed, despite more sophisticated analytic frameworks, gender and politics scholars mostly maintain the presumption that women will be more adequately substantively represented when women representatives sit in our Parliaments. It is just that the story of how this might happen has got messier. No longer is it presumed that women's interests are homogenous and 'out there' ready to be acted on by women representatives. Institutions and wider political environments are acknowledged to matter. They may be more or less conducive to the substantive representative of women; and representatives, within and without elected political institutions, male and female, can and do make representative claims and seek to act *for* women, even if only women can make representative claims and act *as* women. Finally, and no longer either should it be assumed that the substantive representation of women equals the feminist substantive representation of women. Conservatives can and do claim and seek to act for women. Sometimes these claims might well be anti-feminist.

The possibility that anti-feminist claims for women are made by women representatives will no doubt be problematic for those seeking a feminist re-gendering of politics, or those who contend that the substantive representation of women can only ever mean the feminist substantive representation of women. It might be that observing such representation (constitutive and substantive) makes some gender and politics scholars less certain about the relationship between women's descriptive and substantive representation. Accepting as legitimate representative claims and actions for women, forthcoming when women representatives looked like a feminist vanguard (when maybe they are even ahead of women's mass opinion), might be resisted when those acting, do so in an anti-feminist fashion (Dodson 2006). At its most extreme, is the suggestion that feminists could walk away from women's descriptive representation if the women representatives turn out to be conservative or anti-feminist ones.[41] Yet, the presence of women in our political institutions matters irrespective of their attitudes and behaviour. It is something that should matter to all democrats, for simple reasons of justice and equality (Childs 2008; Phillips 1995). But what it does mean is that gender and politics scholars have to walk away from straightforward assumptions about 'what difference' women representatives make when they are present in politics.

Section II

Women's Descriptive Representation in the Conservative Party

2
Women Members and the Party's Women's Organizations

If women [are] going to have voice, they need a women's organization in some guise.[1]

The Conservative party's women members are infamous. Often praised for being the 'backbone' of the party, stuffing envelopes and making tea, they are, frequently at the same time and sometimes by the same people, parodied as the 'blue rinse brigade'. They are the party's embarrassing secret, whose demise would not be mourned. One sitting MP, asked of her views on the women's organization, put her hands up to her face and her body language shrieked 'don't ask me that question'. Party leaders too have been said to be keen, especially under William Hague's tenure (1997–2001), for the women's organization to wither. Indeed, at that time its very existence was questioned and the relationship between it and the wider party was widely acknowledged to have deteriorated. Yet, over the last five years or so, the party's various women's organizations looked to have had something of a rebirth. The Conservative Women's National Committee (CWNC) re-launched itself as the Conservative Women's Organization (CWO), with popular annual conferences, and new activities, formats, and groups: Women's Forums and Summits and the CWO Muslim group. In addition, the party Vice-Chairman for Women position was re-established (2005–2010); a Woman's Officer appointed; and a ginger group, Women2win, focused on increasing the selection of parliamentary candidates was formed. Finally, Theresa May, previously Shadow Minister for Women and Equalities, who was ultimately responsible for a policy review that formed the basis of the 'women's' part of the 2010 manifesto, became, in the coalition government, Minister for Women and Equalities, as well as Home Secretary.

These developments are perhaps surprising given that political parties are assumed to be shifting away from group representation in favour of individual representation (Young and Cross 2002; M. Russell 2005). Yet the current Conservative leadership, mindful of needing women's votes and recognizing women's campaigning capacity, had incentives to reconsider its position *vis-à-vis* the party's women's organizations, even as its primary focus was on the drive for more women parliamentary candidates. Of course, the mere existence of women's organizations within the Conservative party in the contemporary period tells us little about their function and impact, and there are concerns about the continued form that the organizations will take in the years ahead. Nor does it tell us whether the various groups are working in tandem or whether, as previously suggested, latent potential for conflict between them materializes in practice (Childs 2008). The arms-length Women2win might constitute an explicit as well as implicit criticism of, and challenge to, the CWO, for example (Childs 2008). Its founders were reacting to the failure of the party to increase the number of women MPs and candidates in the 2001–2005 Parliament – something that the CWO had been vocal about – but they were also, by their very establishment, questioning the ability of the CWO to enhance the party's supply pool of aspirant women candidates. Women2win also offered the possibility of becoming an alternative organization for Conservative women members, especially for younger ones. Given such developments, questions as to which women's organizations and actors within the contemporary Conservative party are the most powerful, both relative to the others and the mainstream part of the party, were likely to arise.

Analysis of political parties' women's organizations needs to consider two tensions or dilemmas.[2] First, the 'integration versus separation' dilemma. This questions whether women party members are best served by participating in parties' 'women's' organizations' or through mainstream organizations, posing whether separation always equals lesser, or whether it might provide a safe space for women to organize, and act as a pressure group on the party proper? (Boucek 2009). Second, the 'collective versus individual representation' dilemma: should women opt for an organizational form that seeks to substantively represent women *as women* through parties' 'women's organizations', or one that advances the participation of women *as elected representatives*? (Lovenduski 2005b) This choice might, of course, be something of a false one, with parties engaging successfully in both, as elected representatives positively coexist with the women's organization and women party members. If so, women's substantive representation may become formal and, or institutionalized with accountability being secured either formally or informally. Alternatively, elected women representatives may constitute a distinct category from women party members, with different characteristics, attitudes, motives and goals. Here any representative relationship may well be more complex and, or diffuse.

These twin dilemmas beg additional questions: what is the nature of a women's organization's aims and activities? Do they seek to substantively represent women *as women*, constituting what some call quasi-women's policy agencies? (QWPA) Or do they act as 'ladies auxiliaries' engaging in 'political housekeeping', supporting the party in a subordinate and not a 'big P' political fashion?[3] (Young 2000: 134) Historically, the UK Conservative party's women's organization has been considered an auxillary *par excellence* (Campbell 1987).[4] In contrast, QWPAs are understood in terms of the definition of Women's Policy Agencies (WPAs). According to the United Nations, these are bodies 'recognized by the Government as the institutions dealing with the promotion of the status of women' (E/CN.6/1988/3, para.21, cited in Squires 2007). In Beatrix Campbell's (1987: 283) terms one would ask: are women constituted as subjects in their own right? Are they the centre of their own conversation? Then there are questions relating to where a party's women's organization sits within the party's internal structure, and how it relates to other internal organizations. For example, how are the women's organizations officially constituted and are they well-resourced compared with other party groups? Notions of intra-party democracy are relevant too. What power do the women's organizations have, relative to the party leadership and other party organizations and bodies, and in respect of what?

It is, moreover, one thing to document the various structures for women within the contemporary UK Conservative party, and to establish how they relate to each other and how they interact with mainstream party structures. It is quite another to be able to show that they impact on party (and when the Conservatives are in power, governmental) policy making and outcomes. For example, the clearly observable shift from a more collegiate approach to developing women's policy in the earlier years of the Cameron era to one which located this more squarely within the remit of the Shadow Minister for Women, suggests that the party in public office, or more accurately women in the party in public office, have very much acquired women's policy development as their responsibility (even if this is within the terms announced by the party leadership) (see Chapter 5). In so doing, and given the informal relationships between the (shadow) Minister for Women and women party members and their representatives, this suggests only diffuse influence and accountability, at best. Over and above this, the nature of the relationship between the women's policy process and the wider party structures and processes, as well as the broader political/electoral environment, provides the immediate context within which women's policy, as defined by the Women's Minister might translate into party and government policy.

Women's organizations in the 20th century Conservative party

The Conservative party was the first political organization in the UK to give women a major role (Maguire 1998). In the first half of the 20th century women were separately organized, with local and regional women's sections. With integration more in vogue after the Second World War the women's branches were abolished and by the 1960s 'women's constituency advisory committees' were famed for the provision of 'food and drink' provided at social events and for election campaigning (Maguire 1998: 140–1; Kittilson

2006: 78). There was, though, also a tradition of collective representation of women, with a Vice Chairman responsible for women; an Annual Women's Conference; and women's Committees at the regional and national level. However, it was not until Edward Heath's modernizing leadership in the late 1960s that demands for the integration of women's concerns were more accepted. Like Cameron, improving the party's image with women was recognized as means to signal modernization and win women's, especially middle class, professional women's votes (Maguire 1998: 120–2, 137; Lovenduski 2005a: 60). A new Committee of Women's Rights was established in 1973. From 1975 to 1990, the Conservative party was famously led by Margaret Thatcher. Although her impact on women's participation and representation in the wider party is, unfortunately, under-researched, it can be said with some confidence that her era did not witness a blossoming of women's representation (descriptive or substantive) in the party.

Relations between the party's women's organization and the national leadership in the more recent past are widely regarded as poor. Specifically, the 1997–2001 period saw the organization downgraded. Hague's reforms to party organization provided an opportunity to exclude CWO representatives: the CWO 'may' be, but did not have to, be included on all of the mainstream voluntary committees at regional and constituency levels. In some cases pressure was put on Conservative Women Constituency Committees to close down. The CWO, along with party's youth organization Conservative Future, was also repeatedly denied representation on the Party Board. The reason given was this was already of optimum size, despite the fact it was later expanded to include three extra MPs.[5] By the time of the 2005 general election, the women's organization felt itself ignored by the then party leader, Michael Howard. This was despite the fact that under the chairmanship of Pamela Parker the organization had developed comprehensive analysis of how the party should reach out to women voters.[6] Knowing the kinds of policies they wanted[7] they had made presentations to that effect to the party leadership, in the form of the then party chairman Liam Fox, and had meetings with those with responsibility for women. A post-election report restated the call for policies on care packages for the elderly, childcare, maternity, valuing carers, improving pensions and championing equal pay and equal opportunities.[8] In a letter Parker wrote to Howard in November 2005, the chairman's sentiment is baldly stated:

> As national chairman of the Women's Organization we submitted in March 2004 a comprehensive study on the value of the women's vote. Maybe if the party had taken on board our recommendations we would have seen more Conservative MPs elected?...I apologise to sound so absolute but the party has ignored our recommendations for far too long.

The Conservative women's organization today: mission and structures

The CWO exists to assist the Conservative party by:

> Providing a focus for women of all ages, all backgrounds and from all parts of the country within the Conservative party; encouraging and enabling women to participate and stand for office at all levels of the Conservative party, Government and public appointments [through training]; ensuring that party policy takes women's views into account; helping the Conservative party regain the women's vote; making the Conservative Women's Organisation relevant and valued in today's political climate.[9]

Its mission statement is, then, multifaceted: to deliver women's political participation within and for the party; to win women's votes; to impact on policy; and to 'be relevant'. These aims stand as clear indicators against which its organization, effort and impact can be assessed. The CWO leadership is confident. Their entry to the party's 2007 National Excellence Awards, Membership and Affiliation, reads:

> We have fundamentally changed the image of the organization – the CWO is now seen as more approachable, consisting of pro-active women, who do not stand back from any debate, but, on the contrary, are eager to discuss matters of moment, and to highlight and campaign on critical issues, bringing them to public notice.

Membership of the CWO is automatic for women members of the Conservative party. With Conservative party membership estimated to be 60 percent male: 40 percent female this would imply somewhere between 70 000 and 100 000 CWO members – a figure less than half the numbers of twenty years ago.[10] (Overall party member numbers are estimated to be between 250 000 and 200 000, although some suggest membership may be as low as 180 000.)[11] The CWO regularly corresponds in a two-way communication with some 4,000 members,[12] although the leadership prefer to measure member and supporter activism, for example attendance at various events or website activity. Organizationally, Conservative Women Constituency Committees (CWCC) operate at the constituency level, although again there are no central figures on the total number of CWCCs across the country.[13] It is the case, however, that not all constituencies have them. CWCCs are connected upwards into Areas and then the 12 Party Regions. All the Regional Chairmen have, since 2008, been instructed to include the CWO on their committees and, within their Regions, to ask the Area and constituency committees to do likewise, although it was expected to take time to ensure that Constituency Chairmen include CWO representatives and their views. The Executive Committee of the CWO is made up of its Regional Chairman, plus two deputies/ representatives from each region, Officers of the CWO and Co-opted members. The Constitution says that the EC must meet three times a year.

Formally, the CWO links with the mainstream party through the National Convention, which is composed of Constituency Chairman, Regional Chairman, Chairman of Conservative Future and Chairman of the CWO, and other representatives. Currently the CWO has 42 places out of over 800. These are filled by both CWO Officers and Co-optees. The CWO Chairman also sits on the Convention strategy team, which consists of all the senior members of the voluntary party, *ex officio* (Regional Chairman and Chairman of CWO and Conservative Future, and Chairman of Councillors). Critics contend, however, that the Convention is too large to constitute a robust discussion body. The CWO is not directly represented on the Conservative's Board, the party's 'ultimate decision making body'.[14] Fiona Hodgson, ex-Chairman of the CWO is currently on the Board, but she is not a there as a representative of the CWO, and nor is she the formal 'point of contact' for CWO – arguably, a missed opportunity by the Party to institutionalize CWO input.[15] In her appeal for votes, Hodgson did draw attention to the small numbers of women elected to the Board, thereby making sex and gender part of her manifesto, though this is in no way an institutionalized relationship, with any attendant accountability.

Resource wise, the CWO is the only part of the voluntary Conservative party that is a national organization which is self-funding.[16] Fundraising pays for two part-time employees. All other work is undertaken by volunteers. Expenses are not reimbursed.[17] Admittedly, the organization is provided with resources in kind from the centre, something that is said not always to be fully appreciated, as one party worker put it. This includes office space (the CWO 'desk' at CCHQ was removed under Hague and reinstated in 2002), administrative support, IT, postage, printing, and branding.[18] Even so, and despite recognizing that the receipt of resources might come with strings attached, the CWO leadership sees benefit in an administrator to work with the regions, and, or a researcher, to help draft speeches and write briefing papers. As one of its Chairmen put it, 'it really would be nice not to be constantly looking over our shoulders as to how we can move the organization on, because we've got to have the finance to do it'. The CWO Chairman would also benefit from having a parliamentary pass, if not for symbolic reasons, for reasons of efficiency in organizing events at Westminster.[19]

At the national level the CWO hosts its own Annual Conferences and AGMs, holds fringe meetings at the annual party Conference, and engages in various fundraising activities, not least the annual 'Blue ribbon' dinner, as well as more recently holding Women's Forums, Summits and Muslim

Group Forums. In addition to these, information is sought from the CWO members through feedback from the Regions via the local CWO Chairman, and more directly through member questionnaires, the latter of which elicit variable response rates. The organization is supported by a website, email and an online forum. Under the Chairmanship of Fiona Hodgson (2005–2008), the CWO consciously ramped up its central activities, building on her predecessor's efforts to focus the organization more on policy.[20] In March 2006 a trip to visit the Republican Party in the US energized the CWO leadership. David Cameron's call to reach out beyond the party was also enthusiastically embraced, and in 2008 the CWO leadership attended a UN meeting on the Commission on the Status of Women.

In recognition of the CWO's 'rather tired' image and in an attempt to attract younger and working women, as well as women from 'a full range of ethnic backgrounds', the CWO established the new Women's Summits and Women's Forums, and the CWO Muslim Women's group. These groups' events would be open to women 'who had not previously been involved with, or interested in politics' and where not necessarily members of the Party.[21] Other recent developments include the establishment of a University branch at the University of Essex. Less traditional fundraising activities designed to attract younger members, included a Rolling Stones tribute band gig, a joint Summer Party with Conservative Future in 2006, and a fashion show in Edinburgh.[22] Most importantly, during the 2000s CWO Annual Conferences – the organization's most high profile activity – went from a relatively weak and marginalized position to one that, in 2007, reportedly impressed Cameron's team. The Conference filled the big hall of the Queen Elizabeth II conference centre and Cameron made the key note speech.

In addition to expanding its activities, the CWO has, since 2005, although building on the efforts of its previous Chairman, purposefully sought to consider much more extensively policy and set out to address 'edgier' issues 'previously untouched by CWO'.[23] This takes place at the annual conferences, Women's Forums and Summits, and to a lesser extent (in terms of the number of members participating) in the organization's AGMs. The programme for the CWO annual conferences and AGMs is devised by the CWO Chairman and Officers (see Table 2.1 and 2.2). Note that the observation of 1980s women's conferences as ones 'largely addressed by men' (Campbell 1987: 294) no longer holds.[24] The conferences conform to a 'top-down education' model (M. Russell 2005). Whilst there is some opportunity for 'Q&A' sessions, the overarching structure is one of information-giving rather than information-gathering. In the absence of formal resolutions, accountability to the membership occurs through the election of CWO Officers.

Turning to the first of the new innovations, *Women's Summits* adopt a workshop/conference format and engage with outside organizations (Table 2.3). They again reflect efforts by the CWO to reach out beyond its normal party

Table 2.1   CWO Annual Conferences 2005–2010

Year	Topics	Women: Men speakers	Attendees
2005	Leadership contenders; Drugs and youth; Equality	7:3	200[25]
2006	International Women's Human Rights; Successful Women, Supporting British Food & Farming	7:5	300
2007	Africa; Environment; Women as Peacemakers; European Parliament report; Iain Dale Interview	9:5	700[26]
2008	Cycle of Life – the third age; the balancing act; Iain Dale Interview	7:7	350[27]
2009	What Women Want; Iain Dale interview with Eric Pickles	3:4[28]	350[29]
2010	Stepping up to the Challenge	9:1	180[30]

Table 2.2   CWO AGMs 2006–2010

Year	Topics	Women: Men speakers	Attendees[31]
2006	Conservative women go green; new intake of MPs; Environment	5:5	c80
2007	Nurturing the next Generation	6:2	c75
2008	Tackling Violence Against women 'mini conference'	10:1	c80
2009	Entrepreneurs or Political Dinosaurs	4:1	60
2010	The Blight of Boozing Britain	n/a	55

members. Summits take place during the day and include 'groups from all sectors of the community'.[32] The aim is to bring in organizations with expertise in a specific policy area, to explore the 'female perspective' and ensure that this view is 'imparted to senior members of the party'.[33] The 'sixth form summits' for young women are designed to show, through talks with women MPs, what it is like to be an MP, and the various routes into parliament taken by different women MPs. They seek, furthermore, to 'plant the seed of the idea' of participating in politics.

Conservative Women's Forums (CWF) were, as noted above, established in recognition of the ageing membership of the CWO and the changing work/life patterns of women in their late 20s and 30s. Such women are felt

Table 2.3 CWO Women's Summits 2006–2010

Year	Topics	Women: Men speakers
2006	Children	4:1
2006	Charity	2:3
2007	Stalking	6:0
2007	Pensions	2:3
2007	Sixth Form Students[34]	4:0
2008	Prostitution	8:1

to be less likely to be involved full time in the party because of childcare and paid employment responsibilities, and are perceived generally to have less 'inclination' to join formal organizations.[35] Forums would, then, be a new means of connecting with 'busy' and 'time poor' women. They are held on weekday evenings (6pm–8pm, to be compatible with women coming straight from work), mostly in or around Westminster, and usually open with a short presentation by a Shadow Minister and a spokesperson from a relevant pressure group or interested party (see Table 2.4). Women PPCs, women MPs and MPs with relevant portfolios are also invited. Questions and contributions are subsequently taken from the floor. Meetings last approximately two hours. Refreshments are provided and time for networking scheduled in so as to make women 'feel welcome' and show that they party is 'friendly, accessible and caring'.[36] Recall that Forums are open to those who are not party members. On the basis of observing six Forums (2008–2010), attendee numbers range between 10 and 18. Mostly these are women, with a mix of older and younger ones, although with more of the former. Few BME women attended all but one of the observed Forums, with BME men attending Forums on Iraq and gangs.

A CWO steering group was established to identify topics for both Forums and Summits although on occasion Theresa May, as (then) Shadow Minister for Women and Equality and Margot James as (then) VC for Women, asked the CWO to address a particular issue, for example May's request for a Summit on prostitution. Each Forum and Summit is reported back to the departmental teams, via written minutes of the meeting and often through recordings of the event. Senior CWO members report that front bench spokespersons rate the quality of the discussions:[37] The Chairman also claims to disseminate Forum discussions via the talks she gives at regional AGMs and meetings.

The Conservative *Women's Muslim Group* was set up to 'promote greater dialogue and understanding between Muslim and non-Muslim women and to dispel some of the 'myths and misconceptions' that exist in the post

Table 2.4   CWO Women's Forum Panels 2006–2010

Year	Topics	Women: Men speakers	Attendees[38]
2006	Constitutional law reform	1:2	31
	Work and families bill	2:0	28
	Childcare bill	1:1	36
	Violent crime bill	1:1	41
	Education bill	0:2	33
	NHS and hospital closures/health	0:1	c25
	Local govt and communities	1:0	c30
2007	Meet the minister – Andrew Mitchell – International development	1:1	33
	Vision for G7 and EU Transatlantic agreement	0:2	n/a
	Environment	1:2	26
	Cyber-bulling	2:1	22
	Women as entrepreneurs	3:1	c20
2008	Iraq and Afghanistan...and those left behind	2:1	14 women, 2 BME, 2 men[39]
	Women and Taxation	2:1	10, all women, mostly 20s/30s, couple 60+, two BME[40]
	Oxfam	1:0	18
	Disarming Gang Culture	1:2	14, 3 men, of whom 1 BME man and 2 BME women[41]
	Funding the Arts	1:2	21 all female
	Universities – A good investment?	0:3	18 women, of whom 6 older, 3 BME; 3 men (young)[42]
2009	Women and sport		25 female & 1 male
	Social cohesion	0:4	14 women, 2 BME women[43]
	Conference fringe event with Oxfam	3:2	15 women
	Women and Debt, with YWCA and CAP	2:1	15 women
2010	Building Relationships: Understanding the generational Impact of Trauma	3:1	12, all white, one disabled, two men, two or three younger women in 20s
	Meeting new women MPs	7:0	32 female audience

'September 11' and '7/7' environment.[44] It was disbanded in late summer 2010. The Group's origins lie in the fore mentioned CWO trip to Washington where at one reception there were women from Iraq and Afghanistan: 'It made us realise that one of the biggest tensions in the world today is between the West and the Muslim World'.[45] Baroness Warsi, since the 2010 general election the first Muslim woman Cabinet Minister, was critical to getting the idea of such a group off the ground. At the first meeting it was evident, at least to one member, that 'they [CWO] really didn't know what to expect or what would come out of our mouths and perhaps it was the same on our side'.[46] The organization was co-chaired, pointedly, by a Muslim woman, Dr Shazia Ovaisi, alongside Fiona Hodgson, the CWO ex-Chairman.[47] Membership was restricted to Conservative party members, but, like CWO Forums, anyone could attend CWO Muslim group events.[48] Observations of a number of events between 2008–2010 show that attendance numbered between 45–70, on most occasions, with women dominating, and with a more ethnically mixed audience than other CWO WF events – mostly half and half Black and Minority Ethnic (BME) and white. Some meetings, especially those discussing extremism and those not explicitly gendered, looked to be attended by larger numbers of Asian men. On occasions, male invited speakers including male front bench spokespersons, did not always gender their presentations even when topics were themselves explicitly gendered. Sometimes male audience members dominated discussions.

Table 2.5 CWO Muslim Women's Group 2007–2010

Year	Topics	Women: Men speakers	Attendees[49]
2007	Marriage – A woman's Choice	3:1	45 – mostly women – mainly BME
2007	Honour Killings and Violence against Women	5:1	48 – predominately women – mainly BME
2008	Future of Pakistan	2:5	50+, slightly more men than women; mainly BME[50]
2008	Challenge of Extremism	3:1	50, 50:50 women men, mostly BME, handful white women[51]
2009	Female Face of Afghanistan	1:2	60–70; 80% women, 50%+ BME[52]; fewer BME men
2010	Inter faith dialogue	2:3	45; 9 men, of which 4 BME; women 50:50 BME[53]

All CWO Muslim Group Forums took place in London. The group received some administrative support from the CWO, but its organizers were all volunteers, and again like the CWO proper, expenses were not met by the party. Attendance at party Conference was also at their cost. In terms of impact Muslim Group officers talk about the party being 'more sensitive to listening' than in the past, believing that a 'subtle message' was getting through that 'we're not all a bunch of, you know, extremists'. MPs who attended events were claimed to be impressed by the audience diversity. However, the CWO Muslim Group did not seek out a more high profile role amongst the party in the country or in the media. In part this reflected the voluntary nature of the group.

As indicated above the CWO Muslim Group was short-lived. Following what are considered to have been a series of successful meetings on particular topics (see Table 2.5 above), the CWO leadership decided to seek to engage a wider range of minority groups and operate 'without specific labelling' which they felt might be seen as 'exclusive of other faiths and other minority groups'. In other words, they preferred to 'mainstream'[54] the Group's activities. Some CWO members and regional chairman were reportedly less than sympathetic[55] to the group. Given that the Muslim Group was not formally established these changes were easily implemented, but for those critical of its abolition, there is ill-feeling that the group had perhaps been regarded by the party leadership as merely of a symbolic rather than substantive nature – created for reasons of political expedience and something that could be dropped once the 2010 election was over. There are also concerns that mainstreaming will dilute its focus and activities.

A revitalized organization?

Nearly ten years on from fears of abolition, the CWO has showed itself capable of renewal in terms of both membership and activity. In its view new and non-traditional CWO issues were part of its agenda, and its discussions offered substantive insights on policy concerns. The organization also claimed to have made greater connections with non-Conservative women and women's groups. More specifically, on the plus side of the balance sheet for the period until 2010 are, then: (1) higher attendance at the CWO annual conferences, compared with the dark days of the late 1990s and early 2000s; (2) the innovations of Forums and Summits, which were particularly extensive in the mid years of the 2005–10 parliament, when policy was being reviewed; (3) increased website hits – an indicator of larger engagement with the organization, even if internet supporters do not physically attend CWO events; (4) a centrally stronger organization; (5) a new group for women in small enterprises, 'C-Wise' established in autumn 2010; (6) demonstrable, if arguably symbolic, party leadership support with for example, Cameron attending its annual conferences and

the Blue Ribbon Dinner (the latter a year after he had cancelled his attendance at the last minute); and (7) and a development programme, designed
to help those considering standing for public office at any level, inaugurated
in September 2010. On the negative side, concerns include: (1) smaller,
post-2007 conferences – a decline which is explained by the CWO leadership as reflecting a decision to hold more fringe meetings at the Party Conference and to move the Women's Conference to a smaller, more affordable,
venue. There may also be issues of lesser diversity in the more recent years;[56]
(2) limited attendance at Women's Forum, relative to the size of the CWO
itself, with only a few occurring in the regions; (3) a decline in the number
of Summits in more recent years, though this may reflect the election cycle,
as the party moved from policy review to campaigning; (4) broader concerns about the regional organization, not least, the quality of regional
chairman and appreciation that new CWO members are less likely to work
through the regional structures. Note, the CWO leadership consider this a
reflection of the decline of voluntary political participation in the UK more
generally; (5) continuing concerns about funding; and (6) concerns, at least,
from some quarters of the CWO about the abolition of the Muslim Group.

One consequence of the recent transformation of the CWO structures
looks to have been the mobilization of a 'third' type of Conservative woman
– the 'missing generation' as a leading CWO member put it (see also Tessa
Keswick 2000: 9; Maguire 1998: 205). She is likely to be in her mid-40s,
London-based, in paid employment and more interested in issues than in
being an elected representative. She is, in short, neither the traditional Tory
Lady, nor (as yet) the aspirant Parliamentarian. But she is keen on issues
rather than socializing – a school gate politician – and wants to attend
Forums and talk 'big P' politics. If her present existence is not in doubt, it
is not yet clear how numerous she is, and in what ways she might relate
to the two other types of Conservative party woman. She may look to be
more similar in profile to the elected representatives, and might have little
interest in joining the CWO of old, fearful of being shunted off into the
sidelines. The CWO considers her, though, one of theirs.

Meanwhile, the traditional Tory lady demands the continuation of her
coffee mornings and lunch clubs. Such is the reverence accorded her by
CWO leaders, alongside a belief in the party being a 'broad church', that
there is no talk of curtailing her activities. Forums, like other activities for
the third type, are to be 'bolt[ed] on' to traditional CWO activities; this is
to keep the older ladies 'on board', as one CWO Chairman put it. The traditional CWO woman does not, however, always feel valued and she is not
backward in saying so. Observations of CWO annual conferences reveal
such women raising criticism of what they apparently perceive as feminist
(and in their view, problematic) perspectives being articulated by women
Parliamentarians, CWO Officers, and other speakers. This is true in respect
of the role of mothers, paid work, women parliamentary candidates, and the

CWO's focus on international development and violence against women, the latter of which is felt not to impact on 'women like us'.[57] Whilst not representative, the following, have been overheard. At one conference a woman said, 'sorry girls' as she praised the married man's tax allowance.[58] Another disagreed with flexible working. She was a small business owner and a single mother. A third said she did not feel deprived of a career because she did not work and accused the [CWO] conference of making her feel like she had failed. Yet another claimed that, at the party Conference in Blackpool in 2008, women who stay at home were 'almost booed out of room as old fashioned'. There was only a single 'hear hear' when Theresa May's retort centred on women making choices about whether to work or not. Another woman (sitting next to one of the authors at the 2007 CWO conference) failed to understand why Africa was being discussed as the first item on a CWO conference agenda when she considered it more suited to an 'afternoon slot'.[59]

Party member views

Drawing on a specially commissioned survey of party members (see Chapter 4), we can gain insight into the attitudes and activities of CWO members. First, notwithstanding the claim that technically all female party members are automatically members of the CWO, very few actually seem to be aware of the fact. Only 1.7 percent of our respondents claimed to be members of the CWO (3.7 percent of women and 0.3 percent of men). CWO members are overwhelmingly middle class (even more so than the party membership as a whole) with 83 percent coming from social grades AB and C1, with a third being graduates (slightly higher than for the membership as a whole). The average age of CWO members is 56, which is almost identical to that of the membership in general. However, CWO members are far more likely to be committed party activists than non-members if self-reported devotion to party work can be relied upon: some 57.7 percent of CWO members claim to work for upward of six hours a month on average on behalf of the party, compared to just 16.7 percent of non-CWO members.

Attitudinally, CWO members are a little less likely to regard themselves as right-wing than non-members are; when asked to place themselves on a scale running from 1 (very left wing) to 7 (very right-wing), the mean score for CWO members is 4.96 compared to 5.33 for non-CWO members. This difference is statistically significant at the 10 percent level (sig = 0.08), and may well reflect the fact that – as we shall see in Chapter 5 women Conservatives are generally not so right-wing as their male counterparts. In that chapter we provide a detailed analysis of the political attitudes of party members which takes into account their scores on a series of attitudinal scales designed to measure their positions not only in left-right terms, but also in terms of social liberalism/authoritarianism, post-materialism/ materialism, European integration, feminism, and the descriptive and substantive representation of women. By most of these criteria, there are no significant differences between the mean locations of CWO members and other party members. The only areas of significant (though not great) difference are on Europe (CWO members are slightly less hostile than nonmembers, but even so they remain broadly Eurosceptic) and the descriptive representation of women. The latter is the most interesting from our point of view, for the mean position of CWO members on the 'selectreform' scale (see Chapter 7 for details of how this is constructed) is 2.97 compared to 3.29 for non-CWO members, a difference that is statistically significant at the 5 percent level (sig = 0.03). Again, this greater propensity to support measures designed to enhance the descriptive representation of women in politics may simply be explained by the fact that the CWO's membership is overwhelmingly female.

Interestingly, CWO members are significantly more likely to feel that their organization plays an important part in the life of the party. Specifically, in response to the statement 'The Conservative Women's Organization plays an important policy role in the party', some 55.5 percent of CWO members agreed, compared to just 36.2 percent of non-CWO members. This does not simply reflect the fact of the CWO's female profile, for there are no significant differences between men and women party members generally to this question; therefore, it seems to be that only those (very few) who are committed enough to the CWO to be conscious that they are members of it see its impact in positive terms. Similarly, CWO members are much more likely than nonmembers to feel that 'The Conservative party should produce a 'women's manifesto' at the next general election'; some 41.3 percent of them agreed with this proposition, compared to just 5.8 percent of non-CWO members.

CWO relations with the mainstream party

Relations between the CWO and the wider Conservative party have, as widely acknowledged, not been smooth in recent decades. This was especially true of Hague's period as leader, which saw the appointment of Peta Buscombe as Vice-Chairman for Women, and when the women's organization very much fell out of favour. Briefly, Buscombe dropped 'women' from her Vice-Chairmanship title and sought the mainstreaming of women's representation in the party (Bale 2010: 76). This met with resistance from the women's organization (ibid) who felt abandoned and lacking a champion amongst the party hierarchy – something they had considered as an important integrating role that, in their view, a previous Vice Chairman for women, Lady Seccombe, had successfully played for a decade. Subsequently, CWO Chairman decided to stand their ground *vis-à-vis* the mainstream party and this has given rise to accusations of them roughing up people

– of being 'difficult'. Such commentary, which may well come from critics who have their own personal and political reasons to state them, might warrant further qualification. It smacks somewhat of those who do not care for 'uppity' women. It also looks to mask territorial battles between those responsible for women within the party as well as wider debates about intra-party democracy; that the voluntary party is, in the eyes of the party in public office, much less controllable than the latter might hope for. According to the CWO leadership their role is to represent and advance their organization, even as they support the party leadership (Childs 2008). Either way, bridges needed to be re-built – and there is some confidence on the CWO's behalf that this has begun to be achieved. The turning point, as already mentioned, is felt to have been the 2007 CWO annual conference when the numbers of attendees were significantly higher than in previous years. This was one reminder to Cameron and his team that he must not 'forget the women'. Beyond the leader, greater numbers of MPs 'than ever before' are claimed to speak at CWO events. Annual newsletters are produced to improve links with the parliamentary party and under Hodgson 'CWO Champions' amongst Parliamentary members were established as an explicit means to better link the voluntary and the parliamentary party together.[60] Visits to the European parliament were also undertaken; and the CWO worked 'more closely' with 'the Shadow Minister for Women, the Candidates' Department, the Candidates' Association, the Convention and the European Union of Women and Conservative Future'.[61] Speakers for CWO events were said to be forthcoming, as a sign of the organization's importance; and finally, relations with local Chairman are said to have improved, albeit patchily so, with work still to be done.

Direct CWO impact on party policy is much harder to deduce, although admittedly their impact on women's policy and relations with others responsible for women and women's issues looks to have been greater than in the preceding period (the content of the party's policies 'for' women is addressed in Chapter 5). Party spokespersons attend and participate in CWO activities. And, as already noted, it is said that they are impressed with the issues discussed at the various events and take away with them insights gained from CWO speakers and audience comments. But this is all rather nebulous. There is little evidence from *observing* CWO events that Ministers not explicitly responsible for 'women's policy' are integrating CWO perspectives into their briefs.[62] Take one CWO Forum, for example, where a male front bench spokesman considered the financial abuse of women to be a matter for Theresa May, the then Shadow Minister for Women, and not for his team. A response which gave rise to the CWO Chairman stating that such issues 'shouldn't be left to just May'.[63] Admittedly this is only one example, but it suggests (along with evidence put forward elsewhere in this chapter and, indeed, in later chapters) that the party has a long way to go before women's perspectives are fully integrated across the board, and that where this happens it reflects CWO input. Similarly, the influence of the CWO Muslim Group on the mainstream party was only ever diffuse and likely limited in direct policy outcome terms (although the Group would no doubt see their main role as educative, for CWO members, first and foremost). Discussions, for example, were had with Dame Pauline Neville-Jones as part of the policy review process, back in 2007/8, and this, they believe, *may* have fed into her report. But there was no discussion with officers of the Group in respect of the 2010 Manifesto, either in terms of security and social cohesion, or with regard to social exclusion, two obvious areas where the Group would have had something to say.

Parliamentarians' attitudes towards the CWO: Observation of recent CWO annual conferences suggests it is sometimes the case that senior members of the party and elected Members often prefer to treat CWO members as 'cake bakers' who require stroking, rather than dealing with the CWO as the organized voice of women in the party. Illustrative examples include Richard Ashworth MEP who stated, confidently: 'I know I can count on your support [for the European Parliament elections]; Steven Norris, who announced that he was grateful as an ex-MP, to have been given the chance to 'see [a] friendly face, [and] get half decent cup of tea'; and ex-Party leader William Hague who commended the audience for looking 'more intelligent' than the House of Commons. Systematic interviews with Parliamentarians from the 2005 Parliament reveal that MPs and Peers both value *and* question the CWO's campaigning and fundraising contributions; query its very existence, on the basis that it is anachronistic; and for women members, reveal ambivalence if not antipathy towards the organization.

The role of the CWO in campaigning and fundraising, its role as the 'backbone of the party', is widely acknowledged by Parliamentarians, although a few male MPs and Peers question its importance. Two male Peers, with extensive and senior party organization experience, explicitly query just how key it is organizationally, and how much funds it brings in. Indeed, one of them accuses the CWO of having an inflated sense of its own importance. Wider ambivalence about the organization is manifest in terms of whether the CWO is simply a hang-over from an earlier era: 'I am not sure I'd apply euthanasia but I certainly wouldn't imply enthusiasm', is how one younger male MP puts it. For some CWO activities are considered 'harmless' and something to be indifferent about. Others see it as 'a bit of a nightmare' which should be left to 'wither'. One woman called it, 'our little secret' which would be more damaging to the party's reputation if the public were really aware of it. While the organization might offer a potential resource if only the CWO forwent their 'old-fashioned style', there is almost no appetite for reviving the organization, even if that means leaving the party without 'envelope stuffers'. For most Parliamentarians, then, the CWO has a 'Do Not Resuscitate' notice hanging around its neck.

Under David Cameron's leadership, there is, contradictorily, some agreement, even if only amongst a small number of mostly women Parliamentarians, that the CWO has been brought back into the fold somewhat.[64] They see it as being now 'more serious' in its outlook and professional, with women who 'really know their stuff' addressing 'surprising' policy issues like domestic violence and people trafficking. In such accounts May and Caroline Spelman are identified by two male MPs, one with extensive party experience, as those who effected this change, with CWO input institutionalized via Oliver Letwin acting as Cameron's policy coordinator. In this view, the organization constitutes a 'voice' for women in the party even if it is not a policy developing body. A distinction between the CWO in the country and the CWO leadership, who might be considered 'big P' actors, is also drawn by a few women MPs. Hodgson's role as CWO Chairman is identified positively in this respect by the same two male MPs cited above, although one woman MP is more critical. The prognosis for the CWO is, however, according to Parliamentarians, limited. Younger and women new to the party are more likely to seek to join the party proper, avoiding what they would consider marginalization. In any case, at least in the views of three women Peers, younger women do not have the time – because they are likely to be in paid employment – to participate in day-time CWO events.

If the broad views of the CWO by Parliamentarians show mostly little difference by sex or by House, there is a unique contribution to considerations of the CWO by women MPs and women Peers, especially those who are ex-MPs. This has three dimensions. First, four women note that the CWO supported them both as parliamentary candidates and as MPs, suggesting that the organization can offer a resource to would be and elected women representatives. Second, and indicating some kind of reciprocal relationship, a couple of women recounted attending CWO lunches and conferences, thereby showing their support for the organization. And it is clear, observing various CWO events, that more women MPs do attend these events, not least as speakers at CWO annual conferences. Even so – and third – is an apparent personal and political distancing from, if not critique of, the CWO in play amongst some women Parliamentarians. This reveals tensions between the organization and parliamentary women:

> I haven't waged war, I haven't said 'buzz off', and occasionally I go and speak to them and my heart sinks...I do slightly resent it.

In turn, this reflects a perception that the CWO has an image problem and that its members disapprove of working women. The CWO is said to attract the kind of 'women I run a mile from', such as women 'who voted against women in Synod'; who are more interested in the 'raffle' than politics; and who fail to appreciate the 'practical implications, life-threatening' effect that rape has on women. Attending a CWO annual conference is, accordingly, something that is considered by some to be an obligation. Perceptions like these on behalf of women representatives are likely to disrupt relations of representation between women party members and women in Parliament and government. And it is not that these views come from those identifiable as the Conservative party's gender equality activists. Only one of these women MPs belongs to the group of Conservative women MPs most publicly associated with gender equality issues.

The Conservative Party's Women's Officer. Introduced by then party Chairman Francis Maude this, innovative for the Conservative party, part-time post had a chequered history.[65] Liz St Clair, as Women's Officer, shifted from assisting the CWO as part of her job, to working more closely with May (which is said to have disrupted relations with the CWO), and back again to working more closely with the CWO. Her focus similarly shifted overtime, from policy in the earlier years (hence the move to working with May), to outreach and external relations in the middle years, then more towards campaigning pre-election. Crucially, the Women's Officer was not an independent actor for women within the party and she had no role in advising on the general election campaign or in gender proofing the 2010 Manifesto. As is made clear below, policy had by then become the responsibility of the Shadow Minister for Women, and there were those in the latter's team who had reservations about devolving responsibilities to the Women's Officer.

The Vice-Chairman for Women. The position of Vice-Chairman for Women, accountable to the party Chairman, was revived in December 2005. A voluntary and part-time job, she would regularly meet the Party Chairman. Whilst in the past, the Vice Chairman for Women saw herself as a 'standard bearer' for women in the party and worked very closely with the CWO, ensuring links with central office in particular,[66] the most recent holder of the post, Margot James (MP for Stourbridge since May 2010), was responsible for building up relations with women's organizations and women *beyond* party members, supported by the Women's Officer. She was, being a parliamentary candidate, also much less involved in political recruitment than previously. Associated pressure on her time was felt to be one reason for the less than close workings of with the CWO during the mid-years of the 2005 Parliament, although there may well have been issues, once again, over division of responsibilities. Subsequently relations were said to have improved, although post-election, the position of VC for Women lapsed.

Relations between the CWO and Women2win – another key area of interest for Theresa May – looked by 2010 to have come through a somewhat rocky stage. This reflects a clearer demarcation between the responsibilities of Women2win, which is specifically focused on *parliamentary* candidate selection and training, and the CWO who regard themselves as concerned with developing women 'for election or appointment to public positions at all levels but with a particular emphasis on the phase *up to* selection at the Parliamentary assessment board'.[67] In understanding the relationship between the CWO, the Shadow Minister and Women2win, issues of territory again come to the fore. Some in the CWO leadership felt that Women2win might have made it easier for them to attract *as CWO members* those women who attended Women2win events, but who subsequently realized that Parliament was not for them. In addition, Women2win had some troubles of its own. Despite its high profile launch and status, strong leadership support, and positive recognition for its activities in supporting women PPCs by, amongst others, newly elected women MPs (Childs 2008), it is recognized by those close enough to know, that it lost momentum mid way through the 2005 Parliament. With one of its leading founders, Anne Jenkin, departed, and under the leadership of Lorraine Fulbrook, who was herself a parliamentary candidate, the organization, at best, stagnated. One leading member further lamented that despite its hard work, the percentage of women coming forward as aspirant parliamentary candidates was still only around 25 percent. For the future, there is recognition internally that Women2win's approach has to be more focused on women who are 'definitely interested' in a parliamentary career, rather than spreading the support too widely on those who show a more generalized interest in the party. There is, crucially though, no drawing back by its key supporters from the absolute recognition of the importance of a slightly removed organization pressuring the party on women's political recruitment (see Chapter 3) and supporting women aspirant candidates. In effect what is being argued here, and claimed to be appreciated by the party's candidates' team, is that Women2win can provide support for women candidates in ways that the candidates' team cannot, given their duty of care to *all* candidates.

The CWO and the (Shadow) Minister for Women and Policy. If, under Hodgson, policy was more central to CWO activities, in part reflecting her predecessor's criticism of the failure of the party at the 2005 general election to present women friendly policies and target women voters, policy making ultimately shifted to the Shadow Minister as the 2010 election approached. The Women's Policy Group had been established under May's predecessor, Eleanor Laing, and brought together, amongst others, the Vice Chairman for Women and the CWO Chairman. Input from CWO Women's Forums and Summits would feed into the *Women in the World Today (WIWT)* Report, published in Spring 2008 (and discussed in full in Chapter 5). Yet with May's appointment as Shadow Minister, CWO contributions apparently reduced. *WIWT* includes very few references to their efforts. May evidently sought to lead on women's policy, with a clear shift away from policy development as a more collective endeavour. Sure the Women's Policy Group would meet, but May was in the driving seat as she took the women's policy brief to the heart of the Opposition. In so doing, this marks a movement of responsibility away from the voluntary side of the party towards the party in public office. Come the general election, and the writing of the party manifesto, there was no direct CWO input. It did not 'gender proof' the manifesto, a state of play very much regretted by some in the CWO leadership, although others felt that as a voluntary part of the party such a role should not have been expected. Either way, the women's section of the manifesto was ulti-mately the Shadow Minister for Women's baby, albeit with approval, like the proposals of all shadow ministers, of the leadership. If, as will be argued in the next chapter, the Conservative party's 'offer' to women was more competitive in 2010, compared with previous general elections, then much of this repositioning lies with the successful political leadership of May.[68] According to Anne Perkins' writing in the *Guardian*:

> May has almost single-handedly made the Tories get real about women and I hereby apologise for all the times publicly and privately I have doubted her. Sorry, Theresa, and congratulations. ...they are right on-side on all the things that go to the heart of vulnerable women in society – domestic and sexual violence, porn, lap dancing etc. Of course, the Conservatives are still reluctant to use the state to enforce equality – they are Tories after all. But at least, because of May's determination, they are at the table.[69]

As the party's most senior woman, and one with a seat at the top table, a considerably larger team supporting her, and a more substantial reputation within and without the party – albeit of the 'marmite kind'[70] – May was less likely to be marginalized than her predecessors.[71] Her success in all this comes in the face, of those colleagues, media commentators and British Politics scholars who considered her lightweight. And it came from a woman who early in her parliamentary career had had mixed feelings about the desirability or otherwise of a Women's Minister Post.

Conclusion: An 'auxillary plus' model?

In 2010 the case for a separate women's organization for women in the Conservative party is no longer publicly disputed by activist women, nor by the party more widely, even if Cameron's endorsement of the CWO may be less than a principled commitment to its current structure.[72] None-theless, many Parliamentarians, especially and perhaps surprisingly women Parliamentarians, show ambivalence towards the CWO, although those with party organization or Shadow Ministerial experience are more likely to recognize the role that the CWO has played in recent times. Over the last few years, and despite its previous Chairmen taking the CWO more down the policy road, it is becoming clearer that the organization's contemporary focus has become less about 'policy' proper and more about 'issues'; it has also been less about the recruitment of women for parliament and more about 'seed bedding' women's participation in Conservative politics. The former responsibility has clearly shifted to the (shadow) Minister for Women and the latter, arguably, to the new ginger group Women2win, working alongside the Shadow Minister and the Candidates Committee. CWO Forums are perhaps the Organization's greatest success over the 2005 Parliament, with some clearly feeding into the policy work that formed the basis of *WIWT* and, hence, the subsequent Manifesto, as Chapter 5 details. They also appear to offer a form of politics and organization that captures a third type of Tory woman. She is younger than the traditional CWO woman; is more interested in issues; and is likely to be juggling work and family life. Evening meetings to discuss such issues are attractive to her. It is unfortunately too early to say whether the 'third woman' will constitute the Tory woman of tomorrow, but what she does emphasize is an apparent distinction between the CWO at the national level (both officer and activist) who do 'big P' politics, and the more traditional organization and membership in the regions. Only time will tell whether this distinction is maintained and, or, becomes more meaningful. In part this likely reflects the relative importance and number of the first and third type of Tory woman.

Given CWO activities in recent years the question of whether it no longer constitutes an auxillary is begged. A straightforward reading of a Quasi Women's Policy Agency (QWPA) would suggest that it falls short. What it lacks, noting the equation of a Women's Policy Agency with state feminism (Lovenduski 2005b), is an overt commitment to feminism. The CWO is not, and never has been, a site for the advocacy of *women movement* demands inside the Conservative party. And yet, if taking seriously the arguments outlined in the previous Chapter regarding conservative claims to represent women, the CWO may well, whilst not formally fulfilling the definition of a QWPA, constitute something other than an auxillary; what may be termed 'auxillary plus'. Indeed, this possibility is foreseen in Joni Lovenduski's appeal (2005b: 237) for the 'integration of machinery and movement in all of the political parties' as a 'prerequisite for effective state machinery' when a particular party is in power. Informal although its influence most certainly, and most often is, the CWO constitutes a means of transmitting Conservative party women members' views to the party proper, and not least to those with formal responsibility for women – the Minister for Women. Of course, there are substantial qualifications to this. The CWO is under resourced. Its conferences are of the educative rather than the resolution type. The Women's Minister is not formally accountable to CWO officers or women party members. And effective CWO-Women's Minister relations rely too heavily on good personal interactions, which can never be guaranteed, and are clearly mediated by territorial ambition and wider intra-party relations. There are also questions about what form the organization's activities might take in the future, noting the smaller number of Forums, Summits and the recent demise of its Muslim Group.

It is even less clear how the various party women's structures will work together with the party now in government. The party in public office will certainly be dominant, as it was in the years preceding the election. There is, moreover, very little sense that the party's parliamentary representatives see themselves in a direct (delegate) representative relationship with the party's women members, as a group. If, overall, Parliamentarians offer little succour to supporters of the CWO – damning it with faint praise – women MPs in particular, add an additional critique. Even whilst some admit to having themselves received support from the organization as candidates, there is a perceived need to distance themselves from it because, on the ground, at least, the CWO is still felt to inhabit a different ideological space in terms of gender and gender relations.

In the post-general election era the precise nature of, and relations between, the party's various women's organizations and posts, has yet to be settled, although that there is no longer a Vice Chairman for Women is notable. The Women's Minister, as a member of the Cabinet level post, trumps the other organizations, as would be expected in political parties where the party in public office has triumphed. Indeed, with the Conservatives now in government, the Women's Policy Group has become the Women's *Advisory* Group (with the unfortunate abbreviation of 'WAG'). In this a demarcation – and a hierarchical one at that – between May's team who do 'policy' and the CWO who do 'issues' appears to have become settled in the former's favour. The relationship between May and the CWO, is then best considered asymmetric and reliant upon good personal relations.[73]

Appendix

Table 2.6   Conservative Party Organization

	Women % 1992	Women% 2010
Parliamentary party	6	16
National union /National Convention	20	28
Regional Office(rs)	35	23
Regional Chairmen	n/a	40
Constituency Executive Committees	46	n/a
Constituency General Committee	31	n/a
Branch officers	48	n/a
Members	48	n/a

Source: Norris and Lovenduski 1993; Hills, J. (1981) 'Britain', in Lovenduski, J. and Norris, P. (ed.) *The Politics of the Second Electorate* (London: Routledge); informant information.[74]

3
Conservative Legislative Recruitment

The *Daily Telegraph* – a newspaper whose columnists and editorials have often not been shy in being critical of the Cameron Conservative party – heralded the election of 48 Conservative women MPs, on May 6ᵗʰ 2010, as the Party having taken 'huge strides towards gender balance'.[1] The representation of women on the Conservative benches following the general election was, indeed, unprecedented and welcome. At 15.7 percent of all Conservative MPs, women's 2010 presence is a clear advance on the last couple of Parliaments, when their proportion flat-lined around 9 percent. Nevertheless, this advance requires some perspective. To talk of the proportion of women 'soaring' is misplaced. The party was starting from very low numbers, just 18 Conservative women MPs had been elected on general election day five years earlier. For the Tories to more than double its women MPs in 2010 should not have been too difficult. The party needed to select fewer than 20 more women in seats it would hold or win. In the event, they gained 30 more women MPs, but the total number fell short of the party's own, widely-stated projection of some 60 women, as it failed to win an overall majority on election night.[2] They missed doubling the percentage of women MPs too. And in the party's retirement seats, unexpectedly greater in number following the parliamentary expenses scandal of 2009, women were selected for only one quarter of its vacancies. Even amongst the party's newly elected MPs, where expectations could, and should have been greater, the percentage of women is just 22 percent. Compared with the current parliamentary Labour party, who lost 90 seats at the 2010 election, the Conservatives remain in a poor second place. Labour has the highest number *and* percentage of women at Westminster, with 81 women MPs, constituting 31 percent of the parliamentary Labour party – more women MPs not only than the Conservatives, but of all the other parties added together.

Any conclusion that Cameron had made good on his leadership accept-ance speech in 2005 to 'change the scandalous under representation of women in the Conservative party' must then be tempered. Tempered in terms both of the overall outcome and in respect of the efforts expended. The party leader had been unashamedly explicit in his stated desire for more women candidates and MPs, seeking also more Black and ethnic minority (BME) and disabled MPs. Cameron frequently claimed, often to a sceptical party, if a more receptive media, that he sought a parliamentary party that looked more like the UK. He accepted, moreover, the need to encourage greater numbers of women to seek selection as Conservative candidates, even as he acknowledged the existence of 'selectorate discrimination', in effect, that women candidates' merit was not always recognized by those in the party selecting parliamentary candidates. Reforms to the parliamentary selection process were implemented almost immediately on his assumption of the party leadership. These set out to change the nature of the selection pro-cess, ensuring that more women, at the minimum, came before local party selectorates. The hope was that the latter could be persuaded to select more women, especially in the party's winnable and vacant held seats. *Inter alia*, Cameron's reforms created a 'Priority List' of candidates, of whom 50 percent were women; varied the format of the selection meetings; widened the selectorate beyond party activists; and introduced sex short-listing rules. Yet he stopped short of imposing women candidates upon local associations. Cameron's unexpected (and belated) advocacy of All Women Shortlists (AWS) for post-January 2010 selections did not see them materialize in practice.[3]

In all this Cameron was cognizant of the electoral benefits of selecting more women. He believed that women's bodies, or at least the rhetoric of a more sex balanced parliamentary representation, would symbolize party change.[4] That his was no longer the Conservative party of old. Even so, on a practical level, setting out to achieve the greater selection of women was bold, for it is not a commitment that would be easy to deliver on. Local party autonomy prevents this being something he – or any Conservative leader – could guarantee without fundamentally altering central-local rela-tions (Kelly 2003). And that would be an intervention Cameron shied away from. He did not, apparently, want the issue of candidate selection to be his 'Clause IV' moment when he took on, and defeated, his party. Unwilling to face down his party on this issue (as opposed to other policy questions), Cameron's options for reform were limited. Correspondingly, so too was the outcome.

The descriptive under-representation of women

That women MPs are lesser in number than their male colleagues is neither unique to the Conservative party, nor the British House of

Commons. In almost all lower Houses women are numerically under-represented.[5] The UK Parliament currently ranks joint 50th, along-side the Czech Republic, Eritrea, Latvia and Uzbekistan. It is beaten by countries from Africa, Latin America, Australasia and Europe, even as it fares better against the US and France.[6] The picture in the UK Parliament is, to be sure, generally improving over time, as Table 3.1 illustrates, although there was a small dip in 2001 when the percentage of women declined from 18.2 percent to 17.9 percent.[7] The UK parliament in 2010 does, moreover, match the overall European average of 22 percent, although it is prescient to point out that the Conservative make-up of the overall total of women in the UK Parliament is lower, as previously mentioned, at just 16 percent of its parliamentary representation. It is Labour's women MPs that make up the difference. The clear asymmetry in descriptive representation in the Labour party's favour continues, then, in this parliament, despite some recent, inter-party rebalancing. In 1997 Labour women MPs constituted 84 percent of all women MPs; 81 percent in 2001; 77 percent in 2005; and 57 percent in 2010.[8]

The key to increasing the number of women MPs in the UK Parliament at any one election is for political parties to ensure that as many women as possible are selected for their vacant held and winnable

Table 3.1   MPs Elected to the House of Commons, 1983–2010, by Sex and Party

Party	1983	1987	1992	1997	2001	2005	2010
Labour	209	229	271	418	412	354	256
Women	10	21	37	101	95	98[9]	81
% of Total	4.8	9.2	13.7	24.2	23	27.7	31.6
Conservative	397	376	336	165	166	198	305
Women	13	17	20	13	14	17	48[10]
% of Total	3.3	4.5	6	7.9	8	8.6	15.7
Liberal Democrat	23	22	20	46	53	62	57
Women	0	1	2	3	6[11]	10[12]	7
% of Total	0	4.5	10	6.5	11	16	12.3
Other	21	23	24	30	25	31	32
Women	0	2	3	3	4	3	7
% of Total	0	8.7	12.5	10	12.5	9.7	21.8
All MPs	650	650	651	659	659	645	650
Women	23	41	60	120	118	128	143
% of Total	3.5	6.3	9.2	18.2	17.9	19.8[13]	22.0

Source: Ashe et al 2010.

seats – those seats that, all other things being equal, will successfully return MPs to Westminster. Analysis of candidate selection by seat safety in 2005 and 2010 (Tables 3.2 and 3.3) reveals that: (1) both Labour and the Conservatives selected more women candidates in 2010 than they did in 2005; (2) only Labour's overall percentage of women candidates matches or exceeds its percentage of women MPs (31 percent MPs and 30 percent candidates), suggesting that Conservative and Liberal Democrat women candidates were less likely to win than their male equivalents; (3) that Labour was alone in distributing women candidates disproportionately in its held seats, whilst the Conservatives placed most of its women candidates in percentage terms (30 percent) in its unwinnable seats. Furthermore, if one looks only at the retirement seats (Table 3.4) the Conservative party selected women in just 26 percent of these compared with both Labour and the Liberal Democrats who selected women in more than half (Campbell and Childs 2010). Given the absolute number of women candidates the Conservatives had in 2010, 24 percent of all candidates, their failure to be selected in those seats that are most likely to return MPs was a missed opportunity.[14] At best – if all Tory women candidates had been elected – women would make up 24 percent of the Conservative parliamentary party. Whilst this might sound like an unlikely scenario, it is precisely Labour's feat at 2010 general election. This, of course, begs the question why the Conservatives do not seem to be able to select greater numbers of women and, more importantly, return similar percentages and numbers of women MPs.

It is often noted that leftist parties, like the British Labour party, *sui generis*, are more likely to return higher numbers of women MPs to legislatures, primarily because of their ideological commitment to equality (and consequent lesser antipathy towards measures that might enhance women's election) (Kittilson 2006). As Lovenduski makes clear (2005a: 60), Conservative thought, lacking ideals of egalitarianism, offers little in support for parity of women's descriptive representation. Hence, there should be less surprise at the historic inter-party asymmetry in the House of Commons. However, when compared to other 'sister' Conservative parties in Europe, and other comparable Westminster systems, the UK Conservative party is unfavourably ranked in 19th position, as Table 3.5 below shows. As such, the British Conservatives cannot maintain that its record is in line with other political parties on the right of the political spectrum. Note too, that the percentage of women in the various centre-right parties varies from the mid-40s to the low 10s. It is not as if centre-right parties cluster around a similar percentage of women. Seven centre-right parties manage to match the UK Labour party's current percentage of women MPs, at 31 percent. Note too, the lack of a deterministic association

Table 3.2 Women Candidates and MPs by Type of Seat 2005 (men)

	Seats won 2001		Winnable[15] 5%		Winnable 10%		Unwinnable		Total	
	Cand.	MPs	Cands.	MPs	Cand.	MPs	Cand.	MPs	Cand.	MPs
Labour	115(288) 26%	**98(257)** 28%	2(6) 25%	**0(0)**	2(19) 10%	**0(0)**	47(149) 24%	**0(0)**	166(462) 26%	**98(257)** 28%
Consv	14(150) 9%	**14(146)** 9%	4(26) 13%	**1(17)** 6%	7(32) 18%	**1(11)** 8%	93(296) 24%	**1(7)** 14%	118(504) 19%	**17(181)** 9%
Libdem	4(46) 8%	**4(41)** 9%	2(7) 22%	**1(2)** 33%	5(8) 38%	**1(3)** 25%	131(423) 24%	**4(6)** 40%	142(484) 23%	**10(52)** 16%

Table 3.3 Women Candidates and MPs by Type of Seat 2010 (men)

	Seats won 2005		Winnable 5%		Winnable 10%		Unwinnable		Total	
	Candidates	MPs	Candidates	MPs	Candidates	MPs	Candidates	MPs	Candidates	MPs
Labour	118(231) 30%	80(175) 27%	20(12) 62.5%	0(1) 0%	5(8) 39%	0(1) 0%	48(188) 20%	0(1) 0%	191(439) 30%	81(177) 31%
Consv	27(181) 15%	26(179) 14%	12(32) 27%	9(25) 27%	12(36) 25%	7(27) 21%	98(232) 30%	6(26) 19%	149(481) 24%	48(257) 16%
Libdem	12(50) 19%	4(45) 8%	7(9) 43.8%	1(1) 50%	3(11) 21%	1(1) 50%	112(425) 21%	1(3) 25%	134(495) 21%	7(50) 12%

Table 3.4   Retirees and Replacements at the 2010 GE, by Main Parties

	Retirements, all[16]	Women Retirements	Women Replacements
Labour	102	24 (23.5%)	52 (53%)[17]
Conservative	38	5 (13.1%)	10 (26.3%)
Lib. Democrat	7	0	4 (57.1%)
Others	2	0	1
Total	149	29 (19.4%)	67 (46.2%)

Source: Ashe et al 2010.

between parties with higher percentages of women MPs and the presence of some form of sex quota.[18]

Supply and demand models

In seeking to account for women's descriptive under-representation, the extant gender and politics literature identifies various factors. These can be broken down into cultural, socio-economic and political ones. More egalitarian cultures, greater secularization and early women's enfranchisement are all positively correlated with higher numbers of women representatives. The same is true for countries which have more extensive women's participation in the public sphere, in the 'pipeline' professions from which politicians are recruited, and where the state tends towards social democracy. Finally, the presence of majoritarian electoral systems hinders whereas proportional electoral systems, especially those with higher district magnitude, favour greater numbers of women. Importantly, no one condition or factor has been identified as sufficient (see for example, Kittilson 2006; Norris and Lovenduski 1995; Krook 2009a,b, 2010a; Wangnerud 2009). Would that it was so, for then it might suggest a single solution. Unfortunately, politics is messy. The same levels of women's descriptive representation may be the outcome of different combinations of conditions and the effects of individual ones may depend on the presence or absence of others (Krook 2010a). Note that improvements in the descriptive representation of women in the UK Parliament over the last decade or so, have taken place *despite* consistency in the electoral system. The doubling of women MPs overnight in 1997 occurred *without any change* in mode of election at

Table 3.5 Women's Descriptive Representation in Centre Right Parties, in Select European and Parliamentary Systems

Country	Party Name	Nos.	%	Quotas
1. Belgium	New Flemish Alliance	13	44.80%	Legislative
2. Sweden	Moderate Party	42	43.20%	X[19]
3. Netherlands	Christian Democratic Appeal	9	42.80%	X
4. Finland	National Coalition Party	20	40.00%	X
5. Canada	Conservatives	23	36.50%	X
6. Spain	People's Party (PP)	51	33.30%	Legislative
7. Iceland	Independence Party (IP)	5	31.25%	X
8. Bulgaria	Citizens for European Dev. of Bulgaria Party (GERB)	35	30.10%	X
9. = Denmark	Conservative People's Party	6	30.00%	X
9. = Norway	Conservative Party	9	30.00%	X
10. New Zealand	National Party	17	29.30%	X
11. Portugal	Social Democratic Party (PPD/PSD)	22	27.10%	Legislative
12. Luxembourg	Christian Social People's Party	7	26.90%	Party
13. Estonia	Union of Pro Patria and Res Publica	5	26.30%	X
14. Slovakia	Slovak Democratic and Christian Union (SDKU-DS)	7	25.00%	X
15. Austria	People's Party	12	23.50%	Party
16. Lithuania	Homeland Union (TS-LKD) – Lithuanian Christian Democrat	10	22.00%	X
17. Germany	CDU	41	21.10%	Party
18. Italy	The People of Freedom	54	19.90%	X
19. = Australia	The Nationals	8	15.70%	X
19. = UK	**Conservative**	**48**	**15.70%**	X
20. Romania	Democratic Liberal Party	16	13.90%	Party[20]

Table 3.5 Women's Descriptive Representation in Centre Right Parties, in Select European and Parliamentary Systems – *continued*

Country	Party Name	Nos.	%	Quotas
21. Switzerland	Swiss People's Party (SVP/UDC)	8	12.90%	X
22. France	UMP	38	12.10%	Legislative
23. Cyprus	Democratic Rally	2	11.10%	X
24. Ireland	Fine Gael	5	9.80%	X
25. Latvia	People's Party	2	8.60%	X
26. Slovenia	Slovenian Democrat Party	2	7.10%	Legislative
27. Malta	Nationalist Party	2	5.70%	X
28. Hungary	Hungarian Civic Union-Christian Democratic People's Party (FIDESZ-KDNP)	0	0.00%	X

Notes: The parties selected are the largest centre right/right parties in their countries and the European parties are typically members of the EPP group. Poland & Czech Republic and Greece are excluded. Quotas refer to the presence of either legislative or party quotas.
Source: Amended from Ashe et al 2010 and http://www.quotaproject.org/index.cfm

Westminster (Kittilson 2006; see also Krook 2010a).[21] That these improvements have also been party specific limits the value of explanations that consider aggregate figures, whilst ignoring party level data (Kittilson 2006: 8).[22]

The dominant framework in the gender and politics literature for understanding legislative recruitment has, for some time, been the supply- and demand-side model.[23] This operates within the specificities of a particular political system which sets the rules of the game (at the systemic level: the legal, electoral, and party systems) and in the context of political parties' organization, rules and ideology (Norris and Lovenduski 1995; Kenny 2009). In simple language, the outcome of particular political parties' selection processes is understood in terms of the interaction between the *supply* of applicants wishing to pursue a political career and the *demands* of selectors who choose candidates on the basis of their preferences and perceptions of abilities, qualifications and perceived electability (Norris and Lovenduski 1995). Recently, the adequacy of this framework has been questioned (Krook 2009a,b, 2010a,b; Kenny 2009). At issue is, first, the need for a supplementary theory of gender. The model, as constructed by Pippa Norris and Joni Lovenduski (1995), recognizes the 'role of gendered norms and practices and the intervening effects of political parties and electoral systems', as its critics admit (Krook 2009b; Kenny 2009). Thus, it is widely agreed that women are, on average, and as a result of gendered socialization and the gendered division of labour, likely to have fewer resources than men, whether that is the necessary free time to engage in politics, money to fund selection and election campaigns, and, or lower levels of political ambition, confidence and experience (Childs 2008; see also Kenny 2009; Lawless and Fox 2005).[24] On the demand side, women have been found to suffer from negative selectorate discrimination (Shepherd-Robinson and Lovenduski 2002). Direct discrimination refers to the judgment of people on the basis of characteristics seen as common to their group, rather than as individuals. It reflects the attitudes of the selectors, and can be seen where gender discriminatory questions are posed during the selection process (Norris and Lovenduski 1995). Indirect discrimination against women refers to instances where the idea of what constitutes a 'good MP' count against women – where, for example, party selectorates prefer candidates with resources primarily associated with men and masculinity. Negative imputed discrimination is where party members may be unwilling to choose a woman candidate because they are concerned that by so doing they would lose votes. Here, the discrimination reflects what selectors perceive to be the attitudes of the electorate.

The second criticism levelled at the supply and demand model is that because political resources and motivations, as well as candidate abilities and qualifications, are likely to be thoroughly imbued by gender, the political marketplace will be distorted and unlikely to produce an equilibrium solution (Krook, 2009: 4). According to Mona Lena Krook candidate selection should, therefore, be recast 'in terms of the gendered institutions that may inform the calculations of potential candidates and political elites' (see also Kenny 2009). Such an approach 'involve[s] attending to configurations of systemic, practical and normative institutions, as illustrated in Box 3.1 below. How these institutions combine, whether 'they facilitate or hinder the selection of female candidates', will determine levels of women's descriptive representation (Krook 2009b: 707). Importantly, distinct institutional configurations operate 'not only across but also within countries, producing variations in women's descriptive representation across parties', thereby meeting criticism of approaches that focus on aggregate figures of women's descriptive representation (Krook 2009b: 712; Kittilson 2006).

Box 3.1   Systemic, Practical and Normative Institutions

Systemic institutions

Electoral systems:	Majoritarian or PR, candidate or list based vote, open or closed party lists, single or multi-member districts
Party systems	One, two or multi-party systems

Practical institutions

Formal Criteria	Age, citizenship, party membership, term limits
Informal Criteria	Ticket-balancing, skills, experience, prominence, party activism, family ties, money, insider or outsider status
Method of ballot composition	(De)centralized, group rights to nominate or veto, primaries or nominations, secret or open ballots

Normative institutions

Norms of Equality	Equality of opportunity or results (system or party level)
Norms of Representation	'Politics of ideas' or 'politics of presence' (system or party level)

Source: Krook 2009b: 711.

Systemic institutions are already central to most extant studies of women's legislative recruitment; practical institutions are also familiar, they shape perceptions of who is 'qualified' or 'desirable' as a candidate. Normative institutions are perhaps the least acknowledged. They refer to beliefs about 'equality' and 'representation' in the candidate selection process and are gendered to the 'extent that they sustain, and indeed justify, ongoing differences among women and men' (Krook 2009b). For Meryl Kenny (2009: 8) gender relations and norms are 'particularly sticky institutional legacies' and are likely to limit change. Notwithstanding these critical refinements, supply and demand side explanations, coupled with a more explicit theory of gender, remain a useful framework, especially when conceptualized in such a way as to recognize that it is embedded in a wider gendered context and when it is not represented in a straightforward inter-action model but one which recognizes multiple directions of causality (Krook 2010b; Kenny 2009: 27).[25]

The relative importance of supply-side explanations for women's descriptive representation at Westminster has been increasingly downplayed over the last decade or so, as scholars acknowledge the higher number of women candidates selected by each of the main political parties relative to the number returned as MPs. This privileging of demand side factors arguably corrects an assumption of an equal weighting in accounts of the supply and demand model (Kenny 2009: 28). Recognizing this shift does not imply that there are no concerns about supply, especially regarding the absolute level and diversity of women seeking selection.[26] Do they all have to be blonde, as one contemporary Conservative woman Peer put it?[27] Rather, it reflects first, greater cognizance that party demand can help determine supply, and, secondly, that there are sufficient women candidates for all the main UK political parties to select women for at least half their vacant and target seats at each general election, if they so choose. This is only about 50 or so women. The logic here is as follows: unless patterns of women candidates' selection accurately reflect their qualifications for office (and of course, such evaluation is likely to be highly gendered in any case), supply-side explanations and, for that matter supply-side solutions, are less convincing. 'What planet are you on?!' Theresa May (2005) decries of those who suggest that the top 50 Conservative women candidates risk diluting the quality of the party's candidates.[28]

Gone, too, is confidence in the 'incremental track' (Dahlerup and Friedenvall 2003) where women's descriptive representation improves gradually in a linear fashion as a consequence of changes in women's social, economic and cultural position. Impatient for change, advocates of the 'fast track' contend that gender inequality is not historic but likely reproduced in 'modern settings' with parties acting as gatekeepers (ibid; Kittilson 2006). Placing emphasis on women's exclusion from politics and equality of results, responsibility for women's under-representation shifts

Box 3.2   Conservative Reforms to Parliamentary Selection 2005–2010

Date	Reforms
May 2006	(1) the creation of a 'priority list' of candidates, of whom at least 50 per cent would be women, with a 'significant' percentage from black/minority ethnicity and disabled communities. Associations in vacant Conservative-held and target seats would be 'expected' to select from amongst the priority list candidates. (2) a three-month progress review; (3) the use of headhunting, mentoring and guidance of local associations; and (4) the option of holding primaries (either open or closed) or 'community panels' to select candidates.
August 2006	(1) Constituencies Associations with fewer than 300 members are expected to hold a primary; (2) where Associations choose not to employ a primary model, Members will draw up a shortlist of three or four candidates from a list of 12–15. The shortlist would be sex balanced: 2 women and 2 men; the final decision would be made by the EC on the basis of in-depth interviews; and (3) if the EC shortlists an AWS, the existing model of selection could be retained.
January 2007	(1) Associations are permitted to choose from the full list of approved candidates with a requirement that at each stage of the selection process at least 50 percent of the candidates have to be women; (2) Associations could still choose to select solely from the Priority list.
September 2009[29]	(1) All applications were to be sifted by Association Officers along with Party Chairman and a representative from the Candidates' Department; (2) Six candidates were to go before (ideally) a Special General Meeting or Open Primary; (3) The Association Executive may meet to remove the 'completely unsuitable' and add a reserve in 'exceptional' circumstances; the final field could be reduced to four; (4) Any seats where the sitting MP announces his or her retirement after January 1st 2010 will be selected by 'by-election rules'; Associations would simply be presented with a list of three candidates by the party from which to choose.[30]

to political institutions, most importantly political parties, and supports the use of measures that deliver women's inclusion.

If a political party wishes to increase the number of its women representatives, it can adopt one or all of three equality strategies: equality rhetoric, equality promotion and equality guarantees, with the latter the most efficient (Lovenduski 2005a). *Equality rhetoric* refers to the public acceptance of claims for women's representation and may be found in party campaign platforms, party discourse, and leader's speeches and writings. Such exhortations for women to come forward and seek selection, for example, will likely affect both selectorate and aspirant candidates' attitudes. *Equality promotion* covers measures that might provide training, financial assistance and soft targets in an attempt to bring those currently underrepresented into political competition. In other words, these measures seek to provide aspirant candidates with the necessary resources to successfully participate in the selection process. In so doing, they should also affect selectorate attitudes. Finally, *equality guarantees* require an increase in the number or proportion of particular Parliamentarians and, or makes a particular social characteristic *a necessary qualification* for office (Lovenduski 2005a, with emphasis added). Taking the form of party or legislative quotas, reserved seats, or in the UK Parliament case All Women Shortlists (AWS, see below), they create an artificial demand in the political party. Such measures may also indirectly encourage an increase in the supply of women, as women perceive this new demand for their candidacy.

Conservative selection procedures for the 2010 general election

David Cameron was quick to suspend selections on taking over as party leader in 2005. Box 3.2 summarizes the series of reforms introduced between then and the 2010 general election. These reforms variously map onto both supply- and demand-side explanations and constitute examples of both equality rhetoric and equality promotion.

Amongst those active on the issue of women's descriptive representation within the party there was clear acknowledgement that the Conservatives needed to increase the pool of women seeking selection. The Labour party were felt to have a ready-made and larger supply pool of women, especially in respect of women working in the public sector and active in the trade unions.[31] Hence Cameron's and others, not least successive Party Chairman, May, Maude and Spelman, and latterly Eric Pickles', personal exhortations for women to put themselves forward as candidates. This missive went out even to women hitherto not involved in Conservative or electoral politics (in part to counter anti-politics sentiment, following the expenses scandal). There was also explicit leadership support for the activities of Women2win in identifying and supporting prospective women candidates (Childs 2008). 'Over Pinot Grigio and canapés Women2win aims to make breaking into such a male-dominated party less daunting and to ensure female candidates are not relegated to no-hope seats'.[32]

Much of the party's efforts, not all visible to the public, were, however, trained on creating an artificial party demand. In this, the party leadership had three main goals. First, efforts were designed to increase the numbers of women candidates put in front of, and thereby, formally considered by local party selectorates. Initially, a Priority List of candidates (in common parlance the 'A List') was created to identify the party's top 50 women and top 50 men aspirant candidates. The party's held and vacant seats were expected, but importantly not required, to select from amongst these. The same rationale underpinned other and subsequent reforms, such as the 50:50 sex shortlisting rules, the intervention of party head quarters (CCHQ) to help sift applications, and their role in identifying the shortlist under the by-election rules. The premise is straightforward. Faced with the 'best' of the party's aspirant women candidates, local party selectorates could not fail but to select them. Second, the form of the assessment tasks undertaken by aspirant candidates was diversified to further increase women's chances. New types of 'interview' were introduced – the traditional 'big speech' was replaced with a 'Question & Answer' session – and there were independent moderators, such as the journalist and ex-Conservative MP Matthew Parris. A 'selection' DVD was also to be seen by the local association prior to the selection to reinforce the message of the importance of descriptive representation (Childs 2008). Finally, reforms were implemented which sought to transform the composition of the selectorate, whether this was through closed or open primaries, the switching of the roles of the EC (if party activists did not want to lose this power to select they could voluntarily have a shortlist comprised only of women, which would cause them to select women, despite themselves), or the use of community panels. Here, the underlying assumption was that activist members of the party were more likely to be predisposed to select men over women, irrespective of women candidates' merit. In contrast, the general public, upstanding members of the community, members of a local party's Executive Committees (at least, once they have been briefed by the centre), as well as ordinary party members, were felt to be less likely to discriminate against women. In turn, this reflects appreciation on behalf of the party leadership that local Conservative associations are themselves descriptively and attitudinally unrepresentative of their electorates *vis-à-vis* the selection of women (akin to May's curvilinear law) (Norris 1995). An elderly woman party member, and graduate of Durham University in the 1950s, speaking privately to one of the authors at the 2008 Conservative party conference nicely illustrates this perspective. She contended that almost all older conservative women had not been to university, and did not, therefore, have, in her view, 'broad minds'. In the case of the EC there were expectations that they could be 'persuaded', by briefings from representatives of the Candidates' Committee, for example, of the (electoral) case to select more women, even if this went against their own 'better' judgement (read: prejudice).

The one thing Cameron stopped short of doing was imposing women candidates upon local constituencies. He, and all of the leading activists of women's descriptive representation in the party, appeared (publicly at least) content to delay accepting the logic of equality guarantees (Campbell et al 2006),[33] or rather, until too late in the day. To much surprise, Cameron's deposition to the Speaker's Conference,[34] a special parliamentary committee looking at the under-representation of women, BME and the disabled, in the autumn of 2009 included an apparent announcement of the introduction of AWS:

> From January, we move to what we call our by-election procedure...the central party provides the shortlist to the association and it's my intention that if we continue as we are, *that some of those shortlists will indeed be all-women shortlists* to help us boost the number of Conservative women MPs and also to recognise the fact that although about 29 percent of our candidates are women, there are many very, very good women on our priority list of candidates who haven't yet been selected...

This announcement came as a surprise to women with responsibility for women's selection in the party. There had been no consultation with them.[35] On BBC Radio 4's Woman's Hour, Cameron made clear that his apparent conversion to AWS was because the rate of women's selection was 'just too slow'. Women were having to 'jump barriers far higher than any of the men', and that, in the absence of AWS, the parliamentary Conservative party was not 'going to be representative enough'. Mainstream critics felt his timing was poor (Snowdon 2010: 381). Too close to the general election, AWS might just constitute the metaphorical back-breaking 'straw' for unhappy members (discussed more in the next chapter). As it turned out, there were no Conservative AWS. In any case, Tory AWS would not have warranted the label of equality guarantees. There was no systematic strategy or proper plans for implementation. Rather, in a particular seat the 'best' aspirant candidates shortlisted via the party's by-election rules would, by happenstance, be women. For these reasons, Cameron's statement to the Speaker's Conference looks to have been mere rhetoric. He had conceded enough to garner favourable media headlines that week, without committing his party to measures that would guarantee the intended outcome – the *election* of women MPs. Perhaps Cameron felt constrained by the likely unfavourable comment that would likely emerge if AWS were introduced. Criticism was swiftly posted on www.Conservativehome following his Speaker's Conference statement. But with his cover, those in his party who had been active in increasing the numbers of women MPs for many years, and who had previously subscribed to the 'everything short of AWS' position, would surely have accepted the case, and become his Praetorian Guard.

The effectiveness of the Cameron era reforms is, perhaps not unsurprisingly, disputed. Over and above disagreements about the total number of women MPs returned at the general election – of whether the Conservative total is sufficient, in absolute or relative terms – what should be noted is that the total number of Conservative women candidates selected in 2010 at 24 percent is five percentage points more than in 2005 (see Tables 3.2 and 3.3 above). This was, though, less than the then Chairman of the party, the 'bullish', Eric Pickles expected. He was confident the party would have in excess of 30 percent women candidates.[36] There is no way of knowing, unfortunately, whether this increase on 2005 reflects an overall increase in the aspirant candidate supply pool or merely greater party demand that saw more aspirant women candidates selected as PPCs for 2010. (Recall too, that 24 percent remains lower than the Labour party's 30 percent.) It is also the case that at the time of the party's three month review 32 percent of the newly selected candidates were women, a percentage that is higher than at the time of the general election some years later, indicating that subsequent selections were less favourable to women, including, and especially, those unexpected ones created by higher than usual numbers of MPs standing down in advance of the election (see also Bale 2010: 325). If the 2006 leadership review of the selection reforms was an admission that they had to-date fallen short, as Cameron's statement of intent suggests, what plays out thereafter must be considered disappointing in the party's own terms.[37] An internal document in 2008 revealed further concern that the party might lose already selected women and BME candidates. It implied that any problems in this regard would likely lie with the local associations rather than the prospective candidates.[38] Individuals associated with Women2win were also publicly disappointed in the overall numbers of women selected.[39] In private they lamented that the party had not done enough in selecting women particularly for its winnable seats. There was additional concern about the failure of the party to recruit beyond 'City' women, as well as a strong sense that the party would need women as a group to pressurize the party during the 2010 Parliament as it selected candidates for the next general election.

So what of the success of the (in)famous 'A listers'? Research by Ashe et al (2010) confirms that the original list was representative of men and women, as it was designed to be, and that experiences were similar for both women and men (Table 3.6 and 3.7 below). Priority List women were equally successful as Priority List men at getting selected for winnable seats and getting elected to Parliament. Particularly notable is the equal selection of women and men for party held seats and those in the 5 percent winnable category. However, without data on the timing of these individual selections we cannot be sure how candidates' 'A list' status intersected with the various other reforms of the selection process as the party adopted different rules between 2005 and 2010.[40]

Table 3.6 Priority List Selection Progress, by Sex

	Women	Men
Original Priority List 100[41]	53 (53%)	47 (47%)
Withdrawn	15 (58%)	11 (42%)
Selected target	14 (52%)	13 (48%)
Selected Con vacant	9 (50%)	9 (50%)
Never Selected	27 (53%)	24 (47%)

Source: Ashe et al 2010.

Turning to primaries, the second and arguably more high profile of the Cameron reforms to parliamentary selection for 2010, there is little evidence that this highly thought of means of selection disadvantaged women (Table 3.8) (Ashe et al 2010 cf Baldez 2004, 2007). This is despite scepticism amongst those active on women's descriptive representation who feared that local men, especially ones well known in the local party and those with high political and financial resources, would be able to put 'bums on seats'.[42] In 2010 there were 109 primary selections, of one form or another, the majority held in winnable seats (see Table 3.8). Overall, 25 percent of candidates selected by primaries in vacant held Conservative seats were women, and women constituted 30.8 percent of candidates selected in primaries in seats where the Conservatives lost by a margin of less than 5 percent in 2005. This is a higher percentage than the overall percentage of women candidates selected by the party, at 24 percent. However, women did slightly less well when one looks at the seats the Conservatives won: women constitute only 27 percent of MPs in the 5 percent winnable seats compared to their selection in 31 percent of these; in the 10 percent winnable seats, the difference is between 10 and 28 percent.

The key unintended consequence generated by various Cameron's reforms, amidst vocal grassroots unhappiness, was the apparent rise of the 'local' male candidate. Candidate selection is a prized benefit of party membership and Cameron's efforts looked to be perceived on the ground (as will be shown in the next Chapter) as unwarranted central intervention underpinned by political correctness. Critics contended that it was evidence that Cameron spent too much time in West London, a euphemism for metropolitanism.[43] The Priority List, in particular, generated intra-party antipathy at best, if not outright hostility. 'Good men' were said to have

Table 3.7 Priority List Selection, by Seat Safety and Sex

	Seats won 2005		Winnable 5%		Winnable 10%		Unwinnable		Total	
	Candidates	MPs	Candidates	MPs	Candidates	MPs	Candidates	MPs	Candidates	MPs
Priority list candidates	22/208 10.5%	22/205 10.7%	11/44 25%	8/34 23.5%	9/48 18.8%	7/34 20.6%	6/282 2.1%	1/32 3.1%	48(582) 7.6%	38/305 12.5%
Women selected from priority-list	11(11) 50%	11(11) 50%	7(4) 63.6%	6(2) 75%	2(7) 22%	1(6) 14%	5(1) 83%	0(1)	25(23) 52.1%	18(20) 47.4%

Source: Ashe et al 2010.

Table 3.8 Conservative Primaries, by Marginality and Sex

	Seats won 2005		Winnable 5%		Winnable 10%		Unwinnable		Total	
	Candidates	MPs	Candidates	MPs	Candidates	MPs	Candidates	MPs	Candidates	MPs
Conservative	16/208 7.6%	16/205 7.8%	13/44 29.5%	11/34 32.4%	25/48 51.1%	20/34 58.8	57/330 17.2%	18/32 56.2%	111/632 17.5%	65/305 21.3%

Source: Ashe et al (2010).

been left off the list in order to make place for 'less good' women. The list was also in some instances circumvented. Although it was intended to be of 'sufficient size', 'breadth and talent' that it would only 'rarely' be necessary to add a particular individual for a 'specific selection' this was, nonetheless, permitted. Crucially, this happened much more than had been foreseen. In Rob McIlveen's study (cited in Cowley and Childs 2011; see also Snowdon 2010: 232, 245) nearly half of 89 constituencies selected a local rather than a Priority List candidate (44 compared to 45). And these local candidates were overwhelmingly male: if more than half (58 percent) of the candidates selected from the Priority List were women nearly all (86 percent) of the local 'exceptional' candidates were men.[44] In common parlance, what was created on the ground was competition between 'local men' and 'outsider A list women'. Conflated in this way hostility towards the Priority List candidates looks to have masked hostility towards women candidates, *per se*. In such a context of intra-party tension, local associations were reportedly complaining about the quality of the 'A Listers' (Snowdon 2010: 245; see also Evans 2008). Conversing with a party member at the 2008 annual conference, it was said that 'women in Lincoln don't like A-Listers coming around where they think an MP is standing down'. This criticism begs the additional question of whether women are less likely to be local. As one leading party activists put it, for women to be successful in business and in science they will have to move to the cities and hence are less likely to 'be local'.[45]

Conclusion

2010 failed to turn out to be a critical election for women's descriptive representation (Campbell and Childs 2010), despite it constituting a good opportunity for the greater selection of Conservative women MPs, with favourable exogenous and endogenous conditions in place. The demands of those in the party long active on this issue, albeit less publicly so in the past, now chimed with a modernizing leadership. The former, not only gendered the leadership contest that saw Cameron become party leader, but Cameron himself recognized that efforts to (s)elect more women might help change his party's image. Fortuitously, unexpected opportunities to select greater numbers of women candidates in many more vacant held seats than could have been foreseen were one positive consequence of the higher than usual retirements following the 2009 parliamentary expenses scandal. Yet, after general election night the bald statistics tell a less than positive story. Despite increases in the numbers and percentages of Conservative women MPs, the Conservative parliamentary party of 2010 continues to fail to meet the criteria of a feminist political party relating to parliamentary representation: parity of representation amongst its representatives. It also fails to meet this criterion even if one considers only the new intake (L. Young 2000). Thus, while some in-roads have been made into the asymmetry in descriptive representation at Westminster, the now long-established lead for the Labour party continues.

It would be too easy and mistaken, moreover, to date Conservative party efforts to increase the descriptive representation of women from the time of Cameron taking over the party. He is widely considered to be 'onside' by the party's gender equality activists, and he did open the door to women's recruitment when other leaders had not, or might not have, done so. Efforts were limited under William Hague and Iain Duncan Smith, stalled under Michael Howard (Bale 2010), and the prospect of a David Davis led party in 2005 hardly looked promising from this perspective. Crucially, however, intra-party mobilization to increase both the supply of, and demand for, Conservative women parliamentary candidates predates Cameron's leadership by a decade or so (Childs 2008; Kittilson 2006), even if it was less vocal and less public at that time. Lone voices had appealed for limited AWS for the 2001 general election (Keswick 2000) but the 2005 general election was the watershed. A frustrated Trish Morris, then the Party's Vice-Chairman for Candidates, had received little or no support from the previous leader in advance of the election (Bale 2010: 228). At the Conservative Conference that year the Conservative women's fringe meeting heard calls for positive discrimination. Further, Parliamentarians like May, who had spoken out previously, became even more publicly vocal in their demands. Hamstrung under Smith (Bale 2010: 160, 166), and already associated with the idea of creating a Priority List of candidates along with Andrew Lansley MP,[46] May spoke at the launch of the 2005 Hansard Society *Women at the Top* Report in November. It looked as though she was to be the 'Tory answer to Harriet Harman...someone who single-mindedly drives the process of recruitment, mentoring and selection'.[47] With the establishment later that same month of the ginger group, Women2win, the party, moreover, had a new, and very different, organization dedicated to the greater recruitment of women for Parliament (Childs 2008), and importantly one that rejected the incremental track of women's descriptive representation – a view also later accepted by Cameron.[48] In short, women in the party hierarchy, both parliamentary and voluntary, coupled with some male parliamentary colleagues, were making clear and greater demands of their party and its leadership.

These demands chimed with Cameron's goal of returning the Conservative party back to power. In agreeing to seek a more descriptively representative Parliamentary party and implementing reforms to that effect, Cameron was cognizant of the possible electoral benefits of selecting more women. As stated before, women's bodies – or at least the rhetoric of a more sex balanced parliamentary representation – would signal party change. Thus women's recruitment constituted one strand of the wider decontamination process (Bale 2010; Lynch and Garnett 2003b; Evans

2008). Publicly Cameron's arguments drew attention to women's talent and the contribution they would make to good government.[49] Of course, such a transformation of the party's parliamentary representation was unlikely to directly win back the women voters it had lost since 1997 (Campbell and Childs 2010). But indirectly, voters – male and female – who had switched their votes to New Labour might yet return to the Tories if they were to perceive the party more at ease (at last) with modern society (see Chapter 8).[50] According to the *Observer's* Catherine Bennett (3 May, 2009), the party 'will have learnt from its marketing tutorials that it is easier for an organization to flog stuff to women if it also employs them'.[51] Indeed, Lord Ashcroft's (the party's infamous Treasurer) analysis of the 2005 general election defeat (2005: 21–3) included public opinion data showing that 67 percent of voters thought the party 'too dominated by men'; 44 percent wanted it to involve more women, young people and ethnic minorities to make the Conservatives look more like modern Britain.

Cameron's pledge to address, in his terms, women's 'scandalous' under-representation was arguably audacious, given that local party autonomy *vis-à-vis* parliamentary selections prevents this being something he could guarantee, without him fundamentally altering central-local relations. This self-imposed limit restricted his options.[52] But, if the impact the reforms to parliamentary candidate selection adopted between 2005 and 2010 were less than the most vocal supporters of women's descriptive representation within the party had hoped for, the party leadership managed to achieve their goal of making some progress whilst keeping critical party members on board, or at least, not openly revolting, something they clearly thought was a possibility (as is detailed in the next chapter). No doubt Cameron trusted that he had done enough in respect of the publics' perception of change. With plenty of media copy, predictably and unimaginatively coining the alliterative monikers, 'Cameron's Cuties' and 'Dave's Dollies', voters could not have been unaware that the Conservative party had a more female face by 2010. It would be surprising if they were anything other than ignorant of the precise ratio of women to men amongst Conservative candidates in advance of polling day. It would not matter to the leadership if academic and liberal political commentators were less persuaded that the parliamentary party had been sufficiently feminized. Cameron's failing, however, was to not to fully mobilize those in the parliamentary and voluntary party to support guarantees of women's (s)election. Arguably, he could have taken on his party and won. He chose not to. And in the absence of equality guarantees the number of Conservative women elected to the House in 2010 was always likely to be far from parity.

4
Reforming Parliamentary Selection: Party Change, Parliamentarian and Party Member Attitudes

At the end of the day when you have got your list of candidates for a constituency the person you must select is the person that's best for the job.[1]

The coming together of those within the Conservative party seeking the greater descriptive representation of women for principled reasons, together with a new party leadership keen to be electorally competitive, created a favourable moment of opportunity for the selection of many more women parliamentary candidates between 2005 and 2010 (Kittilson 2006).[2] The context within which their endeavour took place included, however, a decentralized parliamentary selection process which made it difficult to force local associations to select women and a party ideology that valorized the principle of merit. On both accounts, the party at large was unlikely to support measures that engender women's (s)election, most especially equality guarantees.[3] The party already had form (Bale 2010: 227–8). William Hague, who was party leader between 1997 and 2001, had wanted a woman placed on every parliamentary selection shortlist but, in the face of activist and MPs' resistance, he had backed down (Snowdon 2010: 51). A poll of party members prior to Cameron taking over, had already established that only 14 percent were in agreement with the idea of an 'A' List of priority candidates (Bale 2010: 291). Cameron's strategy would, then, be multi-pronged: partly it lay in reminding members that local associations remained the *final* arbiter of selection. In response, for example, to questions about two women candidates, Joanne Cash and Liz Truss, who had experienced well publicized problems with their local constituency parties (allegedly over pregnancy and an affair with an MP respectively, although Cash was also widely known to be an advocate of AWS),[4] Cameron challenged the suggestion by Radio 4's Woman's Hour presenter, Jenni Murray, that *he* had selected them, maintaining that they had been '*selected by the constituency*'.[5] Sure, the precise process of candidate selection may have changed – local associations might well be considering fewer candidates and in by-election mode only those chosen directly by CCHQ – but the final choice, even in primaries, rested with the local association.[6] Another approach was to seek to transform party membership with new members more at ease with women's descriptive representation. That advocates of women's representation were unlikely to be popular was acknowledged at the very top of the party.[7] Cameron's 'mandate' for reform was also emphasized. In December 2005, just having been elected leader, Cameron stated that he was announcing his plans 'to give this party what *it* voted for': more women in Parliament (emphasis added). Three years later at party conference he reiterated this view:

> You don't pick more women candidates to try and look good, *you* did it so we wouldn't lock out talent and fail to come up with the policies that modern families need (emphasis added).[8]

But, even if God was on 'Dave's side' in the matter of candidate selections, as the *Spectator's* spoof columnist Tamsin Lightwater put it, illustrative comments from Conservativehome suggested that some party members were anything but:[9] 'robbing – yes robbing – constituency associations of their already limited freedom, the party centre is undermining its own foundations'; 'do you expect people to be happy with this [threatening AWS]?' In the months before the 2010 general election, the 'Tory wars' over candidate selection threatened to turn hot.[10] Commenting on the aforementioned Truss case, in which the Priority List candidate faced deselection over the failure to declare an extramarital affair, Conservativehome's Tim Montgomerie was convinced that 'people who want to disenfranchise the Tory grassroots are exaggerating the level of discontent'[11] and warned that party headquarters must 'learn the lessons' about membership rights.[12] The CCHQ view is telling: 'People do wonder what the next sexist remark will be. You hold your head in your hands sometimes'.[13] Truss herself received full support of the national party, with Cameron reportedly telephoning the former High Sheriff of Norfolk who was to propose her deselection.[14] There were also threats to impose an AWS if she was deselected.[15] Nevertheless, and ultimately, CCHQ apologized for its handling of the matter. The announcement of the retirement from parliament of John Maples MP, Head of Candidates, also created consternation amongst the grassroots. His resignation statement, announced in January 2010 after the party's by-election rules 'kicked in', was perceived by critics as an overt play by someone whom they regarded as a key actor in the centralization of Conservative selection procedures, and someone perceived to be 'ideologically in favour of AWS'.[16] Maples' action would, according to his opponents, disenfranchise his local members in the selection of his successor.[17] His defence – that an earlier announcement would link his retirement to the parliamentary expenses scandal – failed to impress.[18]

Conservativehome and the Tory press might well, however, present only a partial (and largely critical) account of Conservative attitudes towards the party's efforts to achieve a higher number of women MPs for 2010. Here, drawing on both qualitative and quantitative data, we present a more systematic and comprehensive examination of party member and Parliamentarian attitudes. First, via focus group discussions with party members;[19] second, with a survey of Conservative party members; and third, via in-depth interviews with Conservative MPs and Peers. Undertaken during 2008–2009, each of these research components was designed to elicit views on the extent to which Cameron's reforms resonated with the party. In other words, was the media-friendly, and widely reported, Conservativehome postings speaking for more than its online contributors? Would Parliamentarians support Cameron's reforms – enabling him to lead his party – notwithstanding apparent party member antipathy? Amongst both members and party elites attitudinal sex differences were expected in women's favour, especially for younger women. It was also expected that in the focus groups, metropolitan party members would be more favourably disposed than provincial party members; and that the parliamentary elite would be more positive than grassroots party members, given the former's concern with electoral success of the party and the latter's likely concern over local party autonomy.[20]

The views of the party membership:[21] Party member focus groups

> Should the Conservative party seek to look like the land that it represents? Of course it should…50 percent of our MPs should be women. (London male, all-male group)

Most focus group participants consider that the parliamentary Conservative party is under-representative in terms of sex. Members, both male and female, in both London and Bristol, are supportive of the argument, in principle, that there should be more Conservative women MPs. A couple of party members are positive that the situation has already improved. Detractors are only few in number. One London woman in the mixed group relies upon the *reductio ad absurdum* critique, talking of the representation of 'supermarket checkout assistants or waitresses or secretaries'. Arguments articulated in support of greater numbers of women are varied. They include symbolic representation – 'candidates that people can relate to' – and substantive representation – 'a different outlook on certain issues'. There was less discussion of the reasons for women's under-representation than might have been expected, however. It was most extensively discussed by the all-women groups. Some saw an incompatibility between politics as 'set up in the House of Commons' and women's family responsibilities.

There were perceptions too that women were bullied, subject to 'a lot of sexist rubbish', had to 'play games', and needed to be 'aggressive'. Others, however, countered these claims by stating that the women 'knew the conditions' when they decided to enter politics. One contended that 'you can't have a part-time MP can you?' and held that 'some women are aggressive'.

Supply and demand-side explanations

The under-representation of women on the Conservative benches is, overall, best understood by party members as reflecting primarily supply-side explanations.[22] In their view, women are simply not coming forward in the same numbers as men. One London woman illustrated this by claiming that the aspirant candidates 'circling' her constituency, where the Conservative MP was retiring, were all 'young men'. Biological as well as social causes were identified by both women and men. Women give birth and care for children, are less interested in politics and think differently. As one London woman put it, 'women have children, in the nature of things, and I think an awful lot of them actually want to look after their children when they're really young'. Women's increasing tendency to delay motherhood meant, furthermore, that fewer women would be in a position to enter politics at a relatively young age. A brief discussion in the mixed Bristol group about the negative impact of combining motherhood and being an MP ridiculed the effect Margaret Thatcher's political career had on her children. At the same time, there was recognition that recent experience of women MPs having children whilst in Parliament 'seems to work', and that the public see such women as more 'worldly'.

In addition to childcare responsibilities, women were said to lack the 'tunnel vision' of men – they might 'have an ambition when they're young', but they 'don't really bother afterwards'. Men will say 'sod the kids, I'm going to a meeting' or 'shut the doors' and not be 'bothered' by anybody. Men will also prepare differently for a selection – women are 'more creative', but less likely to give a 'learned speech', according to one Bristol woman. Alongside an acknowledgement that the party is dominated by women at the local level (an issue to which we will return) and that women are active in local and what is considered non-party political issues, the stark question 'do they [women] want to do it?' is raised. The answer, according to the Bristol men, is that women are less persistent in selections, having 'better things to do'. Men, or rather middle class men, were regarded as able to participate in politics because they had already built up their business and could therefore enter politics because 'they've got somebody in to manage it'.

Supplementing the claim that fewer women seek selection is the related question of the quality of aspiring women candidates. Women should be promoted strictly 'on their own merits'. Here Labour's women MPs were identified as examples of 'people who simply weren't up to the job'. Women candidates would, consequently, benefit from training and support. Women also need encouragement to seek selection, akin to the Liberal Democrats' perceived efforts in recruiting women. The party should, therefore, 'talent-spot' younger women. Though for one London male this should not go so far as 'dragging them off the street'. That said, one contributor to the London all-male group suggested that if the Conservative party had insufficient numbers of men then the party would 'surely' 'go out and find' them.

For the most part, the focus group participants felt that the only rule the party should follow in candidate-selection was that the best person should get the job. This is about merit, and whilst there was some discussion about the criteria by which to judge this, contributors mostly presumed that merit is an objective criterion in itself. What makes a good MP for these party members? Not somebody who has moved seamlessly from university to Central Office to Parliament. There is a strong hostility towards the professional or lawyer politician. The preference is generally for candidates who have had a 'proper job', with 'business' and 'commercial' experience. For some (Bristol men), local candidates should matter more. The London focus groups were influenced by what might be termed the 'Shaun Bailey' effect. Bailey, a BME male candidate, was supported in the all-male London group because of his ability to 'reach out to all sections of the community', but his selection was also considered a 'real strength' in that he 'can say the most outrageous [Thatcherite] stuff' and 'they can't touch him' because he's black – 'he's bullet proof'.[23] Sex did not seem to matter much in these deliberations, although one London woman in the mixed group felt that women would be more diligent MPs. Another contribution suggested that women would make the party look less 'nasty'. Overall, the feeling was that 'good' women candidates, like Margaret Thatcher, would get through on their merits. Those who do not get through are by definition lacking merit. There is, though, a perception that some parts of the country – Yorkshire is identified – have selected very few women, though no reasons to explain this were proffered.

Most party members did not subscribe explicitly to the selectorate discrimination thesis. Yet, there was at the same time widespread (and paradoxical) support for the view that women, especially older women, discriminate against women candidate: 'I conducted countless selection processes and the only people who were prejudiced against women, from what I could see were women'. Such hostility was acknowledged to have dogged Thatcher's own selections. And one male Bristol contributor recounted his experience of undertaking local government short-listing where the name and sex of the applicant was unknown and admitted that it 'really was quite an eye-opener' – a position which suggests some sympathy with the selectorate-discrimination thesis. Other participants claimed anti-women discrimination by women as deriving from a fear of sexual relationships developing between a woman MP and their husbands (all-male London; mixed Bristol, woman) or because of the aspirant candidates' dress sense (all-male London). Other reasons for selectorate bias included assumptions about voter discrimination – 'they tend to go for men because they thought they would be more electable' – and traditional views of gender roles – 'older women think women should, you know, be in the home'. If women are the discriminating sex, the solution was, at least for one Bristol man, to have more men on the selection committees.[24]

To further probe participants' views on descriptive representation the focus groups were given handouts containing the following two quotes:

> Looking at its elected representatives, you will see a predominantly white, male party. Given that we now see an ethnically diverse society, where women increasingly play a major role, the Conservative party just doesn't look like the people that it is claiming to represent. (Theresa May)

> I don't think it matters if you're a man, woman, young or old – all that matters is that whoever is in charge has got there on their own merit. (Ann Widdecombe)

Two main observations are evident in participants' responses to these two statements. The first is the tendency to question the implied incompatibility of the two positions. This was the case for men in both the mixed London group and all-male London and Bristol groups, and for men and women in the mixed Bristol group. Even so, participants were inclined to reiterate the importance of the distinction between good and poor quality MPs, with the implication that May's position supports the election of women MPs who are 'not up to the job' (while one participant claimed that Widdecombe had herself been over-promoted and should have remained a junior minister). It was also suggested that 'quota women' suffer from a lack of confidence in their own abilities, having got their position 'automatically, without having to work for it'. One contributor in the Bristol all-women group focused on the position of BME women candidates and contended that 'it could take five more years before we have enough, say, coloured women who have achieved, or are brought up abreast the idea that they have a part to play in public life' and that, like the Labour party, the Conservative party should appoint BME women into the Lords in the first instance.[25]

The second main response to the two prompts was, however, to place a generational interpretation on the statements by May and Widdecombe. According to women in the mixed London group, 'Ann's is the old Conservative party and Theresa is the new Conservative party'; 'the older members of the party tend to all to agree with Ann Widdecombe and the young people agree more with Theresa May'. A man in the all-male Bristol group concurs, asking, 'how old is Ann Widdecombe and how old is Theresa May?' Another way of distinguishing the comments was to describe them as pragmatic (Widdecombe) and idealistic (May), and to suggest that 'at the top [of the party] it's Theresa May, but down on the ground it's Ann Widdecombe'. Amongst the all-women London group, there were differences of opinion. One intervention – arguably ironic – questioned whether the House of Commons should be one side female and one side male, whilst another contributor argued that the party should make it easier for women to be elected – not least because 'government wants to benefit from having more women in it'. This link between descriptive and substantive representation is, however, countered by a further claim that the House would only be more concerned about 'shoes' , a direct, albeit, implicit criticism of May. In the Bristol all-male group, contributors, whilst preferring Widdecombe's position, recognized that May's position might reflect what the 'middle ground of the electorate' think, and perhaps should therefore be taken more seriously by the party and themselves.

Equality strategies

Support for the principle of women's greater representation does not, in our focus groups, necessarily translate into support for doing anything to 'fix it'. Unsurprisingly, party members – male and female across both locations – proved to be more comfortable with equality rhetoric and equality promotion measures rather than equality guarantees (Lovenduski 2005a). The party should, therefore, 'announce very firmly that...you're fully supportive of women candidates' and go 'out and bring women in from student groups'. Any 'perceived underlying prejudices' should be removed and training provided, though there was debate about whether training should be provided for women only or for all candidates, with both women and men preferring the latter. When it comes to financial support, there were claims from the all-male London group that (a) the party is making money available; (b) such money should not be available because (to paraphrase) the job is a 'calling', a position that begs the question whether the financial costs of standing permit only rich MPs; and (c) women would use any financial support for a 'dress allowance'.

There is no support for AWS, bar one London woman who admitted that she was 'not too against that' and a woman in the Bristol group who was clear that Labour's AWS policy worked and garnered women's support for the party, a view also supported by some of the women in the mixed London group. The individual London woman stood out from her fellow party members, both male and female, in her group. She made a number of notable interventions: citing selectorate-discrimination against women;

claiming that there are 'fantastic women out there'; and that selecting greater numbers of women has to be 'made a much bigger issue within the party' so that selectors' attitudes change. She added, to qualify her position and to refute, in anticipation, the *reductio ad absurdum* critique, that she was not asking for women to be chosen 'because they've got one leg'. She also made it clear that she was not advocating positive discrimination, not least because she recognized that this invites the charge that a woman 'only got selected' because of her sex and 'she's not that good really'. This woman also raised the question of whether one would want to force particular measures on local associations: 'you see, I'm not too against that, but I'm not sure in what context you would use it, whether we want to force that on a constituency'. The men in her group countered her position with concerns about justice, political correctness and, once again, the issue of the quality of the candidate. Some support for this London woman's perspective was, forthcoming in the Bristol all-women group – though not from all the women in that group. One contributor was concerned that the party's efforts were not 'tackling' the underlying issues of the selection committees, the grass roots who do 'the actual voting'.

Elsewhere, from men and women, opposition to equality guarantees was unequivocal – 'it's a no-no'. The party's Priority List came under fire: 'dreadful...completely and emphatically'. Once again, the *reductio ad absurdum* critique was aired: 'I don't like this idea of a shortlist completely of women, or...of dwarves'. There was also more discussion about the concept of merit and the quality or otherwise of women (and other fast-tracked) candidates: they lacked 'experience', and were 'ill-prepared' – just look (once again) at 'Blair's Babes'. Here the objection to the Priority List was presented in terms of the women on it not being good enough, rather than the mechanism itself (London all-male group).

There was also criticism of top-down imposition by the party's central organization on local constituency associations. One London male asked if the party might be 'using a sledgehammer to crack a nut' in its reforms to parliamentary candidate selection procedure, which stemmed, in part, from the belief that the problem was essentially one of supply rather than of demand. Another contributor accused the leadership of being 'pretty heavy handed'. The Bristol all-male group, in particular, did not pull their punches. The new selection procedures were 'completely undemocratic', an 'absolute disgrace', 'politically correct – it's bloody Labour'; and in any case the selection process was 'already in favour of women and ethnic minorities'. Did the party really want to impose '100 women on 100 constituencies?' They also questioned whether women wanted such measures.

The effect of what was perceived as Central Office imposing women and BME candidates on constituencies was felt to be negative by both women and men, although to a greater extent by the men, especially in the all-male groups and the mixed London groups. For a start, it would 'kill off the grassroots', and reduce campaigning as members will not do 'that extra bit'; it would also 'kill off your fundraising' and create a backlash. 'White middle aged men might get a bit shirty' and there could be a legal challenge. It might also negatively affect turnout amongst core voters, and more generally men, who 'do feel a bit drummed down at the moment'. The party should not look like it had succumbed to political correctness. In short, there was widespread support for the view that 'local members' should have the final say:

> Because the one thing that the Conservative party doesn't like and local parties don't like is being dictated to by the centre all the time on issues which have always been up to the local parties to decide (London all-male group).

Pre- and post-questionnaire Data

In pre and post focus group questionnaires participants were asked about their views on three reforms that Cameron introduced: the Priority List; sex quotas at the shortlisting stage; and party training for women and BME candidates. Only training – the weakest form of equality promotion – gained majority support from the focus group members. Overall, in the pre-questionnaire, 19 were in favour and 14 against. In the post-questionnaire, 24 approved and 11 disapproved, suggesting that the intervening discussion did persuade a few party members to support such initiatives. In contrast, the Priority List and the requirement of a minimum sex quota at the short-listing stage were not supported, even though these measures stop short of equality guarantees. In the pre-questionnaire only 7 members supported quotas at the short-listing stage, although 14 approved of the priority list. By contrast, 30 disagreed with the sex quota and 18 disapproved of the priority list. The comparison of the pre-and post-questionnaire data suggests that the discussion of these issues, for the most part, hardened party members' views against the two stronger forms of equality promotion.[26]

Sex and other differences in party member focus group attitudes

Party members' views on candidate selection are mostly shared across the focus groups. Women as well as men rely on biological and social factors to explain away the differences in the numbers of female and male Conservative MPs. Women and men agree that the 'best person for the job' should be selected. Even so, there are some subtle sex differences. Some women, particularly younger ones, offer more critical viewpoints. For example, one London woman contested a male participant's view that men's dominance as parliamentary representatives reflects the fact that they are able to let their businesses be managed by others, by suggesting that it is a woman who will make sure that such men get to work on time. Here, there is an implication of a gendered critique of the sexual division of labour and the public/private split: men's ability to participate in politics is dependent upon women's domestic labour; it is the difficulties of women establishing their own business that means that, unlike men, they are less likely to engage in politics. Women's unequal domestic responsibilities also influenced suggestions by London women that women candidates and MPs require the full support of their partners in ways that male candidates tend not to. Women, for example, are likely to need familial support for childcare (as one London male also admits). The mixed Bristol group also discussed the necessary support of husbands for women candidates without making any similar claim for men candidates, although the all-women Bristol group contended that being an MP was a family commitment 'whether that's the husband or the wife'.

The sexes generally took different views of the symbolic effect of Margaret Thatcher for the greater descriptive representation of women. For the Bristol men (and one Bristol woman in the all-women group) Thatcher proved that a good woman will win and, by implication, that women who are not selected are, objectively, not good enough. Thatcher also 'opened the door' and was a 'real role model'. Indeed, other 'dominating' and 'scary' women were identified by these men to bolster this argument. But members of the Bristol all-women group were more likely to see Thatcher as having 'put' back the cause of women's descriptive representation, because she 'scared' the party into being thereafter more hesitant about selecting women.

The all-women London group also offered a more lengthy discussion of merit, even if there was disagreement amongst them. One woman neatly outlined the critical perspective:

> [Meritocracy] only works up to a point, because how do you know that's the best person if, in fact, they've had far more opportunities and perhaps...there's some even better person that didn't manage to fight their way into a position to become a candidate or whatever, because it's just been too difficult?

There were also assertions that for 'any woman wanting to get ahead on her own abilities she's got to be probably twice as well qualified as a lot of men'.

> There are a lot of good women who might be equally good, who are less aggressive, that fall by the wayside...nobody goes and recognizes their qualities; they've actually got to push themselves forward to be recognized and they're going to be put down by men anyway, to a large extent.

Another contributor noted that there are 'a lot of good women around...on boards too', although her conclusion was that women do not, therefore, need special treatment. It is only women in the mixed London group who identified 'politics as male' and 'shockingly awful', 'cut throat...full of testosterone' (although one woman admitted to rather enjoying this style of politics). Similarly, the all women Bristol group raised the issue of whether women and men have different styles of politics. They also suggested that the quality of the male candidates is not necessarily without dispute. 'They are not necessarily top notch'.

In respect of selectorate discrimination a Bristol woman who had herself sought selection recounted her experience of having been asked 'completely different questions' to her male competitors and that she was asked about how she would 'manage' her childcare. Such discrimination she saw as specific to her party which 'does not accommodate' women. She noted too that the 'majority of the room is filled with older people...and older women don't like to see a woman in politics'. It was suggested that Central Office needed more women workers too. One London woman in the mixed group summarized it in the following terms: 'I've been involved in the Conservative party for 25 years, since I was a child, and it's still run for – no offence – white middle aged men...the (female) candidates are being selected – they're on councils, but that's as far as women go'.

Women's contributions – where they are different to the men's – fell on the more progressive side of the argument about women's descriptive representation, even if, some women also subscribed to more explicitly traditional views of gender and politics. The London women's focus group briefly discussed the issue of how women MPs with children managed their childcare responsibilities, which slipped into a more general discussion of the role of nannies. The employment of 'another woman' to enable women to be 'free' to undertake paid work was considered to be 'very odd' and 'really funny', although one older woman recognized that her views were 'old-fashioned'. The Bristol women's group discussed the illegality of asking women about their childcare arrangements: 'If you're interviewing a woman who's got young children, you're going to want to know that'. One woman claimed that her male partner would feel 'dreadfully upset if he...wasn't asked about how he would deal with the children because he also...takes a share of the role with me'. Another woman summarized the situation: 'I think sometimes as women we can't have everything'. It is the women too in the mixed groups that contested some of the more old-fashioned claims, though once again this position was not unanimously held amongst the women. For example, in the mixed Bristol group a woman questioned whether women who go into politics should be having children.

Party member survey

Like the Conservative party members who participated in the focus groups, the majority of survey members agree that there are too few women in Parliament, as Table 4.1 reveals. There is, moreover, and again like the

Table 4.1   Should Parliament have More or Fewer Women MPs?

	Men	Women	
Many more	74	66	140
	15.5%	21.4%	17.8%
A few more	211	135	346
	44.1%	43.8%	44.0%
Same as now	158	89	247
	33.1%	28.9%	31.4%
A few less	27	13	40
	5.6%	4.2%	5.1%
Many fewer	8	5	13
	1.7%	1.6%	1.7%
Total	478	308	786
	100.0%	100.0%	100.0%

Cramer's V = 0.08 (sig = 0.24)

focus groups, no significant difference of opinion between men and women on this point. Nearly 60 percent of men and 65 percent of women think Parliament should have either a few or many more women MPs.

Selectorate discrimination

Party member attitudes towards the charge, forthcoming in the focus group discussion and evident in much of the extant literature, that women aspirant candidates are not judged on merit by women members of the party's selectorate, is revealed in Table 4.2. A significant minority of respondents – just over one-third – strongly or tend to agree with such a statement. Note again, that men and women party members think this in roughly equal proportions.

Perceptions of selectorate discrimination, whether by women or men, are, of course, not the same thing as proving that it takes place (Norris and Lovenduski 1995). People can misperceive what is going on. To try to better gauge if there is hidden bias against women candidates amongst the Conservative party membership – some of whom may well participate in candidate selection – a simple experiment was undertaken with our sample of party members, the results of which are reported in Table 4.3. The sample was split in half, and each half was a given a biographical description of three hypothetical aspirant parliamentary candidates. Each respondent was asked to rank the three in order of preference. The only thing that distinguished the candidate descriptions were their names, which implied that the candidates were of different sexes. Thus, split sample A was told that '*Peter King* is a Barrister with a 10 year long record of party office as a local

Table 4.2 'Conservative women members are more likely to discriminate against women seeking selection as parliamentary candidates than Conservative men members'

	Male	Female	
Strongly agree	34	19	53
	4.3%	3.5%	4.0%
Tend to agree	216	141	357
	27.4%	26.0%	26.8%
Neither agree nor disagree	302	198	500
	38.3%	36.5%	37.6%
Tend to disagree	199	147	346
	25.3%	27.1%	26.0%
Strongly disagree	37	38	75
	4.7%	7.0%	5.6%
Total	788	543	1331
	100.0%	100.0%	100.0%

Cramer' V = 0.06 (sig. 0.340)

Table 4.3 Split-sample Evidence of Latent Bias against Women Candidates

	Peter King	Patricia King	John Harrison	Jane Harrison	Leslie Green 'A'	Leslie Green 'B'
1st choice	19.5	19.1	63.2	62.6	17.9	17.7
2nd choice	37.6	42.8	25.6	25.4	36.9	31.7
3rd choice	42.9	38.1	11.2	12	45.1	50.7
Total	100	100	100	100	100	100
n	853	837	853	837	853	837

councillor and as an adviser to a shadow minister. He is seeking selection in a Greater London seat. He currently works and lives in central London but grew up in Yorkshire'. Split sample B was given exactly the same profile – except that the candidate's name was changed to 'Patricia King'. Similarly, split sample A was told that '*John* Harrison has extensive experience as a Human Resources professional; he has been a Conservative member for 15 years, a local councillor for ten years and fought an unwinnable Conservative seat at the previous election, achieving a greater than average swing'. Split-sample B was told that this candidate was called '*Jane* Harrison'. Finally, a control was applied in that each split-sample was also told of a third candidate with a 'gender-neutral' name: 'Leslie Green is 40 years old and has been a party member for two years, although was born and raised in the constituency. Educated to degree level and a small business owner, Leslie has extensive links with the local community, especially with Black and Asian groups'. If there is latent bias against women prospective candidates we would expect that candidates with female names would garner less support than their male counterparts, while the two split-samples should be indistinguishable in terms of their support for 'Leslie Green'. Table 4.3 shows little or no overall difference between the two split-samples, so that one cannot infer from this data there is bias against the selection of female candidates among Conservative members, a finding that might reassure the party leadership (and advocates of women's descriptive representation for that matter).[27]

Equality strategies

Despite the widespread appreciation of women's under-representation by party members, support for specific measures to address this was less than forthcoming amongst our sample of surveyed party members. Respondents were asked Likert-style questions to gauge how far they approved of the following measures: the creation of the party's Priority List; primaries; sex quotas at the short-listing stage; party training for women and BME aspirant candidates; a sex quota in the party's winnable seats; a 'women's manifesto' for the 2010 general election; and the greater prominence of women MPs and candidates in the election campaign. Responses to these questions were coded from 1–5, with 1 representing strong support for these measures designed to enhance the presence of women in Parliament and election campaigns, and 5 representing opposition to them. When responses to the question about whether or not the low number of Conservative female MPs deters women from voting for the party were combined with data on these other seven questions, a reliable attitudinal scale (Alpha = 0.783) was created, on which the overall sample mean was 3.28 (sd = 0.71) – a position slightly more opposed to than supportive of such measures. There is a modest but significant difference between men and women on the scale (which we call 'selectreform'), with the latter more supportive of measures designed to give women greater prominence in Parliament and election campaigns. The mean position of women on the scale is 3.17 (sd = 0.70), while it is 3.35 for men (sd = 0.70), giving a 2-tailed t-test significance level of 0.000 between the two means. A little more of the detail, including these sex differences, can be illustrated by closer examination of the individual scale items. Table 4.4 reports the overall percentage of men and women approving and disapproving of the various measures, and the relevant percentage difference index scores.

The first point to note here is that there is generally only limited support for reform of the parliamentary candidate selection process. Primaries and the Priority List garner the support of both men and women members,

Table 4.4 Support for Individual Measures Designed to Enhance the Descriptive Representation of Women in the Conservative Party, by Sex

		Men	Women	Total PDI	Cramer's v (sig.)
Creation of a 'Priority List' of candidates	% approving	44	47.7	-3.7	0.131 (0.000) n = 1579
	% disapproving	36.5	25.9	10.6	
Primaries in which candidates go through a series of public votes to win nomination	% approving	74.2	74.8	-0.6	0.059 (0.227) n.s. n = 1621
	% disapproving	14.4	12.3	2.1	
Compulsory minimum numbers of women at the short listing stage	% approving	**14.8**	20.9	-6.1	0.207 (0.000) n = 1630
	% disapproving	69.8	52.4	17.4	
Party training programmes for female black and ethnic minority candidates	% approving	31.8	30.2	1.6	0.092 (0.008) n = 1616
	% disapproving	45.4	43.4	2	

Table 4.4 Support for Individual Measures Designed to Enhance the Descriptive Representation of Women in the Conservative Party, by Sex – *continued*

		Men	Women	Total PDI	Cramer's v (sig.)
A compulsory minimum number of women selected as PPCs in winnable seats	% approving	8.7	20.7	–12	0.254 (0.000) n = 1623
	% disapproving	75.5	54.6	20.9	
The Conservative party should produce a 'women's manifesto'	% approving	13.9	20	–6.1	0.130 (0.000) n = 1564
	% disapproving	68	55.8	12.2	
More women MPs/candidates should be used to front election campaigns	% approving	37.4	39.7	–2.3	0.042 (0.587) n.s. n = 1570
	% disapproving	31.6	30.8	0.8	
Overall Means	% approving	32.1	36.3	–4.2	
	% disapproving	48.7	39.3	9.4	

Note: '% approving' = total of % 'strongly approve' + % 'tends to approve'; '% disapproving'' = total of % 'strongly disapprove' + % 'tends to disapprove'.

overall. This was in line with expectations following the focus group discussions. The lack of support for the provision of training for women and BME candidates is perhaps more surprising, given that our focus groups participants had seemed to be more predisposed towards such measures. Secondly, Table 4.4 shows that where sex differences exist these are most evident in respect of sex short-listing quotas. Here, women are more favourably disposed than the men. This finding is consistent, once again, with the focus group findings. Notwithstanding general opposition that many Conservative members evinced towards these measures, some women participants did voice limited support for equality promotion measures. Note in the Table (in bold) the sex differences in support for sex quotas at the short-listing stage; sex quotas in winnable seats; and the production of a women's manifesto, for example.

Conservative party member antipathy to candidate selection reforms reflects wider attitudes about centre-local relations, as in the focus group discussions. Table 4.5 below shows that more than a quarter of our sample felt that the party leadership generally wielded too much influence over the candidate-selection process, even if most thought it was about right. Here the sex difference is in men's favour, with men significantly more likely to hold this view compared with women party members.

Table 4.5 'Do you think that the leadership has too much, not enough, or about the right amount of influence in the candidate selection process?'

	Male	Female	
Too much influence	276	113	389
	29.7%	20.8%	26.4%
About right	612	395	1007
	65.9%	72.6%	68.4%
Not enough influence	41	36	77
	4.4%	6.6%	5.2%
Total	929	544	1473
	100.0%	100.0%	100.0%

Cramer's V = 0.10 (sig = 0.000)

Turning to whether party members saw electoral value in a more descriptively representative parliamentary party – something that might be thought to persuade them of the case for reform – Table 4.6 reveals that only a minority of party members (approximately one fifth) regards the current under-representation on the Tory benches as something which actually discourages female voters from supporting the party. There are no sex differences on this point.

Table 4.6 'The low number of Conservative female MPs deters women from voting for the party – do you agree or disagree?'

	Male	Female	
Strongly agree	19	16	35
	2.1%	2.6%	2.3%
Tend to agree	170	98	268
	18.5%	16.1%	17.5%
Neither agree nor disagree	206	151	357
	22.4%	24.9%	23.4%
Tend to disagree	377	229	606
	40.9%	37.7%	39.7%
Strongly disagree	149	113	262
	16.2%	18.6%	17.1%
Total	921	607	1528
	100.0%	100.0%	100.0%

Cramer's V = 0.06 (sig. = 0.30)

The attitudes of MPs and Peers towards the (s)election of women

Whilst one can find widespread support for the *principle* of women's greater presence in the contemporary Conservative party in the country, both the qualitative and quantitative data tapping party member attitudes suggests that Cameron would very much need to 'lead' his grassroots membership in respect of measures that would engender women's greater descriptive representation. Indeed, he would need to be mindful of the importance of managing centre-local relations and appreciate that party members might not see the electoral reward that he evidently did in changing the face of his party. At the same time, Cameron might be reassured by the potential support amongst some women party members who are more favourably disposed to equality measures. But what of his parliamentary colleagues? Would many of these, over and above those already publicly known for mobilizing on this issue, be sympathetic to his reforming agenda? There is no doubt that some Conservative MPs were, and remained, hostile to Cameron's initiatives (Evans 2008), not least, the vocal and media-savvy Ann Widdecombe and her fellow MPs who proposed legislation to proscribe equality guarantees in 2009.[28] Much of this antipathy reflects concerns about the merit of candidates, but there is also 'lingering resentment' about the *arrivistes* from Notting Hill, perceived to care more about revamping the party's image than ensuring activists were prepared to campaign on the ground (Bale 2010: 300–2).

Supply and demand

For Conservative Parliamentarians the explanation for women's under-representation at Westminster is more an issue of paucity of supply rather than a lack of party demand (Table 4.7 below). That said, our interviews with party elites reveal that the selectorate discrimination thesis garners widespread support, and does so from Parliamentarians from both Houses and of both sexes.[29] Qualifications about perceptions of selectorate discrimination once again notwithstanding (Norris and Lovenduski 1995), there is a widespread view amongst Conservative Parliamentarians that women do not experience a level playing field when seeking selection as parliamentary candidates for the Conservative party. Although sitting Conservative women MPs often appear initially reluctant to admit that women

Table 4.7   Supply and Demand Side Explanations, by Parliamentarian Type and Party

	Women MPs	Women Peers	Men MPs	Men Peers
Demand				
Reject selectorate discrimination	1			
Accept selectorate discrimination	5	5	6	6
Reject 'Old Biddies' discrimination			1	1
Accept 'Old Biddies' discrimination	4	3	3	4
Questions about husbands/ manage/childcare		1	1	
CCHQ 'persuaders'		1		1
Supply				
Childcare/family incompatibility	2	2	2	1
Maternalism/maternal guilt	1		3	
Geographic mobility/constituency demands	1	1	1	
Financial resources	1			1
Public/media scrutiny	1	2		
Supportive husbands/marriages	3	2	1	
Struggle with selection		2	2	
Lack role models/need exhortation		2		1
Risk career		1		
Adversarial politics		1	1	
Less interested				1

are discriminated against, further discussion often reveals a deep-seated appreciation that it does take place. To illustrate: one woman MP admits that local associations often make decisions which are not 'the wisest in the world' and need 'cajoling'. Shireen Ritchie and John Maples are cited as examples of those within the party with responsibility for candidate selection who have succeeded in 'showing' associations how good women candidates can be, a view supported by a PPC who adds the name of Bernard Jenkin as someone who has been willing to champion the cause of female candidates. A woman Peer concurs in praising the role of central party 'persuaders' and argues that Parliamentarians should help better 'inform' local selectorates on the choices before them, in order to 'stop them being quite so certain of what they wanted'. Another Peer, this time male, suggests that once a decision has been made to be more representative, 'talent' which had hitherto not been recognized becomes evident. For some, this makes it imperative that the commitment to reforming the process of candidate-selection continues after the 2010 election.

There is also widespread awareness of the difficulties women face in getting selected. This is true of women Peers (as well as MPs), especially those Peers who had either sat in the Commons or had unsuccessfully tried to become MPs. Prone to being criticized for aspects of their personal lives, such as being divorced, one MP claimed that women need to 'cuddle up' to the selection board, whose instinct is to prefer a 'pinstripe identikit' candidate with whom they wish to 'spend Friday evenings'. Female activists of long-standing service in local constituency associations, unflatteringly referred to as the 'old biddies', were (as in the focus group discussions) frequently identified as the most likely to discriminate against women aspirants, although some interviewees were more inclined to identify older people *per se*. The alleged prejudices of older women in the selectorate were thought to stem from the implied challenge that younger women aspirants present of their own choice to stay at home and raise their families. Older women were felt to be those for whom your skirt must not be 'too short' (again a sentiment shared with some focus group members).[30]

Turning to supply side explanations, differences between men and women, and between MPs and Peers, are sometimes apparent, as Table 4.7 indicates. Whether the problem of women's lack of supply is seen to lie with political institutions (whether the party, parliament or electoral politics more generally) or with women, depends to some extent on one's sex. Broadly speaking, women MPs talk in terms of both these factors, whereas men tend to see greater explanatory merit in the latter. Women Peers sit somewhere in the middle of these groups. In the first place, there is widespread agreement that women's parental, spousal and family responsibilities are difficult to reconcile with the demands of being an MP. Second, all bar women MPs, are more likely to identify deficiencies in women. Whether that is because women are less interested in politics; find the selection process difficult; or because they dislike the mode of political engagement in the House. Women MPs and Peers, in contrast, are more likely to offer a critique of the current system and practices of British party politics. However, while some men may see it as the 'natural order of things' for women to prioritize their families over Parliament, and some women MPs concede that women could be inhibited by a sense of 'maternal' guilt, there is little evidence that they consider the possibility of 'paternal' guilt. Nor do those who identify the tension between dual responsibilities to family and parliamentary career ponder whether this affects men as well as women.

Furthermore, not one woman MP argues that women are not interested in politics, lack role models, struggle with selection, or are not prepared to risk their non-political careers for a parliamentary one. And current selection practices and norms are more problematized. For example, one female Peer notes the woman candidate's dilemma: because she must look confident, but not too confident, in the selection meeting, she may end up presenting in a 'diffident' or 'apologetic way'. A second contends that as the Conservative party selection format has changed (see Chapter 3) women have 'started to do a lot better', implying that the format of selection was hitherto in some way at fault. In contrast, one senior Tory male MP takes the view that women candidates – even the 'top' ones – need extra training to help them succeed in selection meetings, and are put off by adversarial politics. For another male MP the solution is for the party to recruit older women with retired husbands (so that their families do not get in their way). Such a scenario illustrates, once again, a failure to consider why Parliament is apparently incompatible with younger mothers' but not younger fathers' lives.[31]

An additional difference between women and men MPs relates to the principle of descriptive representation. While most male MPs accept the reality of women's under-representation, they do not usually tend to see it as the most significant problem of representation. Age, disability and race may each be identified as important, and even the rise of the professional politician elicits greater concern. But the identity which most animates them is class. There is, moreover, an interesting interaction here between class and sex, with working class frequently equated with men, and middle class equaling women. Selection becomes, then, a zero sum game in which working class men are said to lose out, but where working class women are never in the frame. Further, a few of the male Peers' discussions reveal contradictory positions on women's descriptive representation. One claims that dominance by 'middle aged men with ties and darks suits' is problematic whilst recognizing that this might be the outcome of the individual choices of the different constituencies. A second holds that women's descriptive representation is necessary even though the sex of the candidate does not matter. A third maintains that that it would only be really problematic if the House of Commons was completely unrepresentative, implying that current levels are satisfactory. Finally, only women MPs (but not women Peers nor male MPs and Peers) conceive of party modernization as embracing the greater representation of women in the parliamentary party. Even here it is a minority position, with one woman MP explicitly rejecting the association. Of the three interviewees who do regard better descriptive representation as intrinsic to party modernization, two are senior women publicly known to be active on the issue, and for whom it is also in part a strategy to win back women's votes. Theresa May, speaking in 2005, was explicit on this point: the party 'needs more women to *vote* for us....Labour is far better than we are at speaking the language of the woman voter...focusing on the kinds of issues that matter disproportionately to women'.[32] Recognizing the increasingly feminized nature of inter-party competition in British politics – the terrain of 'mummy issues' – she lamented the lost support of younger mothers and aspirational career women.

Equality promotion measures

There is almost no support for AWS among Conservative Parliamentarians. Only one woman MP and one woman Peer would accept them if they were found to be 'necessary', although one male Peer implicitly, and hesitantly, suggests they might be considered as a temporary measure and a single male MP notes that Labour's AWS worked. AWS are criticized for various reasons: because they treat the symptoms and not the cause of women's under-representation; because they offend against the principle of merit (Labour's women are identified by a male MP, male Peers and a woman Peer, but not by women MPs, as evidence of that);[33] because they patronize women; because they are counterproductive for women as they engender a backlash – a 'full scale revolt', according to one male MP; and because they are a threat from the centre to local party autonomy. In this respect, Theresa May is praised by a female colleague for having not taken the 'easy' option of introducing them when she was Party Chairman, and of going down the harder road of persuading local selectorates to select women.

The 50:50 short-listing sex quota garners a warmer response amongst women MPs. These are not perceived to have caused problems within the party; are examples of equal of opportunity; and there is confidence that they will work, as women candidates will no longer be the 'odd ones out' in the selection meeting. Women Peers tolerate the short-listing sex quota, in that there are no outright rejections, although there are some concerns about the quality of the candidates the quota might produce. In contrast, three male MPs are critical and only one is supportive. Male members of the Lords, like their male colleagues in the Commons, are also less supportive than the women. They find themselves 'uncomfortable' with the quota even when they can see its 'symbolic' value.

Support is once again most forthcoming from women MPs for the Priority List. One describes it as 'brave and radical' while another asks 'what other mechanisms' are there? Women and male Peers and male MPs are more divided amongst themselves and sometimes hold contradictory positions. Supportive women Peers are mostly those that either sat, or tried to win a seat, in the Commons. One male Peer goes so far as to claim it is 'absolutely excellent', though others tend to offer less effusive support. They do not have a 'quarrel with it', or talk of it in de-gendered terms as a means to finding the best candidates. Support from male MPs is rationalized in various ways, for instance, on the grounds that it was 'basically necessary', or because there was no measure that would not have invited some criticism, and because the quality of candidates was exceptionally high. But criticism of the Priority List is also expressed, sometimes by the same men, because it is discriminatory and offends against the principle of merit by excluding good men. It favours 'minor celebrities' and the 'weird...black lesbian disabled' – the *reducio ad absurdum* critique, once again – and because it creates 'centrally' imposed candidates, and causes intra-party conflict.[34] This in turn generates an incentive to select men 'simply' because local associations 'don't like being told what to do'. Take these two examples from male members of the House of Lords and Commons, respectively:

> [Cameron] can squeak 'til he's blue in the face but if you go down to Esher, or somewhere like that, and produce a whole crowd of women as possible candidates, you're going to have quite a struggle.

> The kind of idea that a privileged group of cognoscenti should take the view about what the 'right'...type of person was to be an MP...sticks in the craw, I think, of a lot of party workers.

Local autonomy must be protected in such views because local associations provide the party's foot soldiers and campaigners and it is 'all they have'. It also, in this view, protects parliamentary cohesion:

> The Chief Whip would say in the Commons, "well I'll be on the phone to your Chairman and say how badly you behaved". What worries me is the Chairman's going to go there and say, "what's this got to do with me? You imposed this candidate on me!"

The solution here is to be sensitive to 'local circumstances' and permit local candidates (albeit approved by the leadership/centre). Recall that is what, in effect, was the outcome of the third set of selection reforms, and which, as noted in the previous chapter, resulted in rather a lot of 'exceptional' local men. Many more, indeed, than leading gender equality activists had thought imaginable.

There is no denying that Conservative Parliamentarians are well aware of some party members' unhappiness with Cameron's reforms. It was like the party had 'swallowed a wasp', said one woman MP. Yet, for some women MPs, and a single male Peer, with extensive party organizational experience, feathers 'needed to be ruffled' and need to continue being ruffled. This male Peer is a strong advocate of the 'deeply unpopular' move of centralization because the party membership is not representative of the country and is 'out of tune' with 'contemporary society', and because MPs are responsible to the electorate and not the local party.[35] In contrast, some male and female Peers feel good progress has been made.[36] Whilst one woman MP thought that intra-party tension had eased,[37] with the worst case scenario having been avoided – there had *almost* been 'blood on the floor' – there was a shared perception amongst a number of the women MPs of the potential for it to rear its head once again. One observed that the 'ocean' of the party in the country were not yet fully reconciled to the candidate selection reforms,[38] and criticism was considered especially likely once the grassroots realized such reforms were not going to be a one-off. Chuckling, one female MP stated: 'I think for those people who felt strongly against what was done, they probably thought, you know, when push comes to shove, it was only for one election!'

Conclusion

That some party members and MPs were unhappy with Cameron's reforms of parliamentary selection is clearly not in dispute, whether that is based on readings of Conservativehome website, or deriving from the focus group, survey, and interview data presented here. But the more important question, at least for those seeking the greater descriptive representation of women in the Conservative Parliamentary party, is the nature of Cameron's response to this situation. His most obvious response was the removal of the requirement for local associations to select from the Priority List. This action was importantly perceived as a victory for the grassroots by critical party members and unsurprisingly the Tory commentariat. 'Porter's compromise' (Snowdon 2010: 246)[39] was regarded as a face saving device for Cameron. Admittedly, this move was believed at the time, by those active on women's recruitment in the party, as likely to have little substantive impact as most winnable seats had already selected their candidates (see also Bale 2010: 325).[40] Even so, this was the moment that best epitomizes Cameron's decision to step back from the fight with his members over women's descriptive representation (Snowdon 2010: 246). And when the new vacancies for Westminster did arise unexpectedly in 2009, the party was on the back foot. Cameron's belated advocacy of AWS, in effect, 'missed the boat'.

The attitudes of party members and Parliamentarians were evidently perceived as, and therefore, acted as a constraint on Cameron, even if less so amongst others active on the issue of women's representation in the higher echelons of the party. To be sure there is little in the party members' responses to questions about equality promotion and equality guarantees for Cameron and other gender equality activists to feel reassured by. They could not argue that any reforms *reflected* party member demands. Yet member attitudes are not immutably fixed. Not only are some members, especially younger women, more favourably disposed, but if the party were to attract new members this might see attitudinal change too, as some leading gender equality activists hoped.[41] In any case, party leaders can 'lead' their parties, as Cameron has explicitly sought to do on other issues (Heffernan 2010). Conservative Parliamentarians' attitudes look a little more promising in the shorter term from the perspective of gender equality, at least in respect of some of the existing women MPs and Peers (as well as amongst some leading women in the party's women's organizations, see Chapter 2) and some modernizing male MPs.[42] Here there is greater evidence to suggest that Cameron had the potential to mobilize this support to greater effect, even whilst he chose not to do so.

Those keen to continue, if not re-double the party's efforts on descriptive representation, can take succour from the following: amongst Parliamentarians acknowledgement of selectorate discrimination against women in the party's selection procedures is no longer a 'no-go' area. It is indeed, something that Cameron himself has admitted. And women MPs, women Peers and the wives of Peers who had themselves failed to get selected (at least as told by their husbands) can provide evidence of this, albeit in the form of self-reported claims. From this we might infer – and the party should consider – the need for a more critical take on the concept of merit. Presently merit is too often regarded as an unproblematic and objective concept. Yet one cannot hold that Conservative party selection processes are meritocratic at the same time as admitting the practice of selectorate discrimination. Just as the party redefined the criteria of a good candidate in the last parliament – identifying six key dimensions – it must now act to ensure that these are better appreciated and tested during selections for the 2015 parliament (Childs 2008). In acknowledging the existence of selectorate discrimination, the party should also admit the logical necessity of equality guarantees (Campbell et al 2006). The challenge for the leadership and those active in the party on women's representation, therefore, is to get this message over to its members. Attention also needs to be focused on the problem of central-local relations within the party (Childs and Cowley 2011). Perhaps the spectre of a Tory 'Blaneau Gwent', when Labour lost a rock solid seat after an ex-member stood in 2005 as an independent on an anti-AWS ticket, hung over Cameron (Cutts et al 2008) as he decided to back off from confronting his party, though this Labour example was a 'one off'. And if the pursuit of women's descriptive representation has become negatively associated with the perception of the imposition of 'outsider' candidates, then one response would be for the party to devise measures designed to advance the participation of local women in their Constituency Associations. Alternatively, the desirability of localism itself could be contested: are local candidates necessarily good candidates? (Childs and Cowley 2011) Active constituency MPs do not always translate into good parliamentary actors – pavement politics does not necessarily equate with holding the executive to account (Mullin 2010).

Of course, action in these respects requires the continued focus of the party leadership. Securing women's descriptive representation is shown here, and in the previous Chapter, to be a complex matter which depends on several factors: First, the attitudes of party members and elites; second, inter-party competition over women's descriptive representation; third, gender equality activists' efforts within and outwith the party, not least those of leading party women; fourth, the wider context of electoral and political reform; and fifth, the 'will' of the party leader. Between 2005 and 2010 it is fair to say that there was a favourable configuration of such conditions (Kittilson 2006; Krook 2009b). These may not be so for 2015, not least because of the planned reduction in the total number of MPs at Westminster, and the likely lower turnover of members next time around. Political will on behalf of the leadership will therefore be especially interesting to monitor, for it is likely to reveal the true depth and sincerity of Cameron's initiative on women's descriptive representation. At this election we might question Cameron's reluctance to introduce equality guarantees, given that leadership autonomy is more of a 'reality' than is often recognized (Bale 2010: 14–15). This is not to deny that Cameron's honeymoon with the party wobbled during 2007 (Evans 2008: 301), but in the aftermath of the 'election that never was' of October 2007, and with opinion polls moving in his favour, he could arguably have returned to the issue of women's descriptive representation earlier than the Speaker's Conference in the autumn of 2009. Had he done so, Cameron could have been confident that the party's women's organizations would be with him. Ditto a group of Parliamentarians, mostly women, but also including a group of modernizing men. And a more focused educational effect targeted at party members could have been undertaken – unpacking the concept of merit would have been the critical starting point. Of course, this is not to suggest that the party would have rushed to embrace AWS, but then that can hardly be said of the Labour party (M. Russell 2005; Childs 2004) in the round either.

Section III

Women's Substantive Representation

5
Party Member Attitudes and Women's Policy (by and for women?)

Stealing a march on Labour.[1]

The pre-Cameron Conservative party lacked electoral competitiveness on 'women's issues'.[2] By the 2010 general election this was very much less the case. Policy pledges on maternity and paternity leave and pay, and flexible working, amongst others, suggested substantial reform, if not redirection of the party's position, even if Cameron's public commitment to recognizing marriage in the tax system, at least for some commentators, tempered such appraisals (and may, indeed, have outweighed the other initiatives in terms of the public and media attention it attracted). The party's 'women's' policy commitments were evidently designed to market the party to women voters, especially middle income mothers, as well as others who, whilst not directly affected by them, would see in them a sign that the party was now more in tune with modern life. Some of these policies looked risky in terms of the party's ideological traditions and its core vote, especially those whose dispositions might be expected to favour more traditional gender roles and who might wish to protect business from what they would consider 'costly', in both economic and social terms, social engineering. Indeed, of the 2008 Women's Policy Group Report, *Women in the World Today*, which under-pinned the party's 2010 manifesto commitments, a leading Conservative woman felt sure that some in the Parliamentary party (and one might add too, the party's grassroots) would be concerned that the Tories had 'stolen a march' on Labour.

Analysing the Conservatives' new women's policies in terms of consti-tutive and substantive representation, the focus of the first part of this chapter, reveals just how the party leadership conceived of women's and men's roles, and how they would seek to act for women in government. Analysis of our party member survey data, the focus of the latter part of the chapter, permits examination of party member views of such representa-tions of, and policies for, women. Apparent tensions between traditional and more contemporary understandings of gender roles, and between new policies for women and the party's more traditional policy foci, thereby throw new light on the extent of Tory party modernization in the party in public office and amongst the grassroots, and in so doing, on intra-party relations.

Constitutive and substantive representation: women in the world today[3]

To modernize Conservative party policy David Cameron set up six independent reviews: (1) the competitive challenge; (2) quality of life; (3) public services; (4) security; (5) social justice; and (6) globalization and the global challenge. Women's policy development fell outside this process. The, then, Shadow Minister for Women, Eleanor Laing MP, alongside the Women's Policy Group that she and the VC for Women had established, would seek, however, to gender these reviews. They would make submissions to the Review Groups and they would write their own 'agenda setting' report (Childs 2008). Ultimately, the 2008 report, *Women in the World Today (WIWT)* would go above the Review Groups directly to the Shadow Cabinet and Cameron's policy team, headed up by Oliver Letwin. There were briefings from Theresa May's office (she had become Shadow Minister for Women), and meetings were held with relevant Shadow Ministers, such as Alan Duncan and Dominic Grieve on women's imprisonment (Shadow Minister for Prisons and Shadow Home Secretary, respectively); David Willets on girls' career choices (Shadow Secretary of State for Education); and Damien Green (Shadow Minister for Immigration) on sex trafficking. Accordingly, there was confidence on behalf of leading women in the party that much of their Report would be taken on board in the party's election manifesto, not least because Cameron had himself adopted some of these issues as his own, notably, violence against women. Anything involving financial commitments (for example to do with childcare) were, nonetheless kept out of the final draft of *WIWT*, by a combination of Letwin's and Steve Hilton's (Cameron's Director of Strategy) hand alongside some self-censorship. A too 'cheeky' report would not have been taken seriously, retorted one woman closely associated with the Report. Similarly, direct policy commitments – possible 'hostages to fortune' – were mostly excluded and so statements about individual issues became linked to the organizations that put them forward, rather than presented as 'Conservative party policy'.

Published on St Valentine's Day, 2008 *Women in the World Today* constituted a 'fresh base upon which future Conservative policy will be built'. Under May's tutelage, the Report addressed 'challenges' and 'opportunities' for women, offered a critique of the Labour government's efforts in respect of these, and outlined an alternative Conservative approach to them. It identified five key issues: (1) the workplace; (2) women in their communities; (3) vulnerable women;[4] (4) ethnicity; and (5) international development. The Report was not, however, widely publicized internally. Many MPs and PPCs would likely have been unaware of it and it was not sent to every local association, so the extent to which Conservative party members were aware of its content was minimal too. Even so, it was said that the Report would signal more widely that the party was addressing women's issues than it previously had shied away from, such as equal pay or trafficking.

As a 'women's document' it is not surprising that women are the central focus of *WIWT*, named some 300 times,[5] with mothers named 11 times. In contrast, men are named just 36 times, fathers three times, parents 37 times, and the family on more than 90 occasions. It is clear in the Report that the party considers British *women* to be facing gendered challenges, with BME women facing particular ones. Women are underpaid (relative to men), raped, murdered, trafficked, used by 'Johns' (our term), forced into marriages, and undergo genital mutilation (FGM). In addition, women 'suffer' in respect of pay, as carers, as homeless and imprisoned women, as victims of violence and, for BME women specifically, in terms of access to education, forced marriage, 'honour' killing and violence, and FGM. Women also lack the 'real' choices that they need and should have: with regard to childcare, education, careers and paid employment. Again, some BME women's choices are further foreclosed in these areas. What women do, according to the Report, is care for children, for the home and for other dependents. When they undertake paid work women do so under less favourable conditions than men – they are paid less, are underemployed, work in low-paid, segregated employment, or work at home without health and safety protection and National Insurance contributions. If women in the UK are mostly represented as 'those to whom things are done', the coverage of women's experiences in the developing world constitutes women as important and active agents. They are not simply the passive recipients of pity or aid. Turning specifically to *mothers,* women feel pressure, because of financial constraints, to return to work after having children; suffer reduced earnings and pensions having had children; do three-quarters of the childcare during the week and two thirds at the weekend; and the majority of those with dependent children also do paid work. Sixty-six percent of women prisoners have children, and yet there are only seven prison 'mother and baby' units.

The lot of *men* is very different. Most (but not all) are likely to benefit from the structure and relations of British society, although 'some' from minority cultures are excluded from the labour market. Named over half the time in respect of paid employment, men earn more than women; are less likely to work part-time; and less likely to seek flexible working, although the numbers are increasing. Men are also less likely than women to cite relationship breakdown or parental conflict as a reason for being homeless; gain from the structure of the pension systems; and are in prisons geographically closer to their families. Though more likely to commit suicide overall than women, men are less likely to do so when imprisoned. Men are 80 percent of stalkers (women are 80 percent of stalkers' victims); and users of prostitutes (likely to be deterred from kerb-crawling by fines and being publicly shamed, but not by knowing that the prostitute has been forced into prostitution). BME men, specifically, gain state benefits from polygamous marriage. In the developing world men share the effects of poor healthcare systems, although experience lower rates of HIV infection than women. The three occasions when *fathers* are mentioned relate to two accounts of BME women whose lives were circumscribed or ended by their father's actions.

The Family is ever-present in *WIWT*. Representations take three main forms. The first captures the difficulties families suffer in balancing their domestic and paid work commitments. This includes concerns that the family is in 'breakdown'; a perception that the single-earner family is disadvantaged by the tax system; and the lack of recognition by the Labour government of familial and informal care of children. Such issues are regarded as moving up the domestic political agenda. The second representation looks to the role of the family in the developing world. Here, women's beneficial contributions to maintaining and improving families' wealth and health are stressed. The final representation – the one that receives the most extensive coverage – looks towards British BME families, especially although not exclusively, South Asian families. Put simply, these families are overwhelmingly presented as negative for women.

Parents are constituted in two main ways in the Report. The first depicts women as one part of the parenting couple. In around two-thirds of British families both parents work but lack choices in childcare (though on one occasion the previous sentence notes *women's* lack of choice in childcare). Parents want to spend more time with their children, (though in another example, the previous sentence talks about *women's* lack of work/life balance). Parents who wish to stay at home to care for their children feel discriminated against. Only richer parents have choice. Childcare, especially for disabled children, is noted as yet more expensive. Parents are also constituted as a problem for younger women, for example, in terms of a breakdown in a relationship leading to homelessness. BME parents are particularly problematic. They may seek to protect their daughters, but ultimately they restrict their life choices and, in some instances, threaten their lives. This reflects (mis)perceptions of British society and beliefs about their daughter's interests. Thus, whilst such parents might be entrusted by young women to find a suitable husband, they deceive social services about taking their children out of school; subject their daughters to FGM; and are unlikely to face criminal charges in cases of forced marriage.

Overall, four broad observations can be made about representations of gender in *Women in the World Today*. The first is that the Report 'sees' gender. Women's and men's lives are different, both in the UK and the developing world. Secondly, there is both implicit and explicit feminist criticism. Gender differences are not constituted as natural (and, therefore, to be left alone), but unequal and unfair (and therefore with the potential to be transformed). The Report is, moreover, explicit, at times, in identifying men as the source of some of the 'challenges' that women face. This is most apparent in respect of women's bodily integrity. It is overwhelmingly women who are stalked and men who do the stalking. It is women who are disproportionately trafficked for prostitution, whilst men are the users of prostitutes. It is also male members of BME families who are the perpetrators of 'honour killings' and violence.[6] At the same time, there are many occasions where the Report appears to 'hide' gender differences, inequalities and hierarchies behind the gender undifferentiated institutions of 'the family' and 'parents'. Accordingly, any criticism and prescription is limited. Take, for example, discussions of childcare. Mostly the language is about choices for parents and families. To be sure, criticism levelled at the current tax system does not talk about mothers staying at home. Even so, the Report includes statements that reveal the likelihood that the parent caring for a young child will be female and that this distribution has negative implications and consequences for women: 'by taking the decision to break from their careers...many mothers experience reduced future earnings, reduced pension provision and reduced financial security in the future'. Such statements are revealing. They start with a non-gendered analysis, then adopt a gendered perspective (noting traditional gender roles in society are likely to determine the different experiences for women and men), before moving onto what can be considered a feminist perspective (that these sex and gender differences are likely to have a negative impact for women). Indeed, it is through this language of choice that one can best capture the Conservative approach to such dilemmas. It is an approach underpinned by a belief in equality of opportunity rather than equality of outcome (which is considered both undesirable and unrealistic). A Conservative government offering women 'choice' will therefore 'set a framework' within which women can choose what they do.

The third observation relates to the perception of the different experiences of BME women in the UK. A whole host of disadvantages experienced by BME women are identified. For example, their harsher experiences of paid employment are noted. BME and South Asian women in particular, are in need of 'protection', as is clear to see from news stories, as the Report puts it. Particular focus is given to the 'no recourse to public funds rule' which prevents immigrant women from making use of the 'Domestic Violence Immigration Rule'.[7] At the same time, the Report is explicit in acknowledging that 'not all women in minority communities suffer' such problems and that the Conservative party 'must not paint a distorted or exaggerated picture'.[8] In identifying the basis for BME women's especial challenges, no truck is given to cultural or religious defence for actions that proscribe women's lives. 'Honour killing' is 'no less than murder' and a clear distinction is drawn between arranged and forced marriages. Reference to the UN Declaration of Human Rights is also made. Women's rights are, then, universal. Furthermore, and in a criticism of (a particular definition of) multiculturalism, *WIWT* states explicitly that forced marriage is not a 'cultural' issue that cannot be 'broached'. It is a 'contravention of basic human liberty'. In terms of prescription, parental perceptions need to be transformed. Parents not wanting their daughters to wear make-up is not considered sufficient reason to segregate young women from British society, even if as the Report suggests British society may well be 'too promiscuous'.

The fourth observation of *WIWT* relates to the role of the state in transforming women and men's gendered experiences and gender hierarchies. To be sure, there are examples of legislative pledges that seek to address some of the challenges the party has identified, but the role of the state is often regarded more as the enabling rather than the providing state, and something that should not be telling families and parents what to do. In this the sanctity of the private sphere is maintained. The following Figure 5.1 shows the variable role of the state regarding the gender pay gap.

Figure 5.1   The Gender Pay Gap and the Role of the State

Gender pay gap caused by outright discrimination: women earn less than men for the same work	↑	Activities of the state increases
Gender pay gap caused by the need for women to seek flexible and part-time work		
Gender pay gap caused by differences in human capital, such as education levels and work experience		
Gender pay gap caused by women's career choices		

Source: *Women in the World Today.*

The economic and business case for equality in the workplace relates, in this view, to a perception that 'long term economic growth depends on the skills and talents of all potential workers'. Business is, moreover, claimed to have 'an appetite' to address this issue: for example, recruiting the non-traditional sex to a job would help 'solve skills shortages'. The category of 'good employers' is also brought into play. Five case studies detail how particular businesses have benefited from adopting flexible work, better maternity leave provisions, and the targeting of, and support for, women workers. Underpinning the Conservative approach to gender equality at work is, then, both a belief that there is an economic and business case to be made, and that the Conservative proposals must be, and are, 'proportionate'. The absence of attention given to the benefits of flexible working for workers and especially women workers – there are no case studies detailing how women's lives have been improved by flexible working, for example – suggests, that there are those in the women's part of the party who believe that the business case still has to be made.

If the above summarizes the main ways in which the Conservative party's 2008 Report views women, men and gender relations (the constitutive representation of gender), analyzing the policy pledges contained therein enables evaluation of the substantive representation of women (Childs et al 2010). Only two of the five women's concerns identified in *WIWT* – women in the workplace and vulnerable women – contain explicit policy 'Proposals'. Even so, analysis of the criticism levelled at the current state of affairs, together with criticism of current practices, as well as of the Labour government, is suggestive of what the Report thinks should be the case in the other policy areas too. Criticism relating to polygamous marriages implies that legislative change might be appropriate, and/or, that guidance to immigration officials should permit the refusal of the entry of second wives if officials are suspicious that divorces are bogus. Criticism of the failure to bring into force Section 12 of the Domestic Violence, Crimes and Victims Act 2004 (which allows for the use of 'restraining orders to be extended to any offence, rather than only those committed under the Protection from Harassment Act 1997'), implies that the Conservatives would act on this. Then there is general criticism of the attitudes and actions of public bodies, including the police (who do not take stalking, domestic violence and forced marriages seriously enough), and educational providers (who do not protect vulnerable BME women). Inadequate provision of services and funding is also highlighted, not least in respect of local authority services for women experiencing domestic violence, for women prisoners, and young women victims of trafficking. The paperwork necessitated by certain government provisions is additionally criticized for making claiming benefits and support overly difficult.

The most extensive critique in *WIWT* relates, however, to women's employment and childcare. In particular, the Labour government stands accused of failing to address the gender pay gap and stopping discrimination against women, as well as inequality in women and men's pensions. Regarding childcare, the report criticizes what it sees as Labour's preference for parents to work full-time, and for restricting diversity amongst childcare providers. The Conservatives, in contrast, want to offer parents and families the *choice* of how to manage their family responsibilities through ensuring the tax system does not discriminate against single earner families. Four work pledges are made in the Report, the first three of which are specific/detailed (Childs et al 2010). The party will: (1) introduce compulsory pay audits for employers who discriminate. A business found guilty of sex discrimination in pay is not, currently, required to change its pay policy nor does a tribunal ruling cover other employees; (2) tighten the rules on the 'reasonableness' test for the material factor defence. Section 1(3) of the Equal Pay Act provides that 'an equality clause shall not operate...if the employer proves that the variation is genuinely due to a material factor which is not the difference of sex'; (3) extend flexible working to all parents of children aged 18 or younger; and (4) help women into work and up the careers ladder, via 'independent providers' and better quality careers advice.

Proposals in respect of rape, the first two of which are detailed, will (1) replace Labour's 'annual funding decisions' with three year funding cycles for rape crisis centres; (2) make compulsory the teaching of sexual consent in the sex education curriculum; and (3) review rape sentencing. Eight detailed/specific policy pledges relate to human trafficking and prostitution. To: (1) establish a Border Police Force; (2) introduce tougher border controls; (3) mainstream human trafficking as a 'core' police priority; (4) prosecute more traffickers; (5) increase the number of places at safe houses for victims of trafficking; (6) allow 16 to 18 year olds to be admitted to Poppy Project (safe accommodation) places; (7) set up a helpline for victims of trafficking and establish campaigns targeted at potential consumers and employers; and (8) ratify the Council of Europe Convention on Action Against Trafficking in Human Beings 2005 International Action.

'An invitation to join the conservative government', the 2010 conservative party manifesto

Across the main three political parties' 2010 general election manifestos it was as mothers that women were mostly frequently represented. Much of the parties' policies were mostly about, and for, families, as Box 5.1 shows.[9] The Conservative party would, in developing countries, 'focus particularly on the rights of women...to access' 'clean water, sanitation, healthcare and education; at home, 'deliver' 'up to 15 new rape crisis centres', and give existing centres 'stable, long-term funding'; 'ensure the school curriculum includes teaching young people about sexual consent'; 'crack down' on the trafficking of people;[10] seek single-sex hospital accommodation; permit more free votes for conscience issues;[11] promote equality and tackle discrimination; stop the 'forced closure' of local maternity hospitals and create local maternity networks; and recognize marriage and civil partnerships in the tax system.

Undoubtedly, the key 'women's' battleground was women's work/life balance and other measures to help families (Campbell and Childs 2010). There was cross-party agreement that women suffer from a gender pay gap and that flexible working and greater flexibility in maternity and paternity leave and pay are 'good'. For the Conservatives there would be support for families in the tax and benefits system; and ending to the couples penalty; 'cutting tax credits and Child Trust Funds for better-off families', contending that tax credits are no longer justified for households earning more than £50K; a freezing of council tax; 'support [for] the provision of free nursery care through a diverse range of providers; 'put funding for relationship support on a stable, long-term footing and make sure couples are given greater encouragement to

Box 5.1 Manifesto Pledges for Families, by Party, 2010

Labour

- Expansion of free nursery places for two year olds and 15 hours a week of flexible care
- Free nursery education for three and four year olds
- New national under-fives service
- 'One-stop shops' open to all families
- Expand number of free early learning places for disadvantaged two year olds
- Long-term goal of universal free childcare for two year olds; more flexibility over hours/days
- Retain childcare vouchers
- Raise childcare standards by a more qualified workforce
- Greater diversity in providers of Sure Start Children's Centres
- Toddler tax credit of £4 a week from 2012…to all parents of young children (whether stay home or not)
- Where parents, especially mothers, want to stay at home or work part-time we will do more to help families with younger children
- Reform Job Centre Plus to provide extra help to lone parents, with childcare, training and support to find family-friendly work
- Require those with children aged three to take steps to prepare for work and actively to seek employment once their youngest child is seven years old;
- Ensure that work always pays for hard-working lone parents
- Greater support for maternity services

Box 5.1   Manifesto Pledges for Families, by Party, 2010 – *continued*

Conservative

- Support families in the tax and benefits system
- End couples penalty
- Tax credits no longer justified for 'households earning more than £50K'
- Freeze council tax
- Free nursery care with a diverse range of providers
- Stable, long-term funding for relationship support; increase the use of mediation
- Sure start [taken] back to its original purpose of early intervention for the neediest families
- 4,200 Sure Start health visitors
- Newly created Early Years support team
- Help reverse the commercialisation of childhood
- End closure of local maternity hospitals

Liberal Democrat

- Ending government payments into child trust funds
- Protect existing childcare support arrangements until the nation's finances can support a longer term solution
- Move to 20 hour free childcare for every child, from the age of 18 months
- Introduce a Default Contact Arrangement – dividing child's time between their two parents in the event of family breakdown, if there is no threat to the safety of the child
- Regulating airbrushing in adverts
- End the closure of local maternity hospitals

Source: Campbell and Childs (2010)

use existing relationship support'; 'review family law in order to increase the use of mediation'; 'take Sure Start back to its original purpose of early intervention, with a focus on the neediest families'; 'provide 4,200 more Sure Start health visitors'; establishing Early Years support teams; and 'take a series of measures to reverse the commercialization of childhood'.

In respect of paid employment and the work/life balance, the Conservatives more specifically pledged to: (1) force equal pay audits on any company found to be discriminating on the basis of gender; (2) initially extend the right to request flexible working to every parent with a child under eighteen...extend the right...[to] all those in public sector, recognizing that this might need to be done in stages [and] in the longer term, extend the right to request...to all; (3) oblige JobCentre Plus offices to ask employers if their vacancies could be advertised on a part-time or flexible basis; and (4) introduce a new system of flexible parental leave which lets parents share maternity leave between them.

Whilst avowedly seeking the 'ambitious goal' of making Britain the 'most family friendly country in Europe', the Conservative party 2010 election manifesto offered less for women than the women's part of the party had advocated in its 2008 *Women in the World Today* Report. Commitments are in particular less detailed, although it might be argued that a manifesto is not the place for such detail. Even so, the 2010 manifesto makes it clear that women's (and mothers) entrance into the paid employment market has been widely accepted by the party. There is recognition too that women do not yet achieve equality of pay and that business must be made more 'family' friendly. That a number of the party's pledges, and the analysis that underpins them, might appear contra to traditional Conservative notions of gender and gender relations, further suggests that the party has, at least on paper, been able to move forward (that is, be more electorally competitive). Despite Cameron's personal commitment to ending the 'couples penalty' and recognition for marriage and civil partnerships in the taxation system[12] which is suggestive of more traditional views, the party is formally neutral about how particular families reconcile their commitments to work and family life. Admittedly, there may well be a difference between an abstract 'choice' and that which many women will face in their everyday lives. In the absence of equal pay, affordable childcare, and protection from businesses who might fail to grant flexible working, women are likely to be less able to make the choice they want. Take, for example, the issue of childcare, specifically. Putting in place a framework that enables parents to choose to care for their young children themselves in the early years will not be cheap for any government; nor will it necessarily be cost-neutral to business. Government will also at some point need to reflect on which parent takes care of the child, in practice, and what the implications of this are for those individuals as well as wider society. The party will have, no doubt, to confront this dilemma directly, as one Conservative gender equality activist admitted.[13] Amongst what might be termed the 'women's' part of the party, the approach to such concerns appears to be more inclined towards changes to law and practice that will enhance women's experiences in the paid employment market, rather than transform men's relationships to the home.

Party policy and member attitudes

Establishing that the Conservative party's new women's policies are more electorally competitive is one thing. It is quite another to establish whether they are attractive to party members. To gauge what party members think of the feminization of the party under Cameron we focus on party members' attitudes on specific issues relating to women's policy. First, though, it is important to map their more general political attitudes. Our survey of party members finds them predominantly middle-class, middle-aged and southern, centre-right, socially authoritarian, materialist and Eurosceptic (see Methods Appendix for more details). There are no major sex differences in these characteristics, though women party members tend to be a little less right-wing, slightly more authoritarian, and more materialist. More specifically, and as Table 5.1 below shows, ideologically, the Conservative party membership regards itself as clearly right of centre. The mean location of party members on this 7-point scale, with 1 representing 'very left-wing' and 7 'very right-wing', is 5.32 (valid n = 1601, sd = 1.1). This places the memberships' self-perceived ideological centre of gravity somewhere 'slightly right of centre'. The table also reveals a slight sex difference, in that women are somewhat more likely to identify themselves as centrists, returning a mean score of 5.22 on the scale compared to 5.38 for men.

Table 5.1   Self-placement of Respondents on Ideological Left-Right Scale

	Sex		Total
	Male	Female	
Very left-wing	0.6%	0.3%	0.5% (n = 8)
Fairly left-wing	1.1%	2.3%	1.6% (n = 25)
Slightly left-of-centre	1.5%	4.3%	2.6% (n = 41)
Centre	12.5%	19.5%	15.1% (n = 242)
Slightly right-of-centre	37.1%	28.4%	33.8% (n = 541)
Fairly right-wing	34.8%	32.3%	33.9% (n = 542)
Very right-wing	12.5%	12.9%	12.6% (n = 202)
Total	100.0%	100.0%	100.0% (n = 1601)

Cramer's V = 0.15 (0.000)

The ideological complexion of our respondents can be examined with more sophistication because the survey asked a number of questions of party members that are designed to measure their location in multiple dimensions of attitudinal space (not only standard left-right ideology, but also social liberalism/authoritarianism, materialism/post-materialism, pro/anti-Europeanism and feminism/anti-feminism). The left-right and libertarian-authoritarian locations are derived from a number of indicators first developed by Heath et al (1993) that have by now become the basis of standard attitudinal scales.[14] Tables 5.2 and 5.3 report the individual Likert scale questions and basic statistics from which the scales were calculated.[15] Our members consistently opt for slightly right of centre (mean = 3.25) and generally authoritarian (mean = 3.93) responses to these

Table 5.2 Left-Right Attitudinal Scale Item Statistics

	Mean (s.d)	N
Government should redistribute income from the better-off to those who are less well off	3.65 (1.25)	1663
Big business benefits owners at the expense of workers	3.22 (1.28)	1663
There is one law for the rich and one for the poor	3.06 (1.41)	1663
Ordinary people do not get their fair share of the nation's wealth	3.17 (1.26)	1663
Management will always try to get the better of employees if it gets the chance	3.14 (1.34)	1663

Note: 1 represents the most of left-wing position on this scale, while 5 represents the most right-wing position.

Table 5.3 Libertarianism-Authoritarianism Attitudinal Scale Item Statistics

	Mean (s.d)	N
Young people today don't have enough respect for traditions	4.24 (0.89)	1654
People who break the law should be given stiffer sentences	4.37 (0.88)	1654
For some crimes the death penalty is the most appropriate sentence	3.74 (1.48)	1654
Schools should teach children to obey authority	4.40 (0.83)	1654
The law should always be obeyed even if a particular law is wrong	3.43 (1.08)	1654
Censorship of films and magazines is necessary to uphold moral standards	3.42 (1.29)	1654

Note: 1 represents the most of libertarian position on this scale, while 5 represents the most authoritarian position. s.d = standard deviation.

questions – perhaps unsurprisingly.[16] Table 5.4 below reports sex differences in terms of the overall scales. These differences are statistically significant in both cases. Women party members are a little to the left of their male counterparts, but more authoritarian. The latter characteristic is best illustrated by the much clearer tendency of women to agree strongly with the statement that 'censorship of films and magazines is necessary to uphold moral standards' (33 percent of women compared to 15 percent of men), while the former is most apparent in the somewhat greater tendency of women to accept that 'Big business benefits owners at the expense of workers' (13.7 percent compared to 8.5 percent).

Table 5.4   Positions on Left-Right and Libertarian-Authoritarian Scales, by Sex

	Sex	N	Mean (s.d)
Left-right scale	Male	1012	3.39 (1.03)
	Female	651	3.03 (1.07)
Liberty-authority scale	Male	1001	3.86 (0.71)
	Female	653	4.04 (0.66)

Note: LRscale = left-right scale; LAscale = liberty-authority scale. Independent samples t-tests produce 2-tailed significance levels of 0.000 for the differences between men's and women's mean scores on both scales.

Turning to materialism/post-materialism, only one of the several items that were included in the survey to tap this dimension showed any sign of sex differences. (A variation of the simple but classic measure first devised by Ronald Inglehart, this is a mini-index constructed from four potentially conflicting goals, two of which are materialist in orientation – 'maintaining order in the nation' and 'fighting unemployment'[17] – and two of which are post-materialist – 'giving people more say in important political decisions' and 'protecting freedom of speech'). Respondents were asked to select their two preferred objectives from this list and deemed to be ideological materialist if they select the two materialist goals, post-materialist if they select the two post-materialist goals, and ideological 'mixed' if the select one of each. Table 5.5 reveals that women are significantly less likely to hold post-materialist orientations on this index. However, noting that other measures of post-materialism do not reveal significant sex differences, it would be wise not to infer too strongly from this single finding; at most, we would conclude that there is a slight tendency for women Conservative party members to be slightly less post-materialist than their male counterparts.[18]

The final basic attitudinal dimension concerns Europe.[19] The survey included a single measure – an 11 point scale on which respondents are asked to locate themselves with respect to EU integration, from 0 (representing the view that Britain should 'unite fully with the EU') to 10 (representing the view that the

Table 5.5 Post-materialist Orientation, by Sex

	Sex		Total
	Male	**Female**	
Materialist	223	201	424
	22.3%	30.6%	25.6%
Mixed	612	388	1000
	61.3%	59.1%	60.4%
Post-materialist	164	68	232
	16.4%	10.4%	14%
Total	999	657	1656

Cramer's V = 0.11 (0.000)

country should 'protect its independence from the EU'). As Table 5.6 shows, there is no significant difference between men and women in the party on this issue. Both sexes share a common hostility to the EU, with mean scores very near the Eurosceptic end of the scale.[20]

Table 5.6 Conservative Members' Attitudes towards European Integration, by Sex

	Sex	N	Mean (s.d)
Your views	Male	1012	8.77 (2.61)
	Female	649	8.71 (2.80)

Note: An independent sample t-test produces a 2-tailed significance level of 0.644 for the differences between men's and women's mean scores on this scale.

With respect to gender relations and politics more specifically, our survey focused on three broad types of issue: basic orientations towards gender roles and relations; specific policy measures on the current agenda of British politics which are relevant to the substantive representation of women; and the descriptive representation of women (reported in full in the previous Chapter). In respect of the former, we find that amongst Conservative party members there is the potential for distinct responses by women and men, as women are more likely to be predisposed towards feminism. The survey asked respondents a group of five Likert scale questions in order to get a general sense of party members' views about gender roles and relations. These were coded similarly so that a '1' represented an anti-feminist position and '5' a feminist position.[21] The individual item statistics are reported in Table 5.7 and the locations of men and women on the overall feminism scale are shown in Table 5.8. These show a statistically significant difference between men and women, with the latter being somewhat closer to

Table 5.7   General Feminism Scale Item Statistics

	Mean (s.d)	N
Government should make sure that women have an equal chance to succeed	3.79 (1.14)	1584
Most men are better suited emotionally to politics than most women	3.45 (1.19)	1584
All in all family life suffers when the woman has a full-time job	2.54 (1.17)	1584
Being a housewife is just as fulfilling as working for pay	2.63 (1.19)	1584
A husband's job is to earn money; a wife's job is to look after the home and family	3.35 (1.29)	1584
Women should have an equal role in running business, industry and government	3.81 (1.12)	1584

Table 5.8   Positions on Feminism Scale, by Sex

Sex	N	Mean (s.d)
Male	936	3.1106 (0.72)
Female	648	3.4856 (0.81)

Note: An independent sample t-test produces a 2-tailed significance level of 0.000 for the differences between men's and women's mean scores on this scale.

the feminist pole of this attitudinal spectrum (though we should note that men are also closer to this pole than to the opposite one). The differences between women and men are furthered illustrated by a few of the individual scale item details: whereas 42 percent of women strongly agree that 'government should make sure that women have an equal chance to succeed', only 25 percent of men do; while 33 percent of women strongly disagree with the statement that 'men are better suited to politics emotionally than most women', only 17 percent of men do; or, again, nearly half of men tend to agree that 'family life suffers when women have a full-time job', compared to just a third of women; and finally, while 43 percent of women strongly agree that 'women should have an equal role in running business, industry and government', only 27 percent of men can bring themselves to do so.

Turning to the specific women's issues either advocated by the Conservative party in 2010 or more generally circulating in contemporary British party political debate (Table 5.9), sex differences of opinion amongst our party members are again evident. Crosstabulation analysis of a battery of questions reveal statistically significant differences between men and women on 11 out

Table 5.9 Sex Differences on Current Gendered Political Issues

	Strongly agree	Tend to agree	Neither agree nor disagree	Tend to disagree	Strongly disagree	Total PDI	Cramer's v (sig.)
Tax allowances that can be transferred from one partner to another for married couples	8.2	−4.9	−3.7	0.3	0.2	17.3	0.094 (0.006)
Tax allowances that can be transferred from one partner to another for all couples (ie, heterosexual and gay)	−1.4	−5.4	−4.2	0.8	10.2	22	0.134 (0.000)
Right to request flexible working for parents of children up to the age of 11	−9.3	−5.6	2.7	6.5	5.7	29.8	0.177 (0.000)
Right to request flexible working for parents of children up to the age of 18	−5.2	−6.1	−0.4	−0.9	13.4	26	0.187 (0.000)
Extension of maternity leave and pay to one year	−7.8	−7.1	−2.3	−0.3	16.9	34.4	0.223 (0.000)
Transformation of maternity leave and pay to shared parental (i.e. mother or father) leave and pay	−4.1	−1.6	−1.9	−0.4	7.9	15.9	0.106 (0.001)
The obligation on single parents to seek paid employment or lose benefits when their child is 5 years old	−1.9	4.6	1.7	−3.1	−1.4	12.7	0.065 (0.139) n.s.

Table 5.9 Sex Differences on Current Gendered Political Issues – *continued*

	Strongly agree	Tend to agree	Neither agree nor disagree	Tend to disagree	Strongly disagree	Total PDI	Cramer's v (sig.)
The obligation on single parents to seek paid employment or lose benefits when their child is 11 years old	-0.9	3.3	-0.8	0.9	-2.5	8.4	0.062 (0.177) n.s.
The obligation on single parents to seek paid employment or lose benefits when their child is 16 years old	4.5	-4.4	-1.3	1.5	-0.5	12.2	0.067 (0.115) n.s.
Compulsory audits to check if men and women doing the same work are paid equally in companies previously found guilty of unequal pay	-25.4	-1.6	4.5	10.8	11.8	54.1	0.336 (0.000)
Compulsory audits of *all* companies to check if men and women doing the same work are paid equally	-24	-10.7	1.6	12.8	20.5	69.6	0.388 (0.000)
State provision of financial support for childcare, including care by grandparents	-11.4	-0.4	2.5	0.3	9	23.6	0.184 (0.000)

Note: Each cell is a percentage difference index (PDI) score, calculated as the percentage of females opting for the same response minus the percentage of males opting for a given response; positive scores indicate that men prefer a given position more than women do, while a negative score indicates the opposite. The 'Total PDI' sums all PDIs for each row, without taking direction of sign (+ or −) into account. n.s. = not significant.

of the 12 questions (see Table 5.10) even if these differences are not especially notable in most cases. A 'percentage difference index' (PDI)[22] serves as a simple measure of the extent to which sex differences exist on these questions. With a theoretical range running from 0 (no difference between men and women) to 200 (no overlap whatsoever between the views of men and women), we can see that this confirms both the existence of, and the limits to, sex differences. The smallest PDI is 8.4 (on the suggestion that 'single parents to seek paid employment or lose benefits when their child is five years old'), and the Chi Square test reveals that the difference between men and women on this issue is not statistically different. However, on all but three of these questions, sex differences do prove statistically significant. In particular, Table 5.9 reveals clearly that the issue which most polarizes opinion is equal pay: women are much more likely than men (by 44 percent to 18.5 percent) to agree strongly that compulsory pay audits should be conducted on companies previously found guilty of unequal pay to see if they are paying men and women the same amount for the same work (the PDI between men and women is 54.1 percent on this issue). Further, they are much more likely (by 38 percent to 14 percent) to feel that pay audits should take place in all companies irrespective of whether they have a previous record of transgression (PDI = 69.6). The implications of childcare also produce notable differences in the overall distribution of opinion between men and women, for example, rights to flexible working arrangements, maternity leave, and state financial support.

Responses to these 12 questions on women's policy can be combined into a summary additive scale (Alpha = 0.716). These figures suggest that, on balance, both men and women in the Conservative party are more opposed to, rather than supportive of, such reforms. They also confirm that overall differences between Conservative men and women are significant, with the mean score of men being 2.85 (sd = 0.58), while that of women is 2.52 (sd = 0.59), where 1 represents high support for reform and 5 represents low support.[23]

Sex difference amongst Conservative party members is also evident on abortion. Amendments to the Human Fertilization and Embryology Act 2008 (discussed in more detail in the next chapter) proposed various reductions in the legal time limit for abortion. Echoing these amendments, our respondents were asked whether they felt the current 24-week limit should be increased, left where it currently stands, reduced to 22 weeks, to 20 weeks, to less than 20 weeks, or outlawed altogether except in cases of medical emergency. The difference between men and women was either insignificant or modest with respect to most of these options, but the women were notably more inclined (by 23.5 percent to 14.3 percent) to argue that the limit should be reduced to less than 20 weeks (see Table 5.10) – the less progressive position. This finding contrasts with that for Conservative MPs, where women are more progressive (Cowley and Stuart 2010).

Table 5.10   Sex Differences on Abortion Law, PDI Scores

	PDI
Should the legal time limit for abortion be increased to more than 24 weeks?	2.7
Should the legal time limit for abortion remain at 24 weeks?	7.4
Should the legal time limit for abortion be reduced to 22 weeks?	0.3
Should the legal time limit for abortion be reduced to 20 weeks?	−1.7
Should the legal time limit for abortion be reduced to less than 20 weeks?	−9.2
No legal abortions should be allowed except in cases of medical emergency	0.4

Note: PDI calculated as explained in Note to Table 3. Cramer's V = 0.13 (sig. = 0.000), n = 1506.

Moving beyond bivariate analysis, multivariate analysis permits the demographic and ideological backgrounds of party members to be taken into account, so that we can gain a better sense of what factors might be conducive to more or less feminist orientations among Conservative party members at the individual level. If sufficient evidence was forthcoming from the bivariate analysis reported above to suggest that sex is likely to be a factor which makes a significant difference to respondent's attitudes, several other potentially important standard demographic factors need also to be taken into account: social class, educational experience, age and, given the preceding discussion of the possible biases of older women (and indeed, an established literature about the impact of the 'gender-generation gap' in British politics (Norris 1999b)), a possible interaction between sex and age. In addition, it is important to consider the extent and nature of the impact of the fundamental ideological orientations referred to earlier – left/right ideology, social libertarianism/authoritarianism, and post-materialism/materialism. Our expectations of the relationships between the dependent variables and the predictors in this model are as follows: ideological leftism, social liberalism and post-materialism are all likely to be positive correlates of support for progressive positions on the gender politics scales, as is female sex, higher social status, higher educational attainment and youth rather than age. The interaction effect for the relationship between sex and age should show that older women are hostile to progressive positions, while younger women are not, an effect that requires a multiplicative rather than a simple additive term in the equation. Finally, we regard general orientation toward gender roles and relations as logically prior to attitudes toward the more specific questions of substantive and descriptive representation; for this reason, the general feminism scale will be added as an *independent* variable to the models of genderscale and selectreform.

Table 5.11 OLS Regression Model of General Feminism Scale ('feminism')

Model	Unstandardized Coefficients		Standardized Coefficients	t	Sig.	Collinearity Statistics	
	B	Std. Error	Beta			Tolerance	VIF
(Constant)	3.756	0.209		17.995	0.000		
Left-Right scale	-0.044	0.024	-0.060	-1.791	0.074	0.907	1.102
Liberty-Authority scale	-0.152	0.039	-0.134	-3.947	0.000	0.876	1.142
Sex of respondent	0.372	0.051	0.235	7.316	0.000	0.976	1.024
Age of respondent in years	-0.005	0.002	-0.101	-3.111	0.002	0.950	1.053

Dependent Variable: FEMINISM, Backward stepwise elimination of non-significant factors in 6 steps. Adjusted R-squared = 0.084; Durbin-Watson statistic = 2.041; n = 912.

The feminism scale is designed to give a sense of underlying attitude towards gender roles and relations, so we start here. The key results of our ordinary least squares analysis are reported in Table 5.11.[24] This table only reports the data for those independent variables which are significantly related to the dependent variable after non-significant predictors have been eliminated.[25] As can be seen, only four of the predictor variables emerge as having a significant influence on the dependent variable: respondent's sex, libertarian-authoritarian predisposition, age, and left-right ideology, in that order of impact. The interaction effect between sex and age is not significant. Overall, this model only explains 8.4 percent of the variance in the dependent variable, which is not particularly high. Nevertheless, our expectations are confirmed in as much as the significant coefficients are all signed as we had expected: relatively left-wing and socially liberal attitudes tend to increase an individual's likelihood of holding a feminist conception of gender roles and relations, as do youth and female sex.

Moving onto our model of attitudes towards the substantive represent- ation of women (specific policies as reported in Table 5.9), we see remark- ably similar results: the same four independent variables are once again significant, with the addition of underlying orientation towards gender (the feminism scale). Overall, this model is somewhat stronger, explaining nearly 30 percent of the variance in the dependent variable. The significant coefficients are once again nearly all signed as we had expected, with the exception of the respondent's location on the Liberty-Authority scale. Somewhat counter-intuitively, however, social liberals seem slightly less likely to support these objectives than social authoritarians. While this is theoretically unexpected, a possible empirical explanation is that women are both more socially authoritarian than men in our sample, and also more supportive of reforms designed to enhance the substantive represen- tation of women (see Table 5.9), so it may not be surprising that authoritar- ianism correlates negatively with genderscale. Nevertheless, this pattern was not apparent in the model of the general feminism scale reported in Table 5.12, so it remains slightly puzzling.

Finally, Table 5.13 reports the results for our model of attitude towards the descriptive representation of women. This shows that no demographic factors play a significant role in shaping attitudes towards reforms designed to enhance the presence of Conservative women in Parliament and national election campaigns; it seems that only the underlying ideological predispositions toward leftism, social conservatism (again) and feminist conception of gender roles and relations play a significant part.

Conclusion

On the basis of our survey of Conservative party members, the contem- porary Tory party remains a right-wing party. Yet, it is certainly possible for

Table 5.12 OLS Regression Model of Substantive Representation Scale ('genderscale')

Model	Unstandardized Coefficients		Standardized Coefficients	t	Sig.	Collinearity Statistics	
	B	Std. Error	Beta			Tolerance	VIF
(Constant)	3.365	0.172		19.531	0.000		
Left-Right scale	0.170	0.017	0.294	9.823	0.000	0.896	1.117
Liberty-Authority scale	-0.159	0.027	-0.177	-5.780	0.000	0.854	1.170
Sex of respondent	-0.147	0.037	-0.117	-3.960	0.000	0.922	1.085
Age of respondent in years	0.006	0.001	0.159	5.453	0.000	0.945	1.058
FEMINISM	-0.221	0.023	-0.280	-9.425	0.000	0.913	1.095

Dependent Variable: Genderscale. Backward stepwise elimination of non-significant factors in 6 steps. Adjusted R-squared = 0.297; Durbin-Watson statistic = 1.986; n = 874.

Table 5.13 OLS Regression Model of Descriptive Representation Scale ('selectreform')

Model	Unstandardized Coefficients		Standardized Coefficients	t	Sig.	Collinearity Statistics	
	B	Std. Error	Beta			Tolerance	VIF
(Constant)	3.881	0.217		17.905	0.000		
Left-Right scale	0.175	0.023	0.261	7.707	0.000	0.920	1.087
Liberty-Authority scale	−0.069	0.036	−0.065	−1.922	0.055	0.910	1.099
FEMINISM	−0.278	0.030	−0.302	−9.197	0.000	0.977	1.024

Dependent Variable: Selectreform. Backward stepwise elimination of non-significant factors in 7 steps. Adjusted R-squared = 0.174; Durbin-Watson statistic = 2.010; n = 785.

Conservative party members to hold views consistent with more progressive gender attitudes and objectives, and even 'feminist' ones. With respect to broad views on gender roles and relations, the party members are moderate on the whole, with women showing a significantly greater sympathy than men for the more progressive and feminist positions. Persistent sex differences in outlook reveal themselves on specific women's issues, especially in respect of equal pay and childcare – issues which formed a substantial part of the party's manifesto appeal in 2010. Multivariate analysis shows that age and sex count here: younger members and women generally are significantly more progressive on such matters.

The main (gendered) implications of our survey of party members for the party's leadership are four-fold. First, there is the potential for the party leadership and leading party gender equality activists to mobilize women members in favour of the party's new policies for women, both by proselytizing within the party to garner wider party member support, and beyond the party in terms of electoral competition on the women's terrain. Secondly, if the party was to be successful in recruiting younger women as party members, this 'women's' support base might well be enlarged further. A potential for generational shift in attitudes over time, as party members are replaced, is clear. Thirdly, if we assume that Conservative women party members remain less amenable to the party's policies 'for women' than non-Conservative women (even as they are more at ease than their male party members), then the party leadership might well have been right to feel confident in assuming that its policies would be more attractive to unaligned women voters in 2010, given that some of their own women members were themselves not unhappy towards these policies (see Chapter 8 for a fuller analysis of this). Finally and prior to any membership renewal, the party would likely need to manage those current party members less at ease with party policies for women that appear, at least to them, counter to conservatism. These would include policies such as additional paternity leave and flexible working which both suggest that women and men should engage in caring and paid work. The language of choice, (as suggested in previous chapters) looks to be one means to resolving or limiting any intra-party tensions in this respect. As one of the party's senior woman MPs asked: 'does the government say "this is the sort of woman you should be and this is the sort of thing you should do" or does government say "we will set a framework and you can choose what you are doing within that framework"'.[26] Given that there are Conservatives at the membership level (and the parliamentary level too, for that matter) who think they know what women and mothers should do – namely, stay at home – the language of choice might just permit those in the party who take a different view to 'push the agenda forward', whilst enabling the party to formally 'sidestep' normative questions about what women *should* do.

6
Sex, Gender and Parliamentary Behaviour in the 2005 Parliament

[Working and staying at home] are equally valid choices, and both put mothers under enormous strain.[1]

One could not be sure how the Conservative party would act on women's concerns in the 2010 Parliament; whether its manifesto pledges would be implemented or whether its broader perspectives on gender and gender relations would inform its overall governing actions. Analyzing how the party acted in opposition during the 2005 Parliament is, however, suggestive. Of course, there are qualifications: membership of the Conservative parliamentary party is qualitatively and quantitatively different in 2010. There are many more Conservative women MPs, who may be more likely to be predisposed to gender politics. The newly elected Conservative MPs and newly appointed Conservative Peers might well be members more in tune with 'modern' gender roles, as a result of generational turnover. Coalition politics might be expected to further bolster an emphasis on women's issues, given the Liberal Democrats prior history in this respect (Evans 2011; Childs 2008). Even so, Cameron had had five years in which to refashion his private and parliamentary leadership teams (Bale 2010), and to mould his parliamentary party by the time of the 2010 general election. Hence, if the Conservatives under Cameron did indeed seek to be a different kind of Conservative party, the potential opened up for the party to adopt a correspondingly more progressive position on women's issues during the 2005 Parliament.

Three pieces of legislation are examined here to explore how the Conservative party in the 2005 Parliament constitutively and substantively represented women. All three are explicitly gendered: the Work and Families Act 2006 (WFA); the Human Fertilization and Embryology Act 2008 (HFEA); and the Equal Pay and Flexible Working Bill 2009 (EPFW).[2] Yet each is of different legislative type. The WFA is a piece of government legislation; the HFEA 2008 is a 'conscience' issue; and the EPFW 2009 is a Lords' Private Members Bill (PMB).[3] This variation permits comparison of institutional factors, most importantly party. In the UK's partisan, if not adversarial system, opposition MPs are widely assumed to oppose the government, even if they do not do so, in practice, quite as often as many think (Cowley 2002).[4] The working assumption here is that the WFA 2006 would see inter-party differences, reflecting both the historical association of the Conservative and Labour parties as the party of business and working interests, respectively,[5] and 'New' Labour's claim to be the most 'feminist' party UK politics has seen (Childs 2004; Annesley et al 2007). Expectations of inter-party division would hold too for the EPFW Bill, which as a Lords PMB would be especially short of parliamentary time if there was partisan dissent (H of C 2009: 4, 6).[6] This looked likely. The introduction of the Bill by the Conservative party signals inter-party competition over the terrain of 'women's issues', in turn, supporting wider claims (Childs 2008) of a feminization of British party politics.

Over and above expectations of inter-party competition and intra-party cohesion on legislation in general at Westminster, on explicitly gendered legislation there are additional, if not, competing expectations of sex differences (Norris and Lovenduski 1995; Lovenduski and Norris 2003; Childs 2002; Campbell et al 2010). All other things being equal, the expectation is that Labour MPs will be more predisposed towards gender equality positions than Conservatives – for left/right ideological reasons (inter-party differences). Yet, women of all parties might be expected to be more favourably positioned towards gender equality compared with male colleagues in their respective parties – on the basis of gender consciousness (intra-party sex differences). On conscience legislation expectations alter again.[7] Conscience legislation is often associated with free votes where legislators are not subject to the party whip (Cowley and Stuart 2010; Cowley 2002: 134). This was true for the abortion amendments to the HFEA 2008 despite the Bill's designation as a 'Government Bill' when it was first introduced into the Lords.[8] Parliamentarians' constitutive and substantive representation, might, in this case be said to reveal attitudes and behaviour unconstrained by party identity. Note, however, that even in the absence of the party whip the most important determinant is likely to remain party irrespective of whether that is because of ideological cohesion – MPs of the same party are more likely to agree with each other; that is why they are members of the same political party – or 'behind the scenes' pressure (Pattie et al 1998; Cowley and Stuart 2010; Cowley 2002: 134). Accordingly, our assumption relating to the HFEA legislation is that Labour Parliamentarians will be more favourably disposed to permissive abortion legislation and that women in all parties will vote in the more pro-choice direction than their male colleagues from the same party (Cowley 1998). At the same time, and in a pro-life/anti-choice direction, another identity – Catholicism – is, on the basis of previously observed behaviour, likely to trump both party and sex (Pattie et al 1998).

A second institutional dimension likely revealed by these case studies is the difference between the two Houses of Parliament. This further illuminates the impact of party politics at Westminster. The Lords is widely considered to be a less partisan House than the Commons, or rather was, until the 1999 reforms to the Upper Chamber when it lost its historic Conservative bias. Comparison also highlights the Upper and Lower Chambers' distinct compositions. At present the Lords is comprised, *inter alia*, of appointed representatives, alongside 92 remaining 'hereditaries'. This difference is said to contribute to the Lord's reputation as a House of 'experts', a perception that has, if anything, been enhanced since Labour's constitutional reforms. Indicators suggest its Members are increasingly bold in its scrutiny of legislation (Russell 2009). Accordingly, more partisan politics than previously expected is predicted, and expertise is likely to play a bigger role in parliamentary debates here than in the Commons.

The data are the Bill, associated explanatory notes and regulations, and other official documents, as well as the parliamentary debates and votes that accompanied each Bill's passage. The full analysis is four-staged for each of the case studies. This approach facilitates discussion of both the nature and direction of individual representatives', and the parties' collective contributions, as competitive representative claims are made. First, the constitutive representation of gender is considered in respect of what might be termed the 'official' position. For the WFA 2006 this is the Labour government; in the HFEA 2008 it is a Parliamentary committee, the Science and Technology Committee (STC); and in the EPFW it is the Conservative party, or, more accurately, their Women's Policy Group. Research questions informing the analysis include enquiring as to the nature of 'what it means to be a woman and a man'; the nature of the issues and interests claimed to be 'women's' and 'men's'; the nature of the relations between women and men and whether these are premised upon notions of sex- and gender-sameness or difference, whether they are co-operative or conflictual, and, or, hierarchical or egalitarian, and whether women are constituted in a homogenous or heterogeneous fashion.[9]

Secondly, parliamentary votes are analysed as a surrogate measure for MPs and Peers' preferred policy outcomes, itself taken as an indicator of the substantive representation of women. There was no division on the EPFW Bill,[10] but there is one maternity/paternity division on the WFA 2006 and six abortion divisions on the HFEA 2008.[11] Thirdly, the constitutive representation of gender is analyzed in terms of the Bill's accompanying parliamentary debates. This analysis is a useful, if not necessary, supplement to parliamentary vote analysis, which captures only the end point of the legislative process (Tamerius 1995) and the point in Westminster politics where party cohesion usually dominates (Cowley 2002, 2005). Finally, and because of Squires' (2008) assumption that the two dimensions of constitutive and substantive representation are likely intertwined in practice, even if analytically distinct, the two facets of representation in each of the case studies are compared. Here the focus is on internal consistency between them. Where possible, comparisons between competing constitutive representations proffered by different political actors are also undertaken (Childs 2010; Saward 2006). As argued in Chapter 1, congruency might imply that the substantive representation is a logical response to the representation of gender and might legitimize the particular representative/s' claims, and indicate a substantive commitment to act for women. Alternatively, dissonance might suggest tensions and might undermine the robustness or legitimacy of the constitutive representation of gender, or signal a rhetorical rather than substantive commitment to 'act for' women.

'Fatherhood and apple pie': The Work and Families Act 2006[12]

The aim of the WFA 2006, according to the Labour government, was to enhance the choices of parents in balancing their work and family responsibilities. Its central provisions relate to the 'statutory rights to leave and pay in connection with the birth or adoption of children'. More specifically, and *inter alia*, it extended the period of statutory maternity and provides for extended paternity leave via additional paternity leave (APL). The Bill's provisions touch directly on notions of gender relations. In respect of these, the Labour government favoured, even if it would not prescribe, parental care in the first year. By extending maternity leave, the Act sought to give women more rights. It also gave fathers new rights through APL, although these new provisions are qualitatively different than those for mothers. For example, qualifying mothers are given the right to one year's maternity leave. Fathers have the potential to receive half a year's leave, a right that is dependent upon the entitlements of the mother and her decision to return to work. The Act remains, then, in privileging mother care, underpinned by traditional assumptions about who should care for new born babies. It also suggests that mothers are in need of protection – from their employers, their partners and themselves. It is for these reasons that the first six months of maternity leave is protected for the mother.

Despite cross party front bench support for the principle of the Bill, party differences are apparent. Voting was in the expected direction: Labour MPs voted one way (for) and the Conservatives, with the Liberal Democrats, the other (against). Vote turnout by sex was broadly in line with the percentages of women and men in each of the parliamentary parties.[13] In the Commons debate seven substantive issues and inter-party differences and intra-party differences reveal themselves.

(1) *An unintended consequence of the legislation will be greater discrimination against women* (the 'Alan Sugar defence'[14]) and, to a lesser, extent *'younger' men*.[15] It is Conservative MPs who warn of this. Male Ministers

and women Labour MPs remind the House that such behaviour is illegal;

(2) The presumption that *women need to be 'protected'* (from employers and their husbands) is articulated by Labour MPs, male and female;

(3) That *the legislation privileges working mothers* over 'stay at home' mothers is highlighted by Conservatives, male and female;

(4) That *APL should be more flexible and pay enhanced* is a minority position raised by a Liberal Democrat male and two Labour MPs, one of each sex;

(5) *APL conflicts with the business interest.* Conservative male MPs perceive the legislation as a 'Trojan horse';

(6) *A preference for gender neutral legislation underpinned by notions of gender equality* is articulated by a sole Labour woman MP;

(7) *Prioritizing the business interest* is most vocally advocated by Conservatives. Labour and Liberal Democrat Members are more likely to draw a distinction between good and bad businesses and numerous Labour MPs voice the business case for the principle of the legislation.

In the Lords, substantive discussion centres on four issues, all of which featured in the Commons' debates, although gender equality is more extensively discussed in the Lords. Party differences in the Lords are harder to discern overall relative to the Commons.

(1) *Greater discrimination as an unintended consequence of the legislation* is articulated by Conservative Members;

(2) Male and female Peers, from across the benches, feel that *women need to be protected* from employers and fathers;

(3) *Concern relating to APL* again shows clear difference of direction. Business concerns and the problem of fraud relating to paternity are raised. Conservatives are more concerned about the business interest whereas Peers, predominantly Liberal Democrat ones, seek to maximize fathers' access to paternity leave and pay,[16] while members, male and female, from the Cross benches, the Church of England as well as the Liberal Democrat benches, are concerned about the dependent nature of paternity provision;

(4) *Greater gender equality* is raised by two women Peers (Liberal Democrat and Crossbench).

In the parliamentary debates, maternity leave and pay was relatively uncontentious, even if there were Conservative claims that women would face greater discrimination if the legislation was too burdensome on business (with the implication that the Bill must therefore be limited in some way), and on the grounds that women who stay at home to look after children are either ignored, or disadvantaged, by the legislation. However, the most significant debate across both Houses centred, on the principle and workings of APL – crucially, in terms of the impact on business interests rather than gender relations.[17]

There was near unanimity in Parliament that the legislation widens choice. All but one MP, a Conservative male, considers the legislation as providing greater choice. And Parliamentarians overwhelmingly agreed with the government that this is a choice for families and parents. Some party differences are, beyond this, apparent, although sex differences are harder to discern. Labour and Liberal Democrat MPs, male and female, are more likely to be concerned with balancing women's and mothers' interests. Conservative MPs, albeit sharing with Labour MPs a concern with people's and families' work/life balance, appear more concerned about how work/life balance impacts on business. Conservative MPs and Peers also raise the issue of whether the Bill is itself unbalanced against business. It is Labour MPs, male and female, who highlight women's choice to return to work post-childbirth.

'In the Footsteps of a Redhead from Blackburn...A Redhead from Bolton': The Equal Pay and Flexible Working Bill 2009[18]

The *EPFW Bill 2009*, a Private Members Bill (PMB), was first introduced into the House of Lords by the Conservative Peer Baroness Trish Morris in December 2008 (the 'Bolton Redhead'). The Bill's origins lay in the Women's Policy Group Report *Women in the World Today (WIWT)* discussed in the previous chapter.[19] Unquestionably radical, Morris' PMB would extend the right to request flexible working to parents with children up to the age of 18 and prescribes particular measures that seek to reduce the gender pay gap. In so doing the Bill placed the Conservative party arguably 'ahead' of Labour on these issues, even if the Bill's provisions for equal pay, invited Labour's (and others') criticism regarding the appropriateness and effectiveness of its suggested ameliorating measures.[20] Overall, the Report, the Bill and the parliamentary debate contributions show a clear consensus across the parties relating to women's experiences of paid employment and the work/life balance.

Five main representations of gender relations are evident in *WIWT*.

(1) *Women's and men's lives are different and unequal,* both in general and in respect of paid work;
(2) As an institution *the family is represented as experiencing difficulties in balancing domestic and paid work commitments;*
(3) *It is for families and parents,* and not the state, *to determine who cares for children;*
(4) Women's experience of paid employment is differentiated by *race;*

(5) *Business is represented in multiple, if not contradictory ways.* The business case is said to be clear, but business must not be overburdened, and employees must be protected from the 'unscrupulous' employer.

In the (single) Lords' debate, sex differences are apparent in addition to party ones. Women Members of the Lords are more likely than men to contribute, and contribute extensively, to these debates. It is they, for the most part, who constitute the issues in the EPFW Bill in an explicitly gender equality fashion;[21] talk most about fathers wishing to undertake more family responsibility; and, who are clear that women's interests must not be 'sacrificed' to businesses' in the face of the late 2000s financial crisis. Partisan conflict centres, from the Labour benches, on the failure of Conservatives to hitherto support Labour measures on work/life balance.

'Quicker than a Consultation at the Hairdressers?': The Human Fertilization and Embryology Act 2008[22]

Whilst the Human Fertilization and Embryology Act 2008 did not address abortion, abortion amendments were permitted because it amends the 1990 Act which did. In the Commons the key issue was the time at which abortion is legal, with amendments seeking to reduce this to various points between 12 and 23 weeks and six days, from the current 24 weeks. Other amendments sought to exclude abortion on grounds of sex, race or sexual orientation, provide for 'informed consent' and greater information. Prior to the Bill, the House of Commons Science and Technology Committee (STC) issued a report.[23] Three main representations of women are apparent therein.

(1) The *late abortion seeker who did not know she was pregnant or who faced delay* in securing an abortion;
(2) A preference for *parental decision making in the abortion of a disabled foetus;*
(3) Women *no longer require the protection of two doctors.*

In respect of parliamentary votes, party differences are evident: the majority of Labour and Liberal Democrat MPs are in the progressive lobby while the majority of Conservative MPs vote for more restrictive positions (Cowley and Stuart 2010). Intra-party sex differences in women's favour are also evident in the Commons, although less so in the Lords. Turning to debate contributions, important sex and party differences are, again, apparent:

(1) *Supporters of the 'social abortionist' thesis in the Commons are most likely to be Conservative men.* Critics of this thesis are mostly (Labour) women;

(2) *Men* (on both sides of the debate) *appear to prefer the terrain of science* when discussing abortion;

(3) *Labour women MPs and women from the Cross and Liberal Democrat Lords' benches* dominate contributions that *centre women in any debate* about abortion;

(4) *Explicit supporters of women's 'right to choose' are, all bar one, women, and the majority are Labour;*

(5) It is *Labour women MPs who contest those critics of abortion* (male and female) *who argue that women need protection on grounds that abortion harms their health;*

(6) It is *Labour women MPs who contend that restricting abortion threatens women's health.*

Comparing the parties' representation across the three bills

Men and women, different and unequal

The analysis of the constitutive representation of gender across the cases suggests three broad, overarching findings. First, and perhaps unsurprisingly, given that all three pieces of legislation were explicitly gendered, the Bills/Acts, their associated documents, and accompanying debates all 'see' gender – women and men's lives and experiences are recognized as different. Overwhelmingly, too, and in seeing gender, a critical analysis underpins the representations. Women and men's bifurcated roles are, in nearly all cases, not considered natural but cultural;[24] not to be accepted but to be transformed. Gender relations are also regarded as hierarchical and to men's benefit, at least when men and women's roles at work and in the home are considered. Here there are a few representations of men as seeking greater roles in caring for children – which imply a gender equality approach – but there is no widespread call for greater and independent rights to paternity leave, for example. And for Conservatives there is particular concern that men might become discriminated against in the workplace if they are given greater paternity rights. In terms of women's gender roles there is extensive and an almost universal representation of British women as engaged in paid employment and this is constituted as a good even if they are disadvantaged therein. That women feel obliged to return to work after childbirth for economic reasons is shared by the government and the Conservative party, for example, even if the latter make more of a play of this. Representations which continue to privilege more traditional gender roles for women, not least women's role in post-childbirth childcare, remain. This is true of both the government and the Conservatives once again. There is also concern, even if only a minority one, with the choice of 'stay at home mothers' to be homemakers, although this mostly comes from backbench Conservative men in the Commons. More often, albeit implicitly and by the government and Members in both Houses, is the sense in which women's traditional gender roles will and should continue to be, the outcome of the family and parental choice. Explicit representations of gender equality positions are very much in the minority, for example, in advocating full transferability of maternity/paternity leave, or the privileging of women's choice and bodily integrity in respect of abortion – not forcing women to carry a disabled foetus to term. When they are voiced this is most often by women. In the Commons these are overwhelmingly Labour women, although in the Lords they are from Labour, Liberal Democrat and Cross benches.

Secondly, women are represented as both *sharing experiences* and of constituting an *heterogeneous group*. Class and race feature in discussions of paid employment: educated women return to work whilst lesser educated or lesser skilled women do not. There are concerns too that poorer women and men will be unable to take up additional maternity and paternity leave for financial reasons – it is for this reason that a couple of Liberal Democrats and Conservatives wish to see the total amount of maternity/paternity pay paid over a shorter period of time. Class is the dominant representation in the abortion debate, with race absent, although Northern Irish women are distinguished as the UK's second class citizen, given the illegality of abortion in Northern Ireland.

The representations of women's lot across the three pieces of legislation suggest a *lack of agency* for women, the third observation. Women are those who have things done to them. They have little choice but to accept the conditions and experiences they face. One consequence of this is that women need to be protected. In respect of paid employment, Labour members considered that women need to be protected: from employers (who will exploit them, especially in the face of economic crisis); their partners (who are in competition with them for rights associated with caring); and themselves (for they do not know what is in their own interest). In respect of abortion, critics contend that women need to be protected from doctors, the abortion industry, and once again, from themselves (they do not fully appreciate the risks to their health, both mental and physical). Representations like these logically suggest that legislative protection is needed, for example, to protect the first six months of maternity leave, or to limit the number of days that a mother can work during her maternity leave, and to ensure that women are provided with sufficient information and time to make an informed choice about abortion. Representations of women as needing protection from their partners or husbands not only suggests a similarity of perspective from representatives who might otherwise see themselves on different side of the ideological fence, but also sits uncomfortably with the representations of the family, couples and parents articulated across the parties as a sex-undifferentiated and non-hierarchical unit. Here, then, there is a glimpse of representations that see gender relations as one of potential conflict and hierarchy.

(Mostly) women acting for women in a feminist direction

The actions of MPs and Peers across the three pieces of legislation in respect of how they vote do not proffer unexpected findings. Given the institutional context of UK politics, especially the high levels of party cohesion, there are (1) few sex differences in vote turnout between women and men and (2) party overwhelmingly accounts for Members' vote direction. However, sex plays a greater role in the contributions to parliamentary debates. Across the three cases there is evidence of an *over-representation by women Members* in parliamentary debates relative to their percentages in both Houses, as Table 6.1 below illustrates. Note that both Houses of Parliament at the time had 20 percent female membership. In respect of the EPFW 2009, Labour women Peers constituted four out of the five Labour party contributors. In respect of the HFEA Labour women Members constituted 46 and 56 percent of that party's contributors in the abortion debates (Commons and Lords, respectively). Or consider that Conservative women MPs constituted 25 percent of Tory contributors (including frontbenchers) to the WFA 2006, at a time when Conservative women constituted a mere 9 percent of the Conservative parliamentary party. In the HFEA 2008 women MPs and Peers' greater tendency to contribute overall, masks Tory male Peers' greater tendency to speak on abortion, and Labour's men MPs are notable for their absence across both the WFA and HFEA. The direction of representatives' contributions is important too. Noting who is speaking on women's concerns tells us nothing about what representatives are saying, or what kinds of positions they articulate. In this, women are, overall, more likely to be those contributors adopting the gender equality position. For example, during debate of the EPFW Bill it is women in the Lords who do not wish women's employment rights to be sacrificed at the demands of an economy in recession, whilst in the WFA 2006 it is women, for the most part, who wish to see maternity and paternity leave reformed for reasons of women's equality. Party, of course, plays a role too: these are most often women from the Labour party in the Commons, but in Lords they are also from Cross and Liberal Democrat benches.

Table 6.1 Over-representation of Women Members in Parliamentary Debates

	Men (% of all contributors)	Women (% of all contributors)
WFA 06 Commons	72	28
WFA 06 Lords	66	33
HFEA 08 Commons	74	26
HFEA 08 Lords	40	60
EPFW 09 Lords[25]	40	60

Table 6.2 Legislators' Interests and APPG Memberships, by Sex

	Interests		APPG	
	Men	Women	Men	Women
WFA 06 Commons	Equally divided between business and fatherhood, children, adoption and caring	Overwhelmingly associated women, family, children, carers, adoption	Only two are members of any associated groups – childcare	Eight are members of associated groups: maternity, sex equality, parents, adopting, childcare
WFA 06 Lords	No clear patterns			
HFEA 08 Commons	Health predominates; disability; families, Church/Christianity; Northern Ireland	Health predominates; women are 3 out of the 5 citing equal opportunities/ equality; one woman	Men and women have similar memberships, especially parents and families group	Health predominates; pro-life, pro-choice and equality group have three members each, with all having members of both sex.
HFEA 08 Lords	Single pro-life Peer is a male; one 'gender issues'	Women constitute three-quarters of those with interests associated HFEA; health predominates, couple associated with women's issues/women's equality	Members of health related groups; one member of anti-abortion group	Two members of 'pro-choice group' and one 'sex equality group'; also members of health related groups
EPFW 09 Lords[26]	Business/econ – men more interested, but not by much;	Equalities – Labour/CB women and one LD male	Equalities groups – one woman/one man (lab/LD respectively~)	

Sources: Dod's Parliamentary Guide, Dod's Parliamentary Companion; www.parliament.uk

There are *sex and party differences in Members' interests* in respect of the concerns addressed by these pieces of legislation too. These differences are not absolute, but the broad observation holds whether one looks at legislators' reported interests or their membership of All Party Parliamentary Groups (APPG). Without attempting to identify causal direction, contributing women MPs and Peers are more likely, overall, than male MPs and Peers to be interested in the concerns associated with the content of the three Bills/Acts, as Table 6.2 shows (patterns in the Lords are harder to discern either by party or by sex). In some cases the differences are stark. For example, in the WFA 2006 only two of the ten MPs who are members of the groups associated with the concerns addressed in the Act are men. The other clear sex difference is to do with business – something about which men are more concerned.

Identifying the *critical actors* for each of the three Bills is straightforward if determined on the basis of identifying Members of either House who spoke in most, if not all, of each of the Bills' parliamentary stages. Showing no clear patterns by party or sex, in the Commons, these are Peter Bone, Jim McGovern, Julie Morgan and Charles Walker for the WFA 2006; and Clare Curtis Thomas, Christine McCafferty, Michael Jabez Foster, Jacqui Lait and Iris Robinson in the HFEA 2008. Adopting a qualitative approach and, moreover, controlling for direction establishes that critical actors acting in a gender-equality direction, are mostly Labour women in the Commons,[27] and women from Labour, Liberal Democrat and Cross Benches in the Lords. For example, Morgan MP (Labour) spoke extensively on the WFA 2008 and the HFEA 2008; Baroness Howe (Crossbench) spoke on the WFA 2006 and the EPFW 2009; and Baroness Gould (Labour) spoke on EPFW and HFEA 2008. Other MPs making significant pro-equality contributions include the male MPs Evan Harris and Pete Wishart (LD and SNP) and the Conservative woman MP Lait.

Speaking as... The basis upon which, and the identities MPs and Peers' claim, when they speak in the WFA 2006 debates show some sex differences. Those citing familial experience of, and claims to expertise about, business are, all bar one, male in the Commons, and female in the Lords.[28] References to being a parent in Parliament, and the difficulties of reconciling the House with familial responsibilities, are made by male and female MPs, from both Conservative and Labour sides, even if the women's contributions are more extensive, expansive and, arguably, heartfelt.[29] Representatives explicitly speaking *as* women (or as men or parents for that matter) are rarely present in the EPFW debates, which is surprising given the overlap between this Bill and the WFA 2006, where women and men Parliamentarians were keen to signal their parental identity.[30] Three women Peers (Labour and Crossbench) do however highlight their gender equality expertise. *Speaking as...* A number of women representatives in the debates speak *as women* in the biological sense, as mothers, but also in a more political sense, as advocates of women's equality, or as those who champion the rights of single parents, poor and Northern Irish women. No woman speaks as someone who has had an abortion, although one speaks as a woman who rejected medical opinion to abort. Similarly, no man speaks as someone who was involved in the conception of a subsequently aborted foetus, although a few speak as fathers, husbands and partners, one in relation to a foetal disability diagnosis. Unable to speak as a woman, one male Conservative MP draws on public opinion data, and especially women's mass views, to support his perspective and underpin his contribution in the debate. Pro-choice Labour women MPs contest this, and claim abortion as something uniquely about women, and about which women representatives should speak. For some women 'acting for' women looks, on the basis of what they said in the debates, to derive from both an experiential basis and a political identity: of speaking both *as* and *for* women. Of course, men can only claim the latter, but few do so in terms of gender equality. Rather the men who explicitly claim to speak for women, and, or contest the assumption that only women representatives can and should speak for women, do so on the basis of a more Burkean notion of representation, or employ public opinion data to support their views. To be sure, in the WFA 2006 there was something of a 'Dutch auction' as MPs and Peers claim to speak as mothers, fathers (indeed 'new men'), grandparents, sons and daughters, small business owners, employment lawyers, and/or carers, as if outbidding each other, but this was much less true of the other two pieces of legislation.

Any institutional difference between the two Houses of Parliament revealed in this analysis should not be overstated. The data is limited, not least because fewer Members participated in the debates in the Lords, but also because the debates themselves are less extensive. Comparing the WFA 2006 and the EPFW Bill (recall that this only had a Lords' Second Reading) highlights some institutional specificity of the Lords; fewer sex and party differences. Partisan hostility is also less obvious in the Lords as Peers appear to share views across party and sex more often than in the Commons. Furthermore, it looks like the role of expertise and specialized interests comes to the fore in the Lords to a much greater extent than in the Commons, as expected, not least by Peers seeking to claim this on the basis of gender equality expertise.

Dissonance between constitutive and substantive representation in respect of the WFA 2006 and EPFW Bill 2008 centres on apparent preferences for gender equality as an overarching principle sitting alongside legislative provisions and policy pledges that are underpinned and undermined by preferences, either explicit or implicit, for differences in the roles that women and men undertake.[31] Accordingly, these beg questions about the coherence and robustness of (at least some of) the representative claims. Take the WFA 2006. This piece of Labour legislation gives mothers and fathers important new rights. But these are qualitatively different and, crucially, fathers' are dependent on the decisions of mothers. The six month point at which APL 'kicks in' suggests further tension with the government's agnosticism regarding which parent should care for the child. It also undermines the government's acknowledgement that transferability of leave (which it subsequently dropped from the legislation) will support 'greater equality at home and at work'.[32] Furthermore, it begs questions of the government's acknowledged 'risk' that women will be the main carers of children, 'with the consequential detrimental impact on their careers, pay and pensions'.[33] Similar comments can be made of the EPFW Bill. To be sure, and as stated above, the Bill includes three of the four pledges from Conservative party's Women's Policy Group Report, *Women in the World Today*.[34] However, the implication that women are likely to continue to be the main carers fails to address the negative implications and consequences for women of the traditional sexual division of labour that is also made evident in the Report.

Comparing the representative claims made in the WFA 2006 and the EPFW 2008 as well as the consultation document to the WFA 2006 and *WIWT* Report, reveals an overwhelmingly shared description of women's experiences of paid work and home/work balance between the Labour government and Conservative party's Women's Group. Their overarching depiction of women and men's lives in the UK in respect of paid employment are similar. There is, moreover, consensus across the two Bills and associated debates that the role of government is not to tell parents and families how they should care for their children. Families should choose how best to reconcile work and family life. In this, both parties mostly construct the family as an undifferentiated and non-hierarchical unit even as they recognize that, first, this means in practice women's choice, and secondly, that women need to be protected from their husbands/partners, not least in respect of protecting maternity leave in the post-childbirth period. Where one can see a larger difference between the two main parties is in the Conservative's greater concern with the traditional single-earner model of the family. This is not to say that the right for women to choose to stay home is not articulated by members of both parties – as made clear in the debates associated with the WFA 2006 – but the Conservatives, as outlined in *WIWT*, alongside backbench male Conservative contributions to the WFA 2006 parliamentary debates, are more explicit in the 'unfairness' of any legislative provisions that appear to discriminate against 'stay at home mothers'. Recall too that *WIWT* contends that the Labour government has ignored familial and informal care of children.

Conclusion: Constituting and substantively representing women in a conservative fashion?

One must, admittedly, be cautious in generalizing on the basis of the small number of case studies analysed here, not least by an appreciation of the changing composition of the Parliamentary Conservative party over time and the historic and static picture painted by any study of the 2005 Parliament. Yet, taking three explicitly gendered pieces of legislation and subjecting them to systematic analysis in terms of the Conservative party's underpinning assumptions about gender roles and relations, as well as the particular behaviour of MPs and Peers, reveals how Cameron's Conservatives, individually and collectively, conceived of women's representation when they were faced with particular legislation that was 'for women' in the 2005 Parliament. Indeed, one piece, the EPFW was of their own authorship, permitting greater consideration of the constitutive and substantive representation by Conservative actors. Moreover, both this Bill and the WFA 2006 discuss a key contemporary women's issue – the reconciliation of work and family life and women's experiences thereof. The analysis of the HFEA 2008 additionally provides a case study of the one issue that is popularly regarded as the *sin qua non* women's issue.

In the broadest of terms, the parliamentary Conservative party shares with the other main political parties a view of women and men's gender roles that are more in line with modern rather than the traditionally bifurcated gender roles – a two parent earning family rather than a working husband and father and a stay at home mother. It is, though, also the party that highlights most often the plight of the single earner family. Even so, there is also plenty of evidence that the party, especially its front bench, supports women's greater and better participation in the paid employment market. In the EPFW Bill 2009 in particular, although to a lesser extent in response to the Labour government's WFA 2006, the party advocates legislative intervention that will, in their view, enhance and improve women's experience of paid work. Its measures on flexible working especially, put the Conservative party, at least on paper, ahead of the Labour party. From a gender equality perspective, that is, one that seeks women and men's equal participation in the home and workplace, this is an important development to note. Beyond this bigger picture, intra-party sex differences are apparent. On abortion it is the Conservative party's men who are most vocal in the Parliamentary debates in arguing against current and more progressive abortion provisions and it is they who vote more restrictively. On the employment legislation Conservative women are more likely to participate in parliamentary discussions and more likely to advocate the more gender equality position on these issues than their male colleagues. Conservative Members overall are, to be sure, more likely to be concerned about business interests, the extension of paternity leave of pay, and stay at home mothers, relative to the other two main political parties, but it is Conservative men who are the most concerned.

Such findings beg the question of the extent to which these differences amongst Conservatives matter within the Parliamentary party and front bench. Sure the Parliamentary party contains within it some Members who hold more traditional views of gender roles, revealing ambivalence, and arguably contradictory views, towards women's participation in the paid employment market and their role as mothers and carers of children. But these are mostly back bench men and whilst they may be vocal, and suggest a potential to vote against the party in the future on similar legislation, it maybe that they can be and will be simply ignored and or contained by the 2010 Conservative front bench. And in any case, and like the Labour government, these tensions might be resolved by the absence of prescription. For example, that it will be left to families and parents to choose who works and who cares for children. What probably will matter more for women's constitutive and substantive representation in the 2010–15 Parliament is an appreciation of the interaction between the composition of the parliamentary Conservative party, coalition government policy, leading Conservative representatives, and the wider political environment.

Appendix I: Case I WFA 2006

Table 6.3   Participation in Parliamentary Debates, by Sex and Party

	Women	Men	Total
Commons (all)	12 (28%)	31 (72%)	43
Labour MPs (all)	10 (45%)	12 (55%)	22
Labour MPs (backbench)	7 (41%)	10 (59%)	17
Conservatives MPs (all)	3 (25%)	12 (75%)	15
Conservatives MPs (backbench)	1 (11%)	8 (88%)	9
Lords (all)	5 (30%)	10 (70%)	15

Table 6.4   Peers' Parliamentary 'Interests', Related to the Work and Families Act, 2006, According to *DOD's Parliamentary Companion*

Peer	Interests
Baroness Miller of Hendon (Con)	Women; small business
Baroness Walsmley (LD)	Children
Baroness Howe of Idlicote (CB)	Elderly; equal opportunities
Lord Northbourne (CB)	Children; family policy
Baroness Knight of Collingtree (Con)	Children
Lord Lyell (Con)	Employment & employment law
Lord Bishop of Winchester	Family policy; welfare

Table 6.5 MPs' Parliamentary 'Interests', Related to the Work and Families Act, 2006, According to *Vacher's Parliamentary Profiles*[35]

	Parliamentary Profiles
Alan Johnson L	Fairness at work, working time
Norman Lamb LD	Solicitor specializing in employ law
Mark Prisk C	Chartered surveyor with interest in small business; treasurer of all party group on small business
David Burrowes C	Spoken on equality (defending the diversity of non-fashionable views on morality), fatherhood
John Bercow C	Leading Tory progressive
Alison Seabeck L	Member of Fawcett society; Labour women's network; select committee regulatory reform
Tobias Ellwood C	Was member of London council of CBI
Helen Jones L	Former member of Labour's National Women's Committee; adoption, carers
Gerry Sutcliffe L	Lone parents
Julie Kirkbride C	Defied 3 line whip voted to allow unmarried couples to adopt
Philip Hollobone C	Fatherhood, care of children
Barbara Keeley L	Left of centre feminist; worked for Princess Royal Trust for carers; set up local branch of 300 group; work and families, women and equality
Kitty Ussher L	Attacked gender discrimination over parental leave saying men should have equal time off to care for babies; husband is f/t father
Peter Luff C	Work and families
Julie Morgan L	Feminist; chairs all party group on sex equality; wants universal childcare for those who need it
Jim McGovern L	Member of local concil EO committee; work and families; carers

Table 6.5 MPs' Parliamentary 'Interests', Related to the Work and Families Act, 2006, According to *Vacher's Parliamentary Profiles*[35] – *continued*

	Parliamentary Profiles
Theresa May C	Women in Conservative Party
Liz Blackman L	Feminist credentials; special select committee on adoption
Diana Johnson L	Employment rights; labour women's network; Fawcett society
Eleanor Laing C	Single mother; work life balance; voted in favour lowering age of homosexual consent
Madeline Moon L	Childcare; work and families
Charles Walker C	Employment specialist
Patricia Hewitt L	Keen promoter of alternative families; women's rights; unmarried father's rights
Meg Munn L	PPS to Hodge as Children's Min; adoption
Alan Reid LD	Briefly TI spokesman on IT
Ian Stewart L	Rebelled vs lone parent cut
Stewart Jackson C	Small business
Michael Jabez Foster L	Employment law specialist; adoption
Nigel Dodds DUP	Spokesperson on work and pensions
Robert Smith LD	Selct comm. T&I
Russell Brown L	Childcare
Henry Bellingham C	2002 was shadow small business min; adoption
John Heppell L	Carers

Table 6.6 MPs and Peers Membership of Select All Party Parliamentary Groups

MPs	
Julie Morgan L	Maternity; Carers, Equalities; Sex equality
Alison Seabeck L	Sex equality
Julie Kirkbride C	Parents and families
Meg Munn L	Parents and families
Theresa May C	Adoption and fostering
Liz Blackman L	Adoption and fostering
Eleanor Laing C	Childcare
Barbara Keeley L	Carers
David Burrowes C	Childcare
Russell Brown L	Childcare
Peers	
Baroness Walmsley LD	Children; play
Baroness Howe CB	Parents and families
Earl of Listowel CB	Adoption and fostering; children; Foyers; looked after children and young carers; maternity; parents and families; pro-choice and sexual health
Lord Northbourne CB	Sustainable relationships; parents and families

Case II EPFW 2009

Table 6.7 Lords Contributions 2nd Reading

Name	Party, Position[36]	Sex
1. Baroness Morris of Bolton	Con , Spokes for Children, Schools & Families	F
2. Lord Morris of Handsworth	Lab	M
3. Baroness Howe of Idlicote	CB	F
4. Bishop of Southwark	Bishop	M
5. B. Gould of Potternewton	Lab, Deputy speaker, Deputy Chair of Committees	F
6. Baroness Prosser	Lab	F
7. Baroness Morgan of Huyton	Lab	F
8. Lord Lester of Herne Hill	LD, Spokes for Discrimination Law Reform 2008–	M
9. Lord Hunt of Wirrall	Con, Spokes Bus. Enterprise & Regulatory Reform	M
10. Baroness Vadera	Lab, Min for Economic Competitiveness, Small Business and Enterprise) 2008–, Cabinet Office 2008-	F

Table 6.8 Lords' Interests, Associated with the EPFW Bill[37]

Member	Interests
Lord Morris of Handsworth ,Lab	Social justice, trade unions, the economy, diversity
Baroness Howe of Idlicote, CB	Equal opportunities,
Baroness Gould of Potternewton, Lab	Women's equality,
Baroness Prosser, Lab	World of work, equalities, equal pay
Baroness Morgan of Huyton, Lab	Equality issues
Lord Lester of Herne Hill, LD	Equality and non-discrimination,
Lord Hunt of Wirrall, Con	Business and economy, skills

Table 6.9 Lords' All Party Parliamentary Groups, Associated with EPFW Bill[38]

Member	Interests
Baroness Morris of Bolton, Con ,fb	Vice-chair: Chair Parents and Families Group '07–
Baroness Gould of Potternewton, Lab, fb	Secretary Sex Equality Group 2001–
Lord Lester of Herne Hill, LD, fb	Vice-chair Equalities Group 2004–

Case Study III

Table 6.10 MPs who Spoke on Abortion, by Sex and Party

Party	Men	Women	Total
Labour	15 (54%)	13 (46%)	28
Cons.	23 (88%)	3 (12%)	26
L. Dem	5 (83%)	1 (17%)	6
Other	7 (88%)	1 (12%)	8
Total	50 (74%)	18 (26%)	68

Table 6.11   Peers who Spoke on Abortion, by Sex and Party

Party	Men	Women	Total
Labour	4 (44%)	5 (56%)	9
Cons.	3 (75%)	1 (25%)	4
L. Dem	1 (20%	4 (80%)	5
Cross	3 (30%)	7 (70%)	10
DUP	0 (0%)	1 (100%)	1
Bishops	1 (100%)	0 (0%)	1
Total	12 (40%)	18 (60%)	30

Table 6.12   Peers' Parliamentary 'Interests', Related to the HFEA 2008, According to *DOD's Parliamentary Companion 2007*

Name	Interests
1. Baroness Tonge	Health
2. Baroness Jay of Paddington	Health
3. Lord Jenkin of Roding	Health
4. Lord Walton of Detchant	Health
5. Baroness Emerton	Health
6. Baroness Neuberger	Health
7. Baroness Masham of Ilton	Health, disability
8. Baroness Barker	Health
9. Baroness Finlay	Medical ethics, health and medicine
10. Baroness Knight of Collingtree	Health
11. Baroness Wilkins	Disability

Table 6.13   MPs' Parliamentary 'Interests', Related to the HFEA 2008, According to *DOD's Parliamentary Profiles*[39]

MP	Interests
Judy Mallaber	Equal opportunities
Julie Morgan	Equal opportunities
Dawn Primarolo	Health, equal opportunities
Pete Wishart	Justice and equality
Sandra Osborne	Women
Dr Evan Harris	Health, equality, science, medical ethics, secularism
Andrew Lansley	Health
Nadine Dorries	Health
Paul Willis	Health
Norman Lamb	Health
Brian Iddon	Health
Chris McCafferty	Health
Iris Robinson	Health
Michael Jabez Foster	Health
Mrs Jacqui Lait	Health
Anne Moffat	Health
John Pugh	Health
Dr William McCrea	Health
Mike Penning	Health
Mark Simmonds	Health
Andy Slaughter	Health
Ian Gibson	Health
Jim Dobbin	Health, life issues
Ann Widdecombe	Abortion, health
Desmond Turner	Health, disability science policy
Tom Clarke	Disability rights
John Hayes	Disability
David Burrowes	Family policy, umbilical cord blood banking, treatment and research
Julian Brazier	Families
Edward Leigh	Families
Frank Field	Church affairs
Laurence Robertson	Northern Ireland
Jeffrey M. Donaldson	Northern Ireland, Christian values

Table 6.14 MPs' Membership of All Party Parliamentary Groups Related to the HFEA 2008[40]

MP	All Party Parliamentary Groups
Andrew Lansley	Vice-chair Infertility Group 2003–;
Nadine Dorries	Treasurer Umbilical Cord Blood and Adult Stem Cell Group 2008
Paul Willis	Treasurer Medical Research Group 2006–; Secretary Spinal Cord Injury Group 2008–
Norman Lamb	Vice-chair Epilepsy Group 2001–
John Bercow	Brain Tumours Group 2005–; Secretary Pro-Choice and Sexual Health Group 2007–
Christine McCafferty	Chair:Population, Development and Reproductive Health Group 1999–; Vice-chair Epilepsy Group 2007–
Emily Thornberry	Vice-chair Pro-Choice and Sexual Health Group 2006–; Chair Maternity Group 2007–
Desmond Turner	Chair: ME (Myalgic Encephalomyelitis) Group 2005–; Medical Technology Group 2005–
David Burrowes	Secretary Sickle Cell and Thalassaemia Group 2008–; Chair Umbilical Cord Blood and Adult Stem Cell Group 2008–
Claire Curtis Thomas	Vice-chair: Pro-Life Group 2004–
Dr Evan Harris	Vice-chair Lupus Group 2000–; Chair Kidney Group 2000–; Secretary Equalities Group 2004–; Vice-chair: AIDS Group 2005–; Heart Disease Group 2005–; Brain Tumours Group 2005–; Honorary Secretary Science Group 2005–; Vice-chair: Specialist Orthopaedic Services and Hospitals Group 2006–; Secretary Pro-Choice and Sexual Health Group 2007–; Vice-chair: Medical Research Group 2009–
Dr Richard Taylor	Vice-chair: Cancer Group 2002–; Flood Prevention Group 2002–; Chair Health Group 2003–; Secretary Patient and Public Involvement in Health Group 2005–; Vice-chair: ME (Myalgic Encephalomyelitis) Research Group 2005–; Thrombosis Group 2007–
John Pugh	Vice-chair: Pro-Life Group 2006–
Judy Mallaber	Vice-chair: Sex Equality Group 2006–

Table 6.14 MPs' Membership of All Party Parliamentary Groups Related to the HFEA 2008[40] – *continued*

MP	All Party Parliamentary Groups
Julie Morgan	Chair All-Party: Sex Equality Group 2001–
Dr Nick Palmer	Vice-chair Fibromyalgia Group 2004
Ann Widdecombe	Vice-chair:Pro-Life Group 2002–
Lynne Jones	Chair:Mental Health Group 1997–
Ian Gibson	Chair: Cancer Group 2001–; Secretary Medical Technology Group 2005–; Chair ME (Myalgic Encephalomyelitis) Research Group 2005–; Vice-chair Medical Research Group 2006–; Treasurer Science Group 2006–; Secretary: ME Group 2007–; Umbilical Cord Blood and Adult Stem Cell Group 2008–
John Hayes	Chair Disability Group 2000–; Vice-chair Brain Injury Group 2006–
Mark Simmonds	Secretary Surgical Services Group 2007–
Diane Abbott	Chair: Sickle Cell and Thalassaemia Group
Fiona Mactaggart	Secretary Sickle Cell and Thalassaemia Group 2008–
Jeffrey M. Donaldson	Vice-chair Christians in Parliament Group 2002–; Treasurer: Pro-Life Group 2005–
Jim Dobbin	Treasurer Endometriosis Group 2002–; Chair Pro-Life Group 2003–
Robert Key	Deputy Chair Science Group 2005–; Vice-chair: Population, Development and Reproductive Health Group 2007–

Table 6.15   Lords Membership of All Party Parliamentary Groups, associated with the HFEA 2008

Name	All Party Parliamentary Group
Baroness Tonge	Vice-chair: Pro-Choice and Sexual Health Group 1997–; Treasurer Population, Development and Reproductive Health Group 2005–
Baroness Gould	Chair Pro-Choice and Sexual Health Group 1998–; Secretary Sex Equality Group 2001–
Lord Alton	Vice-chair: Umbilical Cord Blood and Adult Stem Cell Group 2008–
Baroness Masham	Chair Health Group 2001–; Vice-chair: Pro-Life Group 2002–; Patient and Public Involvement in Health Group 2005–; Secretary Patient Safety Group 2005–; Treasurer: Prison Health Group 2005–; Vice-chair: Men's Health Group 2006–; Obesity Group 2006–; Cancer Group 2007–; Treasurer: Primary Care and Public Health Group 2007–; Spinal Cord Injury Group 2008–; Secretary Chronic Pain Group 2008–; Treasurer Continence Care Group 2009–
Earl Howe	Secretary Pharmaceutical Industry Group 2005–; Treasurer: Cardiac Risk in the Young 2006–; Chair Epilepsy Group 2007–; Vice-chair: Prison Health Group 2007–; Cancer Group 2007–
Baroness Finlay	Vice-chair: Medical Technology Group 2005–; Hospice and Palliative Care Group 2006–; Cancer Group 2006–; Vice-chair: Allergy Group 2008–; Parkinson's Disease Group 2008–; Continence Care Group 2009–

Section IV
Feminization and Party Strategy

7
Feminization and Party Cohesion: Conservative Ideological Tendencies and Gender Politics[1]

> *The whole thing has to be looked at in proportion, doesn't it, really? ...equality can be taken too far.*[2]

If David Cameron's strategy of decontamination is widely acknowledged, the importance of feminization to reconstructing the Conservatives as a modern and no longer 'nasty' party is less often noted. Yet, and as previous chapters have shown, efforts to deliver a more representative parliamentary party and to make the party more electorally competitive over women's issues constituted a significant part of Cameron's strategy. In moving the party on this terrain Cameron would be required, at times, to 'lead' his party, just as he had on issues like the environment, education and (whilst tax cuts were resisted) on the economy (Heffernan 2010). With sex differences apparent amongst both party members and party elites on women's issues this would likely be harder to do so in respect of older and male party members and Parliamentarians. Younger party members and women in particular appear generally more comfortable with the party's efforts to 'act for' women, and within the 2005 Parliament, it was Conservative women Parliamentarians rather than men, who, for the most part, acted for women in a more gender equality direction. Here, we seek to shed more light on the impact of feminization on intra-party cohesion, more precisely, to gauge the way in which feminization relates to broader patterns of ideological difference within the Conservative party. Drawing on our survey of party members, three main ideological tendencies are identified. These ideological groupings differ significantly in terms of party member attitudes towards gender politics. *Thatcherites* are hostile to gender-related reforms, and supportive of cuts in tax and spending that bear upon these reforms. *Liberal Conservatives,* the youngest and most male of these tendencies, are distinguished by being the least hostile to feminist values. *Traditionalist Tories,* the largest, most working class and most female of the intra-party tendencies, are surprisingly progressive on a number of specific proposals and issues relating to the descriptive and substantive representation of women. Overall, these findings suggests that, in so far as Cameron has sought to push the party in a generally more progressive direction on gender issues since 2005, he has sometimes been able to work with the grain of grassroots opinion, not least among the Traditionalist Tories. That said there is clear scope in the future for intra-party tension over the Coalition government's agenda of spending cuts, as this will most likely undermine prospects for progressive reform on women's issues.

The significance of intra-party tendencies

The Conservative party has always accorded its parliamentary leadership a wide degree of autonomy in policy matters. Even so, grassroots members play a significant role in establishing a 'mood' to which the party leadership is, or should be, sensitive in shaping its course of action (McKenzie 1955). Every political party is, moreover, a marriage of different actors (for example, MPs, local representatives, party members, party workers, activists), whose aims and interests may differ. Differences in attitudes mediate how different actors conceive of politics and how they respond to particular political issues that confront them. The importance of this was highlighted nearly half a century ago when Richard Rose (1964: 36) asserted that 'the realignment of policy groups within and across party lines has been as significant, if not more significant, than shifts in government caused by general elections'. The significance of intra-party relations is also apparent in the damage to parties that have, from time to time, been done by major internal divisions. With such observations in mind, it makes sense to examine whether pre-existing intra-party cleavages within the Conservative party structure party members' positions on women's issues. Note, that the key intra-party groups we identify can best be regarded as 'tendencies' in Rose's sense of the word (1964: 37): 'a stable set of attitudes, not a stable set of politicians'.[3] It is based upon a more or less coherent ideological position, and may take in a range of policy issues, but it lacks the discipline, consciousness, organization and behavioural cohesion of a true faction.[4]

A fairly extensive literature on the internal groups of the Conservative party exists. Among the more well-known are Philip Norton's (1990) sevenfold typology of the parliamentary party under Margaret Thatcher, and Norton and Aughey's (1981) six-fold account of the party in the country. The former is a time-bound piece designed to provide an informed account of the alignments and fault-lines of Conservative MPs in the last years of Thatcher's premiership. The latter is intended to be of more enduring significance, based on a fundamental distinction between 'Tories' and 'Whigs', and various sub-divisions thereof. Since our intention is to draw a picture of basic party tendencies defined in terms of two main ideological dimensions (left-right and libertarian-authoritarian), the Norton-Aughey typology does not provide a useful cue, for it conflates these and other attitudinal characteristics (for example, 'pessimistic', 'combative') in ways that our dataset cannot engage with. Whiteley et al's (1994) analysis of the party membership in the early 1990s is, in some ways, akin to our purpose, but their method for distinguishing intra-party attitudinal dimensions (factor analysis) generates three scales (labelled traditionalist, progressive and individualist) without identifying the actual groups of party actors that might be associated with such terms. Whilst these and a number of other typologies are undoubtedly instructive in various ways (Seawright 2010; Beech 2009), Valerie Bryson and Tim Heppel's analysis (2010), which identifies three major intra-party tendencies – Traditional conservative, Liberal conservative and Thatcherite – is more useful. For reasons that will become clear, we have adopted this terminology, even though we arrived at this tripartite account of the party by a very different route to them. Our method is primarily inductive, and relies on the statistical technique of cluster analysis.

We assume that the most fundamental underlying dimensions of political belief for the electorate as a whole are the left-right and liberty-authority axes which are now widely employed in comparative studies of electoral and party behaviour, and so we define our intra-party tendencies in terms of these. These dimensions are operationalized in our data set as the additive scales which are described in Chapter 5. Here, we identify the main intra-party tendencies in respect of these basic ideological predispositions through cluster analysis. This statistical technique enables us to identify homogeneous groups (or clusters) of members by measuring their Euclidian distances from each other on the left-right and liberty-authority scales (see Webb 1997, 2000, 2008). The details of our approach to cluster analysis can be consulted in these sources, but it is useful to emphasize two basic points here. First, it is important to understand that cluster analysis does not necessarily produce any single statistically 'correct' solution to our problem. Rather, it provides a range of statistically acceptable solutions, and allows the researcher to select among them in the light of substantive and theoretical knowledge. In this chapter, a number of these statistical and substantive criteria are applied.[5] Secondly, we have been guided by that earlier research to focus on a model of intra-party alignment composed of three main ideological clusters.[6]

This inductive approach to classifying Conservatives is complemented by the more *a priori* approach adopted by Bryson and Heppell (2010) in their recent discussion of conservatism and feminism. They too distinguished three types of actor in the contemporary Conservative Party. *Traditional conservatives* are classic Burkean style conservatives who are sceptical of human reason and social engineering; see various inequalities and hierarchies as natural; and value long-established social institutions and conventions for producing social stability. While clearly located in the authoritarian half of the liberty-authority dimension, they are not as economically liberal as other intra-party groups, and are willing to see intervention as a mechanism for social integration and order.[7] *Thatcherites* are generally further right on economic affairs though just as socially authoritarian as Traditional conservatives, if not more so. As Bryson and Heppell (2010: 35) point out 'the 1979–97 Conservative governments therefore confirmed not only the neoliberal rejection of state intervention and tax subsidies but also the neoconservative suspicion of social engineering'. The final category is that of *Liberal conservatism*. Like the Thatcherites, Liberal Conservatives are economically right-wing, but unlike both Thatcherites and Traditional conservatives, they are socially liberal. While agreeing with the traditionalists that people are naturally unequal in their abilities, the Liberal Conservative 'stress on individual rights and opportunities and the rational calculation and competitive pursuit of self-interest in the free market economy' leads to the 'Darwinian logic of...a full meritocracy' (ibid: 33).

A cluster analysis of our sample of Conservative party members shows, in essence, that the tripartite model works well in meeting statistical and substantive criteria, and generates the results reported in Table 7.1 and Figure 7.1. In the terminology previously employed by Webb in cluster analyses of party actors in Britain, we find a group on the Conventional Right (25.3 percent of the sample), another on the Authoritarian Right (36.7 percent) and – more surprisingly perhaps for the Conservative party – a third one on the Authoritarian Left (38.0 percent).[8] If we wish to understand these in Bryson and Heppell's terms, then the Authoritarian Right clearly lie in Thatcherite territory, while the Conventional Right most

Table 7.1   Three-Cluster Model of Ideological Tendencies within the Conservative Party Membership, 2009

Cluster	Left-Right Scale	Liberty-Authority Scale
Liberal Conservatives (conventional right) 25.3%	3.74 (0.64)	3.05 (0.49)
Thatcherites (authoritarian right) 36.7%	4.04 (0.55)	4.23 (0.40)
Traditionalist Tories (authoritarian left) 38.0%	2.12 (0.6)	4.23 (0.52)
Sample Total 100% (n = 1636)	3.25 (1.06)	3.93 (0.70)
Eta Squared	0.69 (sig. 0.000)	0.54 (sig. 0.000)

Note: Cell entries = scale mean scores, standard deviations in parenthesis. Significance statistics represent the probability of the null hypothesis – that all cluster group means within the population are the same – holding true. Eta squared is a measure of the proportion of variance in the dependent variable (ie, the attitudinal scale) explained by difference between the three clusters.

Figure 7.1   Ideological Clusters of Conservative Party Members in Two-Dimensional Ideological Space

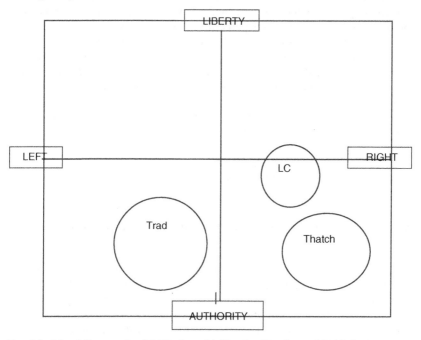

Note: LC = Liberal Conservative (25.3% of sample); Thatch = Thatcherite (36.7%); Trad = Traditionalist Tory (38.0%).

nearly approximates Liberal conservatism, and the Authoritarian Left, in its combination of social conservatism and an undogmatic approach to market economics, bears closest resemblance to Traditional conservatism. Although this latter group espouses a solidly traditionalist position in terms of its basic values, it is also willing to embrace interventionist and often progressive measures on specific issues in order to balance the needs of diverse sections of society, especially women. Note, we find little evidence for the existence of any group in (centre) left-liberal territory; at one time, this might have been considered classic territory for some One Nation actors. However, just as commentators have noted the demise of One Nation Toryism within the parliamentary party (Beech 2009:21), we find few respondents among our sample of party members who approximate to a left-liberal identity.[9]

There are a number of significant demographic differences between these attitudinal clusters. For one thing, the Liberal Conservatives are significantly younger than the others with an average age of 50, compared to 58 for Thatcherites and 57 for Traditionalist Tories; 29 percent of Liberal Conservatives are under 35 years of age, compared to just 13.6 percent and 12.2 percent respectively for the other two groups. There is also a sharp difference between the three groups in terms of sex, with 71 percent of Liberal Conservatives being male, compared to 65 percent of Thatcherites and just 51 percent of Traditionalist Tories. The Traditionalist Tories are considerably more working class than the other groups, with 29.9 percent coming from the manual grade C2-E, compared to just 10.4 percent of Thatcherites and 6.8 percent of Liberal Conservatives. The latter are somewhat more inclined than the others to claim that they are active in the party, with 44 percent seeing themselves as very or fairly active, compared to 35.9 percent of Thatcherites and just 19.5 percent of Traditionalist Tories. The Thatcherites are the most likely of the tendencies to perceive themselves as right-wing; on a scale running from 1–7, where 1 is left-wing and 7 is right-wing, their mean self-perceived location stands at 5.62, compared to 5.13 for the Liberal Conservatives and 5.15 for the Traditionalist Tories.

Conservative party ideological tendencies and attitudes towards gender

Acknowledging different overarching ideological tendencies within the Conservative party begs questions of how these 'fit' with member attitudes towards gender. Turning first to the descriptive representation of women, our analysis, both qualitative and quantitative, reported in previous Chapters (3 and 4) revealed some antipathy towards Cameron's efforts to reform parliamentary candidate selection in order to deliver more women MPs at the 2010 general election – whether evidenced through media reports of particular constituency unhappiness or conflict, or through our party member survey and focus groups, where, and despite most members applauding the principle of a more descriptively representative parliamentary party, there was little appetite for measures that would guarantee an outcome using what they regard as 'politically correct' measures. In this, and as stated before, tensions between local party autonomy and central party intervention were key.[10]

To investigate how the various intra-party tendencies among the members marry with, (or not), measures to enhance the descriptive representation of women, we refer again to the additive scale that we encountered in Chapter 4. This scale, *selectreform*, measures the overall position of respondents on a range of issues relevant to the enhanced descriptive representation of women. The mean scores of the three party tendencies on this scale are reported in Table 7.2.

There are modest but significant differences between the tendencies on the scale, with the Traditionalist Tories being most supportive of measures designed to give women greater prominence in Parliament and election campaigns. The mean position of Traditionalist Tories on the scale is 3.07,

Table 7.2   Positions of Tendencies on Gender-related Attitudinal Scales

Tendency	Selectreform	Feminism	Genderscale
Liberal Conservative	3.37 (0.67)	3.39 (0.68)	2.89 (0.58)
Thatcherite	3.43 (0.68)	3.13 (0.80)	2.84 (0.58)
Traditionalist Tory	3.07 (0.71)	3.31 (0.80)	2.50 (0.59)
Sample Total	3.28 (0.71)	3.26 (0.78)	2.72 (0.60)
Eta-squared (sig.)	0.053 (0.000)	0.019 (0.000)	0.082 (0.000)

Note: Selectreform = scale measuring attitudes towards descriptive representation of women, running from 1 (high support for reform) to 5 (low support for reform); Feminism = scale measuring general attitude towards gender roles and relations, running from 1 (antifeminist-traditionalist) to 5 (feminist-progressive); Genderscale = scale measuring attitudes towards specific reforms that further the substantive representation of women, running from 1 (high support for reform) to 5 (low support for reform).

while it is 3.37 for Liberal conservatives and 3.43 for Thatcherites. As will become clear, it seems that the Traditionalist cluster – recall, that these are the most female of the party's ideological tendencies – is not particularly feminist in the abstract, but when it comes to specific measures designed to enhance the descriptive or substantive representation of women, it is the one most likely to offer its endorsement. The eta-squared statistic confirms that the overall differences between clusters on this scale are significant, albeit not strong.

Addressing women's substantive representation, our analysis draws on two different kinds of questions in the party member survey to gain insight into members' views. First, in order to get a general sense of party members' views about gender roles and relations, the survey asked respondents a group of five Likert scale questions that are combined into the additive scale we call *feminism* that is described in Chapter 5 (see Tables 5.7 and 5.8). Table 7.2 (middle column) shows that Liberal Conservatives hold the most progressive views on this general feminism scale, while Thatcherites are the most traditional. Traditionalist Tories are closer to the Liberal Conservatives in terms of this somewhat abstract view of gender roles and relations, but, and as before, they are inclined to a more progressive take on things when confronted with specific proposals on gender issues. By contrast, Liberal Conservatives are closer to the Thatcherites on the specifics. This is demonstrated by the evidence reported in the final column of Table 7.2, which shows that the Traditionalist Tories are generally the most supportive intra-party group with respect to particular proposals for substantive reform for gender equality. This is based on the summary scale *genderscale* which is constructed from respondent' answers to 12 questions about issues germane to the substantive interests of women on the current agenda of British politics (see Table 5.9 for a reminder of the specific issues). The differences between the party's main ideological clusters on this summary scale are once again significant. Interestingly, the pattern that emerged in respect of the descriptive representation of women repeats itself. While there is little, overall, to distinguish Liberal Conservatives from Thatcherites, the Traditionalist Tories are once again notably more inclined to see things from the more gender equality perspective. This is generally evident from the higher average percentage of this cluster in favour of the gendered propositions put before them, and is particularly apparent in their support for some of the detailed proposals, such as pay audits to check that companies are not discriminating against women, and for state financial support for childcare. Even so, they cannot simply be regarded as instinctively or unproblematically 'progressives' (or feminist for that matter). Table 7.3 reveals the morally traditionalist aspect of their make-up. Here we see that they are significantly more inclined than the other party tendencies to take the view that abortion should be illegal.

Table 7.3 Attitudes towards Abortion, by Tendency

	Liberal conservative	Thatcherite	Traditionalist Tory	Total
Time limit should be increased to more than 24 weeks	6.7%	7.1%	5.1%	6.3%
Should remain at 24 weeks	40.4%	38.3%	32.6%	36.7%
Should be reduced to 22 weeks	9.9%	7.3%	8.1%	8.3%
Should be reduced to 20 weeks	17.4%	16.1%	14.70%	15.9%
Should be reduced to less than 20 weeks	17.1%	17.20%	19.2%	17.9%
No legal abortions should be allowed except in cases of medical emergency	8.6%	13.9%	20.3%	14.9%
Total	100.0% n = 374	100.0% n = 546	100.0% n = 546	100.0% n = 1466

Cramer's V = 0.103 (sig. = 0.001). Question wording: 'Do you personally believe that the period during which a legal abortion can be performed should remain at 24 weeks or should it be changed?'

Our survey also asked respondents a number of questions relevant to the institutional reform of British politics, two of which are pertinent to gender. These relate to proportional representation for Westminster elections and the adoption of more 'family-friendly' working hours in the Commons. While the latter is of obvious relevance and is something that some women MPs have long argued for (and winning some, but by no means all reforms) (Lovenduski 2005a; Childs 2008), the former bears on women's descriptive representation, given the widely recognized, albeit not certain, relationship between proportional electoral systems and higher numbers of women representatives (Norris 1997a). While there can be no denying that Conservative members are broadly against both of these reforms, Table 7.4 shows that there is a pronounced difference between the Traditionalist Tories and the other tendencies. Once again, the Traditionalists are much more willing to embrace reform than their counterparts.

Finally, we think it relevant and important to consider how these intra-party tendencies within the Conservative party vary with respect to taxation and public expenditure, something which has once again become the overriding issue on the current agenda of British politics. In the context of the fiscal crisis which has emerged since 2008, the question of how far the UK should rein in expenditure on public services, and how far tax might need to be raised to protect public provision, dominates the political agenda. The gendered aspect of these issues has been neatly and publicly voiced by the Fawcett Society (the leading UK women's equality pressure group),[11] the Women's Budget Group (who promote gender equality through economic policy),[12] and the ex-Labour Minister, and Shadow Foreign secretary, Yvette Cooper.[13] In sum, critics argue that women face a 'the triple jeopardy': slashed benefits, jobs cuts, and a reduction in the core public services that women rely on for themselves and those they care for. Indeed, Fawcett point out that women make up 65 per cent of the public sector work force, and thus are likely to bear the brunt of the 500 000 job losses that are predicted to result of the coalition government's October 2010 Comprehensive Spending Review. Three quarters of all local government employees are women, so the reductions targeting this part of the public sector is also likely to have a particularly heavy impact on women. At the same time, cuts to spending would hit many services and benefits that women and families rely on, including Child Benefit, Child Tax Credit, Working Tax Credits, and Housing Benefit. The skewed gender impact of welfare cuts is illustrated by the last of these, for one million more women than men claim Housing Benefit, many of them single parents. The Fawcett Society further argues that women tend to access services such as the NHS more frequently and more intensively than men, because of pregnancy, longer life expectancy and lower earnings. Moreover, women still do the bulk of caring for children and elderly parents, and so would be

Table 7.4 Attitudes toward Political Reform, by Ideological Tendency

		Liberal conservative	Thatcherite	Traditionalist Tory	Cramer's v (sig.)
Proportional representation as first preference for Westminster elections	% agreeing	8.3	7.2	22.6	0.214 (0.000) n = 1558
	% disagreeing	91.7	92.8	77.4	
Proportional representation as second preference for Westminster elections	% agreeing	17.7	22.9	30.9	0.124 (0.000) n = 1260
	% disagreeing	82.3	77.1	69.1	
More family-friendly working hours for Parliament	% agreeing	20	21	36.4	0.153 (0.000) n = 1596
	% disagreeing	49.6	52.9	31.2	
Average % agreeing		15.3	17	30	

Note: '% agreeing' = total of % 'strongly agree' + % 'tend to approve'; 'disagree' = total of % 'strongly disagree' + % 'tend to disagree'.

most affected by reductions in childcare and social care that help them meet these responsibilities. All in all, many gender activists will agree with the Fawcett Society's view that spending cuts of the scale and nature set out by the coalition government would represent a huge setback for gender equality in the UK.

Table 7.5 reveals a pattern of attitudes amongst Conservative party members that is not surprising in view of the patterns identified with regard to previous questions of women's substantive representation. Once again, the Traditionalist Tories stand out from the other two clusters as being more hostile to cuts in tax and spending – more left-wing, if you will. Put at its simplest, among our Traditionalists there is a majority (51.8 percent) that either 'tends to' or 'strongly' disagrees with cuts, while only a third (34.3 percent) agrees with them. By contrast, a majority of the both other clusters (52 percent of Liberal Conservatives and 51.7 percent of Thatcherites) 'tend to' or 'strongly' agree with the need for cuts. These observations suggest the possibility of a revival of the 1980s tensions between 'wets' and 'dries', with the Traditionalists being the most likely source of the former sentiment, while the other two clusters seem destined to be economically drier. This reflects, in turn, the sex and class profiles of these different components of the party's grassroots.

Having examined the bivariate relationships between ideological tendency and the Conservative membership's attitudes towards gender politics, we turn to multivariate models of these attitudes. As in Chapter 5, we deploy each of the three gender attitudinal scales that we have devised as dependent variables: 'feminism' (measuring underlying orientation towards gender roles and relations), 'genderscale' (tapping the substantive

Table 7.5 Attitude to Tax and Spending, by Ideological Tendency

	Liberal conservative	Thatcherite	Traditionalist Tory	Total
Agree strongly	15.4%	17.3%	10.3%	14.2%
Tend to agree	36.6%	34.4%	24.0%	31.0%
Neither agree nor disagree	12.2%	10.0%	13.9%	12.0%
Tend to disagree	29.5%	27.0%	34.7%	30.5%
Strongly disagree	6.3%	11.3%	17.1%	12.3%
	100.0% (n = 410)	100.0% (n = 601)	100.0% (n = 613)	100.0% (n = 1624)

Cramer's V = 0.137 (sig. = 0.000). Question wording: Some people feel that government should cut taxes a lot and spend much less on things like health and social services. To what extent do you agree or disagree?

representation of women through issues on the current agenda of politics) and 'selectreform' (gauging support for the descriptive representation of women). In addition, we have run a fourth model in which attitude to taxation and public expenditure is the dependent variable. As in Chapter 5, these models incorporate standard demographic factors among the independent variables: sex, social class, educational experience, age and, given the possible biases of older women (and indeed, the established literature about the impact of the 'gender-generation gap' in British politics), a possible interaction between sex and age. In addition this time, we add dummy variables for cluster membership. Specifically, dummy terms are included for membership of the Liberal Conservative and Thatcherite clusters, while membership of the Traditional Tory tendency is the reference category. Our main objective is not so much to build models that are good at predicting location on the attitudinal scales in question, as to check if a respondent's ideological tendency has a significant influence on his or her location on these scales when all other independent variables are controlled for.

The short answer is yes. In each and every case, at least one of the dummy variables for the intra-party clusters proves significant. Indeed, in most cases the cluster variables are among the most powerful of the independent variables in most of these models. Moreover, all the significant independent variables in these models are correctly signed in terms of the direction of their relationship with the dependent variables. Thus, running from Table 7.6 to Table 7.9 in turn, the models show that: older party members are significantly more likely to hold anti-feminist views than younger members, while women are more likely to hold pro-feminist views than men, as are Liberal Conservatives compared with members of the other tendencies (Table 7.6). Female respondents are more likely to support reforms designed to enhance the substantive representation of women, while older people are more likely to oppose them, as are Thatcherite and Liberal Conservatives compared to Traditionalist Tories (Table 7.7). The same pattern holds for measures that might enhance the descriptive representation of women, and in addition, working class respondents are more likely to support reforms of this nature compared to those from higher social grades (Table 7.8). Finally, women, older and lower social grade party members are all more likely to disagree with the need to cut taxation and public expenditure, while more educated people, Liberal Conservatives and Thatcherites are all significantly more likely to support such measures (Table 7.9).

Conclusion

Three distinct ideological tendencies can be identified among today's Conservative party members. These tendencies differ significantly across a range of contemporary political issues. The Liberal conservatives are the

Table 7.6 OLS Regression Model of General Feminism Scale ('feminism')

Model	Unstandardized Coefficients		Standardized Coefficients	t	Sig.	Collinearity Statistics	
	B	Std. Error	Beta			Tolerance	VIF
(Constant)	3.022	0.126		24.058	0.000		
Gender	0.377	0.051	0.238	7.463	0.000	0.984	1.016
Age of respondent in years	−0.006	0.002	−0.118	−3.676	0.000	0.976	1.025
LibConDummy	0.137	0.058	0.076	2.360	0.018	0.969	1.032

Dependent Variable: FEMINISM, Backward stepwise elimination of non-significant factors in 6 steps. Adjusted R-squared = 0.076; Durbin-Watson statistic = 2.039; n = 923.

Table 7.7 OLS Regression Model of Substantive Representation Scale ('genderscale')

Model	Unstandardized Coefficients		Standardized Coefficients	t	Sig.	Collinearity Statistics	
	B	Std. Error	Beta			Tolerance	VIF
(Constant)	2.475	0.097		25.643	0.000		
Gender	-0.233	0.038	-0.185	-6.057	0.000	0.971	1.030
Age of respondent in years	0.006	0.001	0.162	5.319	0.000	0.974	1.027
LibConDummy	0.423	0.048	0.303	8.811	0.000	0.764	1.309
ThatcheriteDummy	0.329	0.043	0.264	7.741	0.000	0.780	1.282

Dependent Variable: Genderscale. Backward stepwise elimination of non-significant factors in 4 steps. Adjusted R-squared = 0.162; Durbin-Watson statistic = 2.005; n = 927.

Table 7.8 OLS Regression Model of Descriptive Representation Scale ('selectreform')

Model	Unstandardized Coefficients		Standardized Coefficients	t	Sig.	Collinearity Statistics	
	B	Std. Error	Beta			Tolerance	VIF
(Constant)	3.202	0.062		52.006	0.000		
Social Grade	-0.043	0.017	-0.087	-2.493	0.013	0.938	1.066
LibConDummy	0.262	0.064	0.161	4.108	0.000	0.749	1.336
ThatcheriteDummy	0.322	0.056	0.223	5.719	0.000	0.752	1.331

Dependent Variable: SELECTREFORM. Backward stepwise elimination of non-significant factors in 5 steps. Adjusted R-squared = 0.054; Durbin-Watson statistic = 1.973; n = 828.

Table 7.9 OLS Regression Model of Attitude towards Taxation and Public Spending ('taxspend')

Model	Unstandardized Coefficients		Standardized Coefficients	t	Sig.	Collinearity Statistics	
	B	Std. Error	Beta			Tolerance	VIF
Constant	1.581	0.283		5.594	0.000		
Gender	0.510	0.083	0.192	6.182	0.000	0.960	1.042
Age of respondent in years	0.016	0.003	0.192	5.775	0.000	0.838	1.193
Social Grade	0.054	0.029	0.062	1.850	0.065	0.830	1.204
At what age did you finish full-time education?	-0.062	0.030	-0.071	-2.054	0.040	0.763	1.310
LibConDummy	-0.230	0.108	-0.077	-2.136	0.033	0.703	1.423
ThatcheriteDummy	-0.296	0.093	-0.112	-3.181	0.002	0.742	1.348

Dependent Variable: TAXSPEND (scale running from 1–5 with 1 representing strongest agreement, and 5 the strongest disagreement with the view that '...government should cut taxes a lot and spend much less on things like health and social services'). Backward stepwise elimination of non-significant factors in 2 steps. Adjusted R-squared = 0.109; Durbin-Watson statistic = 2.015; n = 966.

youngest, most likely to be male, and claim to be the most active of these tendencies, and are distinguished by being the least hostile to general feminist values. However, the Traditionalist Tories – the largest, most working class and most female of the intra-party tendencies – are more progressive on a number of specific proposals and issues, including taxation and public spending, the descriptive and substantive representation of women, and gender-relevant institutional reforms of politics. This suggests that, in so far as David Cameron has sought to push the party in a generally more 'centrist' and progressive liberally feminist direction since 2005, he has by no means always been going against the grain of grassroots opinion. Traditionalist Tories, in particular, would appear to endorse the thrust of these more centrist elements of his strategy, as well his efforts to transform the descriptive representativeness of his parliamentary party. That said, as the Conservatives find themselves in government, there is clear scope for intra-party tension over cuts in public expenditure, as the primacy of economic policy comes to the fore. Accordingly, government policy is likely to generate intra-party tensions about the differential impact of spending cuts and the restructuring of the state on men and women and on different social classes. A very significant proportion of the party's support base is female, and/or working class and holds to a more One Nation traditionalist view of what it means to be a citizen in modern Britain.

8
The Feminization Strategy and the Electorate

'I've never voted Tory before' .... Julie is voting Conservative at the next election because of our plans to help families.[1]

If the Conservative party was out of favour with much of the British electorate during the New Labour years, its failure to appeal to women was also much remarked upon. The Conservative party, long renowned for attracting the votes of women, found itself apparently struggling to attract them. In particular, and in common with other advanced democracies, the party experienced the effects of a new gender-generation gap, whereby younger women gradually shifted to the left of their male counterparts (Inglehart and Norris 2000; Norris 1999b). A strategy of feminization – of presenting the Conservative party as more descriptively representative in Parliament, as well as offering up more attractive policies for women – might be one means of garnering support from these lost women voters who had over the last decade or more turned their backs on the party. Such a strategy was, in our view, an integral part of David Cameron's wider decontamination process that sought to replace the 'nasty' party image with one of 'compassionate conservatism'.

There are two ways in which feminization might have helped the Conservatives at the general election of May 2010. First, it could have done so *directly* by successfully addressing the substantive concerns of women voters and thereby attracting them to the party in greater numbers at the 2010 election than in previous recent elections. Second, it might have done so *indirectly* by enhancing the general image of the party such that its appeal to the electoral centre-ground was strengthened. In order to assess the effectiveness of feminization we analyse British Election Survey data (BES 2010) to look at the impact of sex (the gender- and gender-generation gap) on vote choice in 2010. To capture 'direct' feminization effect, we examine, in particular, the relative swing to the Conservatives of women and men during the election. If the swing was greater among women – or at least, among some generations of women – than among men, this can be regarded as a prima facie indication that feminization might had borne fruit for the Conservatives. To further substantiate this, we examine the attitudes of women and men on particular issue dimensions, drawing both on survey data and on our focus group discussions with voters who lacked strong partisan affinities prior to the election. The possibility of an indirect impact on voters is examined through considering the contribution that feminization might have made to the party's general image. This draws on survey data on party images in 2010 and once again on our focus group data.

Sex and electoral choice, 2005–2010

2005 was the first UK general election in which the Labour party had a greater lead over the Conservatives among women than it did among men (Campbell 2006: Table 7.2). Younger women, in particular, embraced concerns for health, education and public services – issues that were successfully 'owned' by Labour. Five years on, British Election Study data reveal that the more traditional pattern between sex and vote choice had reasserted itself by 2010: the gender gap once again showed itself to the advantage of the Conservatives in the form of a larger Tory lead over Labour among women than among men (Tables 8.1 and 8.2). Note that this does not seem to reflect a heavier swing to the Conservatives from Labour so much as a gain on the part of both major parties in 2010 at the expense of minor parties. In the BES samples, the percentage of the vote that went to parties other than Labour, the Conservatives or the Liberal Democrats was 9.7 percent in 2005 and 8.8 percent in 2010. The interesting point from our perspective is that women were far more likely to desert the minor parties for either Labour or the Conservatives than men were. As Table 8.3 shows. 51.7 percent of men who chose a minor party in 2005 stuck with them five years later, whereas only 38.4 percent of women did. A quarter of women who voted for a minor party in 2005 defected to the Tories in 2010, whereas only a fifth of men did. There were swings to Labour from the minor parties as well in 2010, and again women were more likely to shift than men (15.7 percent compared to 11.3 percent), but the greatest rate of defection was from women to the Conservatives. Similarly, women were also more likely than men to defect from the Liberal Democrats to the Tories. While 9.9 percent of males who voted for the Liberal Democrats in 2005 opted for the Conservatives in 2010, 13.9 percent of their female counterparts did. This is consistent with the possibility that Cameron's Conservative party held a special appeal for certain groups of women in the electorate, though more, it would seem, for third-party supporters than for Labour voters.

We can further break down the data in terms of the interaction between sex and age. Specifically, the gender-generation gap phenomenon is relevant

Table 8.1   Gender by Party, 2010

	Labour	Conservative	Liberal Democrat	
Male	1642	1873	1643	5158
	31.8%	36.3%	31.9%	100.0%
Female	1735	2187	1781	5703
	30.4%	38.3%	31.2%	100.0%
Total	3377	4060	3424	10861
	31.1%	37.4%	31.5%	100.0%

Notes: Significance = 0.079, Cramer's V = 0.22.
Source: British Election Study 2010, post-election weighted sample.

Table 8.2   The Conservative-Labour Gender Gap

Year	Gender Gap
1992	–5.8
1997	–4.5
2001	–1.1
2005	6
2010	–3.4

Note: Gender gap = (Conservative percentage of the vote-Labour percentage of the vote among men) – (Conservative percentage of the vote-Labour percentage of the vote among women). A positive figure means that the difference between Labour and the Conservatives is greater among men than among women; a negative figure implies that the gap is greater among women.
Sources: 1992–2005, Campbell 2006, Table 7.2; 2010, BES 2010.

here. It was identified by Campbell as an advantage that Labour enjoyed over the Conservatives among younger generations of women in 2005 – broadly speaking, those under the age of 54, and more particularly those under 34 (Campbell 2006: Table 7.1). What of 2010: had the generation gap disappeared even among these groups? Table 8.4 reveals that the pro-Labour gap between women and men shrank dramatically among the two youngest age categories in 2010. In the case of the younger of these groups, the 18–24 year olds, this was not because there was a strong swing to the Tories from Labour. Rather, both men and women swung from Labour to the Liberal Democrats, but women especially so. Thus, by 2010 the two-party gender gap was no longer very great, although the chi-square test still reports a statistically significant difference between men and women, thanks to the greater propensity of women to support the Liberal Democrats. However, among 25–34 year olds we find a pattern much more consistent with the possibility that Cameron's Conservatives might have had a particular

Table 8.3 Vote in 2005, by Vote in 2010

Gender			Vote 2010				Total
		Labour	Cons	LibDem	Other		
Male Vote 2005	Labour	1299 62.3%	224 10.7%	445 21.4%	116 5.6%		2084 100.0%
	Conservative	15 1.0%	1236 83.5%	128 8.6%	101 6.8%		1480 100.0%
	Liberal Democrat	60 6.8%	88 9.9%	664 75.0%	73 8.2%		885 100.0%
	Other	54 11.3%	95 19.8%	83 17.3%	248 51.7%		480 100.0%
	Total	1428 29.0%	1643 33.3%	1320 26.8%	538 10.9%		4929 100.0%
Female Vote 2005	Labour	1325 63.2%	235 11.2%	440 21.0%	97 4.6%		2097 100.0%
	Conservative	35 2.2%	1396 86.1%	126 7.8%	65 4.0%		1622 100.0%
	Liberal Democrat	65 6.8%	134 13.9%	702 73.0%	61 6.3%		962 100.0%
	Other	71 15.7%	117 25.9%	90 20.0%	173 38.4%		451 100.0%
	Total	1496 29.2%	1882 36.7%	1358 26.5%	396 7.7%		5132 100.0%

Gender	Cramer's V	Significance	Valid n
Male	0.571	0.000	4929
Female	0.551	0.000	5132

Table 8.4 Voting by Sex and Age: The Shifting Gender-Generation Gap, 2005–2010

Age	Sex	VOTE 2005					VOTE 2010				
		Labour	Conservative	Liberal Democrat	Total	GG/Sig	Labour	Conservative	Liberal Democrat	Total	GG/Sig
18–24	Male	37.5%	34.4%	28.1%	100.0%	−18.0*	30.4%	29.5%	40.1%	100.0%	0.1*
	Female	43.7%	22.6%	33.7%	100.0%		25.9%	24.9%	49.2%	100.0%	
25–34	Male	37.5%	36.0%	26.5%	100.0%	−19.2***	29.7%	31.1%	39.3%	100.0%	−7.9
	Female	41.3%	20.6%	38.1%	100.0%		25.4%	34.7%	39.9%	100.0%	
35–44	Male	41.4%	34.0%	24.5%	100.0%	−10.2	34.1%	34.3%	31.5%	100.0%	−5.5
	Female	44.4%	26.8%	28.9%	100.0%		37.3%	31.6%	31.2%	100.0%	
45–54	Male	40.5%	32.3%	27.3%	100.0%	5.7	41.10%	30.4%	28.6%	100.0%	−12.1**
	Female	37.4%	34.9%	27.7%	100.0%		34.3%	35.7%	30.0%	100.0%	
55–59	Male	38.2%	35.9%	25.8%	100.0%	−5.1	32.8%	37.3%	29.9%	100.0%	−9
	Female	41.0%	33.6%	25.4%	100.0%		29.6%	43.5%	26.9%	100.0%	
60–64	Male	35.3%	41.7%	23.1%	100.0%	9.1	25.5%	43.4%	31.1%	100.0%	0.6
	Female	42.5%	39.8%	17.7%	100.0%		28.7%	45.4%	25.9%	100.0%	
65>	Male	35.6%	41.3%	23.1%	100.0%	−4.7	25.5%	49.8%	24.7%	100.0%	3.2
	Female	33.0%	43.4%	22.2%	100.0%		28.5%	49.6%	21.9%	100.0%	

Notes: 2005, n = 4493; 2010, n = 1645. ***Male/Female differences significant at 0.001 level; **Male/Female differences significant at 0.01 level; *Male/Female differences significant at 0.05 level.

'GG' = Gender Gap (ie, Conservative percentage of the vote-Labour percentage of the vote among men) – (Conservative percentage of the vote-Labour percentage of the vote among women).

Sources: Campbell 2006, Table 7.4; BES post-election weighted sample 2010.

appeal for women. Here we find that Labour lost support among both sexes, but while men swung mainly to the Liberal Democrats (like the youngest women in our sample), their female counterparts opted heavily for the Tories. A similar pattern holds for the next oldest age category, the 35–44 year olds, and indeed, middle-aged women and older women (that is from 55 and upwards), though in some cases (for instance, the 65 year olds and over) they were not especially distinct from men in this pattern of behaviour. Overall, this means that the gender gap figures eroded and were no longer statistically significant for some age groups, but it does not mean that an important change had not occurred. To the contrary, it seems that women who were largely past their student days, members of the working population and often raising families, saw something in Cameron's Conservative party that they were prepared to vote for.

We can assess the overall importance of gender and age for voter choice in 2010 more systematically by running a multivariate model of Conservative vote at the election. The logistic regression analysis is reported in Table 8.5. A number of standard demographic factors along with sex and age are included (occupational class, educational background, ethnicity and whether people work in the public or private sector), plus an interaction term for sex and age, which is designed to capture the gender-generation effect.[2] Our purpose here is to demonstrate that sex, age and the gender-generation interaction are significant when the other main demographic factors are controlled for, rather than to construct a strong overall explanation of voter choice in 2010. The overall statistics confirm that the model as a whole explains significantly more than a baseline (that is, a constant-only) model would.[3] In addition, the individual regression coefficients accord with normal expectations in so far as they are signed appropriately.[4] Most importantly from our point of view, the model confirms that men are significantly less likely to vote Conservative than women are, even when all other terms in the model are controlled for, and that the gender-generation interaction has some significance.

Sex and issue attitudes: Did Cameron's conservatism appeal to women?

It is apparent that sex was a significant factor in the 2010 general election, and that some age categories of women – in fact, all except the very youngest group and the 45–54 year olds – were particularly moved to shift their allegiance to the Conservatives. This is consistent with the possibility that the party's adoption of policies and strategies regarding the descriptive and substantive representation of women, or compassionate conservatism more generally, might have effected this shift of support. However, the evidence presented so far cannot be regarded as definitive, so we now turn to a closer examination of the attitudes of women voters on certain relevant issue dimensions.

Table 8.5 Logistic Regression Model of Conservative Vote, May 2010

Variable	b	Significance	Exp (b)
OCCUPATIONAL CLASS (comparison = working class)			
Salariat (senior white collar and professional)	0.639	0.000	1.895
Routine non-manual	0.346	0.000	1.414
Petit bourgeois (small self-employed business people)	0.617	0.000	1.853
Manual Foremen and supervisors	0.236	0.056	1.266
SECTOR (comparison = voluntary sector)		0.000	
Private sector	0.640	0.000	1.888
Public sector	0.080	0.474	1.082
EDUCATIONAL QUALIFICATIONS (comparison = non-graduate)		0.000	
Graduate	0.250	0.000	1.282
ETHNICITY (comparison = 'other')		0.001	
White	−0.176	0.508	0.838
Mixed	−0.297	0.391	0.743
Asian or Asian-British	−0.636	0.048	0.529
Black or Black-British	−1.289	0.002	0.276
GENDER (comparison = female)		0.050	
Male	−0.200	0.050	0.815
AGE CATEGORY (comparison = 65+)		0.000	
18–24	−0.880	0.000	0.415
25–34	−0.536	0.000	0.585
35–44	−0.728	0.000	0.483
45–54	−0.551	0.000	0.576
55–59	−0.340	0.002	0.712
60–64	−0.155	0.134	0.856

Table 8.5 Logistic Regression Model of Conservative Vote, May 2010 – *continued*

Variable	b	Significance	Exp (b)
AGE CATEGORY * GENDER (comparison = 65+ female)			
18–24 * male	0.357	0.014	1.429
25–34 * male	-0.012	0.083	0.988
35–44 * male	0.219	0.932	1.244
45–54 * male	-0.216	0.131	0.805
55–59 * male	-0.167	0.135	0.846
60–64 * male	-0.137	0.316	0.872
		0.367	
CONSTANT	-0.950	0.002	0.387
MODEL STATISTICS			
2 log likelihood	12825.100		
Omnibus test of model significance	0.000		
Hosmer & Lemeshow significance	0.280		
% correctly classified	66.700		
Cox & Snell R^2	0.040		
Nagelkerke R^2	0.060		
N	10640		

Women born after the Second World War have been found to be significantly to the left of men and more feminist (Campbell 2006: ch. 3). They are also more likely to prioritize health and education as salient political issues, whereas men tend to emphasize the economy. All of these features of women's attitudinal preferences – leftism, feminism, and the salience of health and education – help explain why, as a sex, they have become more disposed to support Labour over the years. In simple terms, such findings suggest that a party in the Conservatives' position at the time of Cameron's accession to the leadership – one with a reputation for being economically right-wing, socially conservative, and grudging in its support for public services and the welfare state – would have to address each of these problems if it wished to enhance its appeal to female voters. Cameron's 'de-contamination strategy' aimed at doing precisely this, among other things. The strategy initially entailed a new emphasis on descriptive representation within the parliamentary party, as outlined in Chapter 3, and a turn towards a policies addressing social justice, epitomized by the work of Iain Duncan Smith,[5] combined with a downgrading of the rhetoric of economic liberalism. The banking crisis of 2008 complicated things somewhat. The prospect of a new age of austerity might well have undermined the decontamination strategy by unnerving electors, many of whom remembered the experience of Thatcherism with little affection and feared that the party's right-wing might exploit the crisis in order to re-engineer the state as Margaret Thatcher had once sought to do (Bale 2010; Bale and Webb 2011).

To establish whether there is evidence that women were especially drawn to the policies and leadership offered by Cameron's Conservatives we consider first the issues that women regarded as salient for electoral choice in 2010. Table 8.6 reports the responses given to BES questions about the relative importance of major political issues at the start of the 2010 election campaign. Respondents were given a list of eight issues and asked to rank the three most important of them. In the table we record the relative frequency of top-ranked issues and of top-three ranked issues for men and women. In view of Campbell's previous findings on issue salience in 2005 it is a little frustrating that education did not appear in the list of options that was set before respondents. Nevertheless, it is immediately apparent from the table that – unsurprisingly given the economic context – both men and women were overwhelmingly inclined to see economic affairs as the most salient concern. Immigration also features prominently for both, although women rank health as somewhat more important than men. Overall, the table does not suggest any great difference between the sexes, but implies a need to examine the feelings of women in particular about the economy, immigration and health. Given Campbell's research, views of education should also be examined. As a prelude to this analysis, however, we start with an overview of synoptic indicators of position on the two major spectra of ideological belief that political scientists generally regard

Table 8.6 Most Important Election Issues for Men and Women, 2010

	Most Important Issue Only		Total of Most Important Three Issues	
Men	**Women**	**Men**	**Women**	
Economy (47.0%)	Economy (41.9%)	Economy (26.2%)	Economy (24.2%)	
Immigration (16.8%)	Immigration (16.9%)	Paying off state debt (15.4%)	Immigration (16.0%)	
Paying off state debt (14.4%)	Health (10.4%)	Immigration (15.3%)	Unemployment (15.5%)	
Unemployment (6.7%)	Unemployment (9.8%)	Unemployment (13.8%)	Health (15.3%)	
Health (5.9%)	Paying off state debt (8.9%)	Health (12.3%)	Paying off state debt (9.1%)	
Environment (3.8%)	War in Afghanistan (4.2%)	Terrorism (6.0%)	War in Afghanistan (7.7%)	
Terrorism (3.3%)	Terrorism (4.6%)	War in Afghanistan (5.7%)	Terrorism (7.0%)	
War in Afghanistan (2.1%)	Environment (3.3%)	Environment (5.2%)	Environment (5.1%)	

Note: Table is constructed from responses to the question: Please rank what you think are the most important, the second most important and the third most important issues by dragging them to the list on the right. (If you wish to skip this question please simply click on the arrow): The Economy Generally; The Environment; Health care; Unemployment; Immigration; The War in Afghanistan; Terrorism; Paying Off The Government Debt.
Source: BES 2010.

as relevant to party competition: the left-right and the liberty-authority dimensions.

With respect to the first of these, we can examine voters' attitudes towards taxation and public expenditure – to gauge underlying ideological predisposition on the general left-right dimension, and attitude towards the central issue of short-term relevance to the 2010 election. Table 8.7 reports the position of respondents on a 10-point scale (with 0 representing a preference for cutting taxation and public expenditure and 10 a preference for raising taxation and expenditure), and their perceptions of where the main three political parties lay on this scale in 2010. Four observations stand out. First, women as a whole are, once again, significantly to the left of men on tax and spending. Secondly, men and women both see Labour as the furthest left, the Conservatives as the furthest right, and the Liberal Democrats as the centre-party (but closer to Labour) on this issue. Thirdly, women locate themselves slightly closer to Labour on taxation and spending, whereas men place themselves closer to the Tories. Finally, while women generally see the Conservatives as well to the right of Labour on this scale, they do not see them as far to the right as men do. This might suggest that the de-contamination strategy counted for something in respect of women voters, although in general they remain closer to Labour.

With respect to the second major ideological dimension of party competition, that of social authoritarianism versus social liberalism, the BES only has one indicator on which we can draw: how far would respondents prioritize the need to fight crime or prefer to defend the rights of the accused? And where do they perceive the parties to be on this question? Table 8.8 reports the results. Again there are several features worthy of note. First, both men and women locate themselves near to the authoritarian end of the scale (ie. prioritizing the attack on crime over the defence of individual rights), women especially so. Secondly, they both regard the Conservatives as much more authoritarian than either of the other parties, and there is no significant difference between women and men here. Both feel themselves closer to the Conservatives than to either Labour or the Liberal Democrats on this issue, albeit with men even closer than women. This, then, is an area on which the Conservatives would seem to have obvious appeal for women – but no more so than for men. In any case there is unlikely to have been any change in 2010 in this respect as the Tories have long been the party of law and order, and to that extent, Cameron's Conservatives are unlikely to have represented a new attraction for women.

What of voters' more specific attitudes on the four most salient issues that we previously identified – economic management, immigration, health and education? Tables 8.9a–j report evaluations of how the Labour government handled each of these issues and how respondents felt that a Conservative government *would* handle them.[6] With respect to economic management and the financial crisis (clearly the most important matters

Table 8.7 Attitude towards Taxation and Expenditure, 2010

Attitude	Sex	Mean position (sd)	Significance	N	Mean distance from respondent on scale
Cut taxes & spending – Respondent	Male	4.91 (2.23)	0.000	6082	0.00
	Female	5.34 (1.99)		6120	0.00
Cut taxes & spending – Labour	Male	5.85 (2.30)	0.019	6000	0.94
	Female	5.75 (2.10)		5861	0.41
Cut taxes & spending – Conservative	Male	4.08 (2.34)	0.000	5941	−0.83
	Female	4.67 (2.27)		5808	−0.67
Cut taxes & spending – Liberal Democrat	Male	5.42 (2.15)	0.013	5701	0.51
	Female	5.52 (1.88)		5271	0.18

Note: Dependent variable = scale running from 0 (preference for cutting taxation and spending on health and social services) to 10 (preference for raising taxation and expenditure on health and services). Significance = 2-tailed T test for difference between male and female mean scores.
Source: BES 2010.

Table 8.8 Attitude towards Crime and the Rights of Defendants, 2010

Attitude	Sex	Mean position (sd)	Significance	N	Mean distance from respondent on scale
Attack crime vs. rights of accused? Respondent	Male	2.78 (2.61)	0.000	6409	0.00
	Female	2.56 (2.39)		6047	0.00
Attack crime vs. rights of accused? Labour	Male	4.96 (2.92)	0.001	6409	2.18
	Female	4.80 (2.80)		6047	2.24
Attack crime vs. rights of accused? Conservative	Male	3.16 (2.42)	0.391	6409	0.38
	Female	3.20 (2.31)		6047	0.64
Attack crime vs. rights of accused? Liberal Democrat	Male	4.92 (2.67)	0.000	6409	2.14
	Female	4.46 (2.35)		6047	1.90

Note: Dependent variable = scale running from 0 (prioritizing the reduction of crime) to 10 (prioritizing the rights of the accused). Significance = 2-tailed T-test for difference between male and female mean scores.
Source: BES 2010.

on voters' minds in 2010) Tables 8.9a–d show a consistent pattern; there are no great differences between men and women, with both rather skeptical on balance that *either* party could handle these issues well. Women are marginally less skeptical of the Conservatives' prospects for economic management than Labour's, but the differences are not great. The lack of differentiation between the sexes is even more obvious with respect to immigration, where neither men nor women as groups seem able to decide whether either of the major parties handles the issue well or badly (Tables 8.9e–f).

Tables 8.9g–h are more interesting from our point of view because they do show a clear difference between men and women. While men continue to rate Labour higher than the Conservative party on health (with 40 percent thinking it handles the NHS well or very well, compared to only 27 percent thinking the Conservatives do), women see little or no difference between the two parties. In fact, they are slightly more likely to rate the Conservatives highly, although admittedly they are not overly impressed by either party. Still, given the traditional strength of Labour with the electorate on this issue, this seems to represent a degree of progress for Cameron. Could it be that this is an area in which his form of conservatism resonated with voters and with women in particular? If so, this should perhaps not surprise us in view of the party's pledge to protect NHS budgets if it were returned to power at the election, regardless of other spending cuts that might be made. A similar pattern holds with respect to education (Table 8.9i–j). For men, there is little difference between the two parties on their handling of this issue. On the whole, they are more negative than positive about both. However, while women take a similar view about Labour, they are far more disposed to believe that the Tories could handle education better, with 38 percent rating them positively and only 34 percent rating them negatively. Once again, this is consistent with the possibility that Cameron's positioning on public services found a special appeal for women.

The final element of our quantitative analysis of BES survey data concerns voters' views about the relative merits of the main party leaders themselves. Quite apart from the details of specific policy shifts, it is conceivable that Cameron personally might have had an appeal which drew women's support back to the party once again. It is increasingly commonplace for political scientists to argue that in the age of partisan dealignment and weakened class politics, individual leadership evaluations count for more than hitherto in the reflections of voters (Clarke et al 2004; Poguntke and Webb 2005). Table 8.10 reports voters' evaluations of the three main party leaders in 2010 using a scale running from 0 (indicating intense dislike of a given leader) to 10 (indicating intense liking). We also report the evaluations of the main three parties on a similar scale, as it important to take into account whether the leaders seem to have been more or less well liked than their parties, as this is the only way that we can gauge how

Tables 8.9a–c Attitudes towards Key Issues in 2010

a. Labour Handle Financial Crisis

Cramer's v = 0.10 (p = 0.000)	Very well	Fairly well	Neither well nor badly	Fairly badly	Very badly	Total
Male	10.0%	26.3%	16.5%	20.3%	26.9%	100.0% (n = 6328)
Female	6.0%	22.2%	17.9%	24.4%	29.5%	100.0% (n = 6785)

b. Cons Handle Financial Crisis

Cramer's v = 0.06 (p = 0.000)	Very well	Fairly well	Neither well nor badly	Fairly badly	Very badly	Total
Male	7.3%	25.7%	21.2%	23.0%	22.9%	100.0% (n = 6007)
Female	6.1%	27.6%	23.9%	23.6%	18.8%	100.0% (n = 5867)

c. Labour Handle Economy Generally

Cramer's v = 0.08 (p = 0.000)	Very well	Fairly well	Neither well nor badly	Fairly badly	Very badly	Total
Male	5.8%	25.1%	16.1%	21.7%	31.3%	100.0% (n = 6345)
Female	4.3%	20.1%	18.1%	26.4%	31.1%	100.0% (n = 6787)

Tables 8.9d–f Attitudes towards Key Issues in 2010

Cramer's v = 0.06 (p = 0.000)

| d. Cons Handle Economy Generally | | | | | |
	Very well	Fairly well	Neither well nor badly	Fairly badly	Very badly	Total
Male	7.9%	27.8%	20.3%	23.5%	20.4%	100.0% (n = 6030)
Female	6.7%	29.5%	22.9%	23.8%	17.2%	100.0% (n = 5954)

Cramer's v = 0.06 (p = 0.000)

| e. Labour Handle Immigration | | | | | |
	Very well	Fairly well	Neither well nor badly	Fairly badly	Very badly	Total
Male	1.9%	12.7%	15.9%	23.2%	46.3%	100.0% (n = 6309)
Female	1.2%	10.8%	17.4%	26.3%	44.3%	100.0% (n = 6681)

Cramer's v = 0.02 (p = 0.382)

| f. Cons Handle Immigration | | | | | |
	Very well	Fairly well	Neither well nor badly	Fairly badly	Very badly	Total
Male	9.5%	30.4%	21.2%	19.4%	19.5%	100.0% (n = 5983)
Female	9.5%	30.0%	22.0%	20.2%	18.4%	100.0% (n = 5805)

Tables 8.9g–j Attitudes towards Key Issues in 2010

g. Labour Handle NHS

Cramer's v = 0.10 (p = 0.000)	Very well	Fairly well	Neither well nor badly	Fairly badly	Very badly	Total
Male	9.7%	30.3%	22.7%	21.8%	15.4%	100.0% (n = 6300)
Female	5.4%	26.5%	24.4%	25.6%	18.1%	100.0% (n = 6718)

h. Conservative Handle NHS

Cramer's v = 0.07 (p = 0.000)	Very well	Fairly well	Neither well nor badly	Fairly badly	Very badly	Total
Male	4.30%	22.20%	26.80%	23.20%	23.60%	100.0% (n = 6038)
Female	5.30%	27.20%	25.50%	22.40%	19.60%	100.0% (n = 5924)

i. Labour Handle Education

Cramer's v = 0.07 (p = 0.000)	Very well	Fairly well	Neither well nor badly	Fairly badly	Very badly	Total
Male	5.9%	26.6%	24.3%	23.9%	19.3%	100.0% (n = 6199)
Female	3.8%	24.2%	27.1%	26.4%	18.5%	100.0% (n = 6522)

j. Cons Handle Education

Cramer's v = 0.06 (p = 0.000)	Very well	Fairly well	Neither well nor badly	Fairly badly	Very badly	Total
Male	6.1%	26.4%	29.2%	21.1%	17.2%	100.0% (n = 5962)
Female	6.3%	32.0%	27.3%	19.1%	15.3%	100.0% (n = 5862)

Table 8.10 Attitude towards Main Party Leaders and Their Parties, 2010

Attitude	Sex	Mean position (sd)	Significance	N	Mean estimation of leader's party
Feelings about Gordon Brown	Male	3.74 (3.15)	0.021	6291	4.12 (−0.38)
	Female	3.86 (3.02)		6647	4.05 (−0.19)
Feelings about David Cameron	Male	4.36 (3.08)	0.000	6247	4.23 (0.13)
	Female	4.74 (3.01)		6519	4.56 (0.18)
Feelings about Nick Clegg	Male	4.97 (2.24)	0.001	5824	4.97 (0.00)
	Female	5.11 (2.09)		5698	5.27 (−0.16)

Note: Dependent variable = scale running from 0 (dislike) to 10 (like). Significance = 2-tailed T test for difference between male and female mean scores.
Source: BES 2010.

far they had an appeal which is separate from that of their parties. This shows a number of things. First, although Clegg was the most popular, and Brown the least popular leader with the electorate, Cameron was the only leader who was more popular than his own party. This is significant, for it implies that he is the only one of the leaders who might have succeeded in enhancing the appeal that his party might otherwise have had. The differences between males and females are statistically significant in all cases. On this evidence Brown was notably less popular than the Labour Party and might well have deprived it of some votes, especially among men, while Cameron had the opposite effect, especially on women. Some caution should be exercised in interpreting this, however, because the 'Cameron effect' was only slightly weaker among men. Nevertheless, this evidence is consistent with the possibility that Cameron had a positive impact on women's support for the Conservatives in 2010.

In summing up the quantitative evidence reviewed here, it important to emphasize that none of it can really be considered as incontrovertible proof that Cameron's strategy succeeded in winning the support of women in particular. We have seen that women generally remain to the left of men and closer to Labour than to the Conservatives, but they do not regard the Tories as being so far to the right as men do. This might reflect a 'softening' of the 'nasty party' image in the eyes of female voters, though we cannot be sure. On law and order, the Tory advantage over Labour is clear-cut, but is neither new nor specific to women voters. Men and women generally had similar views as to the most important issues at the 2010 election, although the latter gave a little more prominence to the NHS. They did not differ greatly in their evaluations of party performance on economic management or immigration, but on health and education – traditional strongholds for Labour – women proved significantly more favourable to the Conservatives than men did. Along with Cameron's personal appeal, this is probably the strongest suggestion that the data provide of the positive impact of the compassionate Conservatism strategy on women voters. All of this evidence relates only to what we have referred to as the 'indirect' effect of Cameron's re-positioning of the Conservatives on women voters – that is, an enhanced appeal achieved through shifts in general party or leader's image, or through policies which do not directly relate to gender politics. Indeed, the survey data on which we have drawn does not permit us to gauge the direct effect on women of the Conservative party's initiatives on the substantive and descriptive representation of women. However, our qualitative data can shed light on this.

Qualitative data: Floating voter focus groups

Our focus group research with floating voters was undertaken at the end of 2008, some three years after Cameron was elected leader of the Conservative party, and 17 months before he became Prime Minister. The aim was to guage the assessment of non-aligned voters of the Conservative party following Cameron's various reforms and overall positioning. The point was to focus on the type of voter that would be critical to the outcome of the forthcoming general election – those who were 'electorally available' in the sense of not being habitual supporters of any particular party, and who resided in the sort of marginal constituencies that might change hands in the election.[7]

In terms of issue salience, our participants did not generally regard women's concerns as among the most important on the current agenda of politics. Indeed, just one woman indicated that women and politics was a priority for her. Overall, health, education and the economy outrank all other issues, and we can see from Table 8.11 that the group most likely to nominate the first two of these issues was the all-woman one (group 2). These findings, then, are broadly consistent with survey research results in recent years, including BES 2010. But what do our floating voters think about gender equality in general terms?

Some women claimed that gender inequality was either not significant or at least that they were 'so strong as women that we don't allow that [sexism] to faze us'. To them such a focus was patronizing and unnecessary since they believed that the opportunities were available for women to pursue their chosen lifestyle or career. In their view, there are more opportunities for women now and there is less pressure on women to be home-makers and more freedom to pursue their chosen paths. There is also seen to be less of a stigma surrounding men who take more responsibility domestically than in previous generations as well.

> A lot of women are out working now...years ago; you never used to have that, you used to stay at home and the husband would work. (Female, C2DE)

That said, women in general, and women from the manual group in particular, seemed more likely to feel that gender inequality is still an issue. They feel women need to work harder to succeed, get paid less, struggle to break through the 'glass ceiling' to senior positions, and often have to conform to male notions of work place behaviour. The C2DE group of women, in particular, perceived a variety of challenges that they did not believe men encountered to the same extent:

> Still, women are still seen as second rate virtually...Yeah, I think women are in big trouble in the pensions...You end up by dipping in and out of employment in a way much more often than men do because you're busy with family responsibilities. And I think, I just thought of it at the back of my mind but occasionally there's something on the radio saying

Table 8.11 Focus Group questionnaire responses to question 'In your opinion, what issues, if any, would be most important in deciding who you would vote for if there was a General Election tomorrow?' PLEASE WRITE UP TO THREE ISSUES BELOW IN ORDER OF PRIORITY'

	Total	Group 1	Group 2	Group 3	Group 4
Healthcare/NHS	12	2	5	1	4
Education	9	2	5	2	
Economy	6	1	3		2
Police/Law and Order/Crime	5	2		1	2
Housing	5			3	2
Tax/Interest rates	5			3	2
Unemployment statistics	3		1	1	1
Benefits policies	3				
Youth	3	3			
Pensions	2			2	
Political Trust	2	2			
Environmental issues	2	1		1	
Recession issues	1	1			
Helping the homeless	1	1			
Immigration	1		1		
Looking after old people	1	1			
Good solutions to help credit crunch	1	1			
Congestion charge	1	1			
Incapacity health	1		1		
Ending warfare in Middle East	1	1			
Licensing	1		1		
Women in Governance	1		1		
Poverty	1		1		

Table 8.11 Focus Group questionnaire responses to question 'In your opinion, what issues, if any, would be most important in deciding who you would vote for if there was a General Election tomorrow?' PLEASE WRITE UP TO THREE ISSUES BELOW IN ORDER OF PRIORITY' – *continued*

	Total	Group 1	Group 2	Group 3	Group 4
Food prices	1			1	
Nutritional health	1			1	
Security	1			1	
Respect for existing institutions	1				1
Quality of life	1				1
Patriotism	1				1
Social issues	1				1
Don't know	2	1			

Note: Results are based on 32 self-completion questionnaire among floating voters (Groups 1, 3, 4 and 7) December 2008. All results based on all respondents, though as some participants skipped questions the 'total' column does not always add up to 32. Group 1 – ABC1, 2 males/7 females, 2.12.2008; Group 2 – C2DE, 8 females, 3.12.2008; Group 3 – C2DE, 9 Males, 8/12/08; Group 4 – ABC1, 3 males/4 females, 15.12.2008. Efforts were made to recruit participants from a mixture of inner-London, outer-London and non-London areas, as well as from marginal constituencies (ie, where the margin between the first and second place in the 2005 election was less than 15%) such as: Hemel Hempstead, St. Albans, Watford, Croydon Central, Battersea, Harrow West, Hendon, and Eltham.

if you haven't done a certain number of years of NI subs, and basically most women haven't compared to men, and I hadn't realized that and then I hear that and I get terrified and then I just don't know what I'm going to do (woman C2DE).

I do think there is discrimination. It does come down to choice but I also do think there is discrimination in there as well...I think it was said earlier that, gosh, women are less favoured for jobs because of pregnancy and whatever, but that should mean nothing. That should mean nothing (woman C2DE).

People are saying there's no more sexism, but if you actually examine the percentage of people in the highly paid, powerful jobs, in most areas the 'glass ceiling' is still there (Woman C2DE).

Table 8.12a confirms that a broad consensus existed among our participants about the need for greater equality between the sexes, while Table 8.12b shows a similar agreement about the responsibility of government for facilitating such equality. Table 8.12c shows that this is rooted in a common acceptance that traditional conceptions of gender roles only apply to a few participants, although Table 8.12d shows that the perspective is essentially liberal here; the traditional home-maker role for women is regarded as a perfectly appropriate and fulfilling option for women if they choose it. There is, however, a sense of the dilemma arising from the challenges to families if women do decide to pursue full-time careers outside the home. The participants are collectively ambiguous in their reactions to this question (Table 8.12e). Finally, it is interesting to observe that a majority of our focus group members reject the view that women are emotionally less well-suited to politics than men are (Table 8.12f). This is relevant to the question of the descriptive representation of women in Parliament, of course, and bears directly on the Conservatives' candidate-selection reforms.

In this respect there was overarching agreement among participants that politics is very male-dominated and it was widely felt that more women should be encouraged to enter the world of politics. They saw the adversarial nature of party politics as one the key factors most likely to deter women from attempting to become MPs. Female participants themselves argued that women are not on the whole adversarial by nature; they believed that women naturally look more to achieving agreement and a consensus, which in the current male dominated environment is not always possible. As one ABC1 woman stated: 'we are always looking for compromises and consensus's rather than 'I win, you lose'.

The under-representation of women in politics may not be generally regarded as a high political priority overall, but it was far from unimportant, especially to women (see Table 8.13a & b). Moreover, the need to do

Table 8.12 Focus Groups Participants' Attitudes towards Gender Equality

A. Attempts to give equal opportunities to women in Britain have gone...?

	Total	Group 1	Group 2	Group 3	Group 4
Much too far	0				
Too far	3				1
About right	17	2	3	4	
Not far enough	31	6	4	4	5
Not nearly far enough	2		1		
Don't know	3			1	1

B. Government should make sure that men and women have an equal chance to succeed

	Total	Group 1	Group 2	Group 3	Group 4
Strongly agree	23	8	6	4	5
Tend to agree	7	1	2	4	
Neither/nor	0				
Tend to disagree	1				1
Strongly disagree	0				
Don't know	1				1

C. A husband's job is to earn money: a wife's job is to look after the home and family

	Total	Group 1	Group 2	Group 3	Group 4
Strongly agree	2	1	1		1
Tend to agree	1				2
Neither/nor	5		1	2	1
Tend to disagree	5			4	1
Strongly disagree	18	8	6	2	2
Don't know	1				1

Table 8.12 Focus Groups Participants' Attitudes towards Gender Equality – *continued*

D. Being a house wife is just as fulfilling as full time paid employment

	Total	Group 1	Group 2	Group 3	Group 4
Strongly agree	8	2	3	1	2
Tend to agree	4			2	2
Neither/nor	8	3	2	2	1
Tend to disagree	4	1	1	1	1
Strongly disagree	6	3	2	1	
Don't know	2			1	1

E. All in all, family life suffers when the woman has a full-time job

	Total	Group 1	Group 2	Group 3	Group 4
Strongly agree	1		1		
Tend to agree	8		1	3	4
Neither/nor	8	2	2	3	1
Tend to disagree	7	3	1	2	1
Strongly disagree	7	4	3		
Don't know	1				1

F. Most men are better emotionally suited to politics than most women

	Total	Group 1	Group 2	Group 3	Group 4
Strongly agree	0				
Tend to agree	5		3	2	
Neither/nor	7	3		3	1
Tend to disagree	10	1	2	3	4
Strongly disagree	9	5	3		1
Don't know	1				1

something about it was felt to be a particular issue for the Conservative party to address (if still a relatively low priority overall). While there is no consensus on why the Conservative parliamentary party is under-representative, some attribute the asymmetry in women's descriptive representation to the Labour Party's use of sex quotas, as well as the latter's general reputation for greater concern with all forms of inequality, including gender inequality. While initial reactions to the idea of employing equality guarantees in order to increase the number of women in Parliament often echoed those of the earlier focus groups of party members reported in Chapters 3 and 4 – that is, an instinctive concern that such positive discrimination might undermine the quality of candidates and MPs by offending against the merit principle, and would cause dissent within the party – further discussion revealed that women in particular thought it might be the only way to achieve the goal. Witness this exchange between C2DE women:

> It's what I said earlier. They had all women shortlists, it was quite an unpopular concept but they forced it through and it brought in an enormous influx of female MPs. And at that point, if you compared the percentage of female MPs from the Labour Party to the Conservative Party, it was...there was a huge disparity....

> It's positive discrimination.

> Yeah, but if the end result you're seeking is a massive change, it will bring about a massive change.

The results reported in Table 8.13c confirm that opposition to quotas was far from clear-cut. It should be further noted that the problem of women's descriptive representation in Parliament was not simply one of under-representation of women *per se*, but one also of the representativeness of the women who are elected to the House of Commons. The Conservative women MPs already in Parliament did not strike the women C2DE focus group participants as representative of 'real women'. Mrs Thatcher was often invoked in the focus-group discussions as an example of how unrepresentative of women in general Conservative women MPs tend to be. This is partly about the difference in social background, and partly about resentment of the Conservatives' reputation for antipathy towards public services and their preference for private provision. That that this may have left a lasting legacy for the party amongst women voters is illustrated by the following focus group exchange by C2DE females:[8]

> So much of the bad stuff now is traceable back to Thatcher's policies in the '80s.

Table 8.13 Focus Group Participants' Views on the Descriptive Representation of Women in Parliament

a. To what extent, if at all, does the number of female MPs in Parliament matter to you personally?

	Total	Group 1	Group 2	Group 3	Group 4
A great deal	3	2	1		
A fair amount	9	3	5		1
Not very much	15	4	1	6	4
Not at all	4			3	1
Don't know	2		1		1

b. To what extent do you believe that parliament should have more or fewer female MPs?

	Total	Group 1	Group 2	Group 3	Group 4
Many more	9	7	1		1
A little more	14	1	5	4	4
Same as currently	2			2	
A little less	1		1		
Many less	1		1		
Don't know	3			2	1

c. To what extent do you agree or disagree that the UK political parties should adopt 'positive discrimination' for certain groups when selecting candidates to stand for election?

	Total	Group 1	Group 2	Group 3	Group 4
Strongly agree	2	1		1	
Tend to agree	7	3	1	3	
Neither/nor	12	3	6	2	1
Tend to disagree	5	1		1	3
Strongly disagree	4			2	2
Don't know	3	1	1		1

I just think to myself, what experiences have they gone through and how can they represent me?

It looks like she's got a husband that earns lots and lots of money.

I don't think she's ever had to worry whether she'd be able to feed the children.

They all either have got a wealthy man or wealthy husband and they're all like second wives, got married again and got themselves a man who's rich.

But (if) they've lived, they know what it's like to have hard times, good times, had to struggle to get where they are, you're more inclined to want to respect them and listen to them. But if someone's just textbook or a boring housewife or someone that's been to Harvard, they don't know what it's like to want, and then go to come and dictate to you...

Such discussions point towards a credibility problem for the Conservatives under Cameron in respect of changing the policy content, emphasis and image of the party. Even when initiatives such as Cameron's attempt to get more Conservative women into Parliament seem to take the party in a direction which many women in the electorate would approve of, there are doubts about how authentic or meaningful such changes are. This goes for action on both descriptive and substantive representation of women, and our focus group participants generally recognized that Labour had a head-start over the Tories in such matters and were therefore more meaningful:

Moderator: So talking hypothetically, if the Conservative Party were to really start making a strong focus on what we might call women's issues and really start focusing a lot on that...how would you react to that?

ABC1 Woman: I just think that they'd be...it would be just looking for an extra vote. They wouldn't...I don't think they'd be genuine about it.

Moderator: Do you think that there's anything the Conservative Party could be doing to appeal more to women?

ABC1 Woman: If they do now we know it's lip service. That's the problem.

Another ABC1 woman contrasted Labour and the Conservatives on the substantive representation of women by citing the example of Peter Mandelson's actions on flexible working arrangements for women when he was Business

Secretary in Gordon Brown's Labour administration. That he was prepared to proceed with such policies even whilst under pressure from the business lobby not to do so at a time of economic hardship, was a position she doubted the Conservatives would have maintained had they been in government. None of this is to say that Conservative policies 'for women' would not be welcomed by many women, but it leaves one doubting how far they might be noticed or regarded as credible. For the record, however, Table 8.14 shows that, with the exception of tax allowances for married couples (which the mixed-sex ABC1 group was generally against, and which recall came from Cameron and not the women's part of the party), most of the policy that the Conservatives have developed in recent years met with widespread approval or at least acceptance. This is at least consistent with the possibility that the party's pledges for women in this regard may have something to do with the higher than average swing of women back to the party in 2010.[9]

Conclusion

Having reviewed a substantial body of both quantitative and qualitative evidence relating to the electoral appeal of David Cameron's Conservatives to women voters – in particular, whether or not the party's recent initiatives on the descriptive and substantive representation of women might have succeeded in winning back the votes of women – we find that sex is relevant to understanding vote choice in 2010. We found that sex and gender-generation effects on voting behaviour remained significant in 2010, and that the gender gap once again showed itself to the advantage of the Conservatives in the form of a larger Tory lead over Labour among women than among men. While the youngest women in the electorate swung from Labour to the Liberal Democrats, most female age groups, from 25 upwards, switched more heavily to the Conservatives than their male counterparts. This pattern is consistent with the possibility that Cameron's Conservatives might have had a particular appeal for some groups of women. At the same time, and overall, women generally remain to the left of men and closer to Labour than to the Conservatives, but they do not regard the Conservatives as being so far to the right as men do. In turn, this might suggest that amongst women the Conservative party is seen as less 'nasty' than it once was. Men and women generally had, however, similar views as to the most important issues at the 2010 election, although the latter gave a little more prominence to the NHS and probably education. On both of these issues – traditional strongholds for Labour – women proved significantly more favourable to the Conservatives than men did. Coupled with Cameron's personal appeal, this is probably the strongest suggestion that the data provide of the positive impact of his 'compassionate conservatism' strategy on women voters. The qualitative evidence

Table 8.14 Focus Group Participants' Views on Conservative Initiatives regarding the Substantive Representation of Women

A. Tax allowance for married couples

	Total	Group 1	Group 2	Group 3	Group 4
Strongly agree	5		4	1	4
Tend to agree	8		1	5	2
Neither/nor	9	4	2	3	
Tend to disagree	1	1			
Strongly disagree	2	1			
Don't know	4	3	1		1

B. Tax allowance for all couples whether they are married, or not, gay or straight

	Total	Group 1	Group 2	Group 3	Group 4
Strongly agree	7	1	3	1	2
Tend to agree	13	3	3	5	2
Neither/nor	6	2	1	2	1
Tend to disagree	1	1			
Strongly disagree	3		1	1	1
Don't know	3	2			1

C. Rights to request flexible working for parents of children up to the age of 11

	Total	Group 1	Group 2	Group 3	Group 4
Strongly agree	7	3	2	1	1
Tend to agree	17	5	4	6	2
Neither/nor	4		1	1	2
Tend to disagree	2		1		1
Strongly disagree	1			1	
Don't know	2	1			1

Table 8.14 Focus Group Participants' Views on Conservative Initiatives regarding the Substantive Representation of Women – *continued*

D. Rights to request flexible working for parents of children up to the age of 18

	Total	Group 1	Group 2	Group 3	Group 4
Strongly agree	7	4	1	1	1
Tend to agree	14	4	2	5	3
Neither/nor	7	2	4	1	
Tend to disagree	4		1	1	2
Strongly disagree	1			1	
Don't know	2	1			1

E. Extension of maternity leave (for mothers only) and pay to one year

	Total	Group 1	Group 2	Group 3	Group 4
Strongly agree	7	2	3		2
Tend to agree	13	4	4	2	3
Neither/nor	6	1	1	3	1
Tend to disagree	5	1		3	1
Strongly disagree	1			1	
Don't know	1	1			

F. Transformation of maternity leave and pay to shared parental (i.e. mother or father) leave and pay

	Total	Group 1	Group 2	Group 3	Group 4
Strongly agree	6	2	2		2
Tend to agree	13	4	3	5	1
Neither/nor	9	2	3	2	2
Tend to disagree	1				1
Strongly disagree	3			2	1
Don't know	1	1			

Table 8.14 Focus Group Participants' Views on Conservative Initiatives regarding the Substantive Representation of Women – continued

G. The obligation on single parents to seek paid employment when their child is 5 years old

	Total	Group 1	Group 2	Group 3	Group 4
Strongly agree	4	1	1	1	1
Tend to agree	11	2	3	2	4
Neither/nor	10	2	2	5	1
Tend to disagree	7	4	2		1
Strongly disagree	2				
Don't know	1			1	

H. The obligation on single parents to seek paid employment when their child is 11 years old

	Total	Group 1	Group 2	Group 3	Group 4
Strongly agree	6		1	3	2
Tend to agree	10	2	2	4	2
Neither/nor	10	2	3	2	3
Tend to disagree	4	4			
Strongly disagree	1		1		
Don't know	0				

I. The obligation on single parents to seek paid employment when their child is 16 years old

	Total	Group 1	Group 2	Group 3	Group 4
Strongly agree	11	4	1	4	2
Tend to agree	6		3	1	2
Neither/nor	9	2	3	2	2
Tend to disagree	5	2		2	1
Strongly disagree	1			1	
Don't know	0				

Table 8.14 Focus Group Participants' Views on Conservative Initiatives regarding the Substantive Representation of Women – *continued*

J. All employers to be audited for equal pay between women and men

	Total	Group 1	Group 2	Group 3	Group 4
Strongly agree	14	7	3	2	2
Tend to agree	8	1	2	3	2
Neither/nor	6	1	2	1	2
Tend to disagree	4		1	2	1
Strongly disagree	1			1	
Don't know	0				

K. The state providing financial support for childcare, including care by grandparents

	Total	Group 1	Group 2	Group 3	Group 4
Strongly agree	8	2	2	3	1
Tend to agree	12	5	3	1	3
Neither/nor	7		3	2	2
Tend to disagree	2			1	1
Strongly disagree	0				
Don't know	0				

L. The state providing financial support only for state or privately provided childcare keep

	Total	Group 1	Group 2	Group 3	Group 4
Strongly agree	6	1	2	3	
Tend to agree	5	1	1	1	2
Neither/nor	12	5	3	2	2
Tend to disagree	5	1	1	2	1
Strongly disagree	1		1		1
Don't know	1				1

Table 8.15 Voters Positions on Key Themes and Policies, May 2010

	First	Second	First-Second
David Cameron changed the Conservative Party. OR			
The Conservative Party has not changed very much.	46	50	–4
I'm more worried that we will go too far in cutting social spending and public services. OR			
I'm more worried that we won't go far enough to cut spending and reduce the debt.	57	40	17
To reduce the debt, we will need to make major cuts in spending and public services. OR			
To reduce the debt, we must raise taxes broadly and do less cutting of spending and services.	45	46	–1
It is time to cut taxes. OR			
It is not the time to cut taxes.	30	66	–36
We must start cutting the national debt right away. OR			
We must wait to cut the debt until the economic recovery is underway.	49	48	1
I'm more worried that we will do too little to regulate the financial community and allow for another era of speculative booms and busts. OR			
I'm more worried that we will go too far in regulating the financial community, which will harm the British economy.	58	38	20
This is a time for government to get more involved. OR			
This is a time to depend more on markets.	71	22	50

Table 8.15 Voters Positions on Key Themes and Policies, May 2010 – *continued*

	First	Second	First-Second
We need policies to create greater opportunity. OR We need policies to bring less inequality and more fairness.	48	48	0
To get future economic growth, the British government will need to encourage investment in new industries and sectors. OR To get future economic growth, Britain will have to create an environment with less regulation and more freedom of enterprise.	65	30	35
If government gets the right policies, Britain can do well. OR If society is strong, Britain can do well.	57	39	18
Britain will need new immigration, which can strengthen Britain. OR Immigration undermines Britain.	51	42	9
Britain needs to be more involved in the EU. OR Britain needs to be less involved in the EU.	32	64	-32
Britain should be more independent of the United States. OR Britain should be a strong ally of the United States.	54	43	12

Note: Responses are to the following question: Now I'm going to read you some pairs of statements about what should happen in Britain. As I read each pair, please tell me whether the FIRST statement or the SECOND statement comes closer to your views, even if neither is exactly right.
Source: 'The change election – what the voters were really saying'. Greenberg Quinlan Rosner (http://gqrr.com/articles/2445/5678_ukeu05182010charts.pdf, accessed 9 June 2010).

Table 8.16   The Three Most Important Reasons for Voting for the Conservative Party

The Conservative Party has changed	8
Cameron's qualities	26
Time for a change	48
The economy	40
The national debt.	36
Labour's planned tax increases	20
Pro-family policies	19
Done with Gordon Brown	35
Idea of small government and big society	10
Political expenses and corruption	16
Usually vote Conservative	28
(Other)	3

suggests further, that, while women's issues do not rank as highly salient in electoral terms, it is certainly not true to suppose that these things do not matter to voters, especially women. In general terms, the feelings expressed by focus group participants suggest that it made good sense for the Conservatives to adopt the measures that they did in respect of women's descriptive and substantive representation, even if it is not possible to show that these directly contributed to the rise in support from women voters in 2010. In sum, while there may be a credibility problem for the Conservatives in this issue domain, we cannot rule out the possibility that they were helped electorally by their initiatives in 'decontaminating' the party's image that had seemed to dog it since 1990. However, given the likely gendered impact of public spending cuts that the Coalition government embarked upon in the autumn of 2010, one is bound to wonder how enduring the Conservatives' electoral gains among women voters are likely to be.

Conclusion

Becoming a Little More Female would be a Great Start.[1]

At the time of the 2010 general election, the Conservative party had been out of power for more than a decade. Swept out of power in 1997 by the New Labour tide, they ended up losing two more elections in 2001 and 2005, with three different leaders (William Hague, Iain Duncan Smith and Michael Howard). For much of the first decade of the 21ˢᵗ century the party seemingly looked, to many voters, commentators, and political scientists, out of touch: 'male, pale and stale', to use a popular gender and politics phrase. Having lost its reputation for economic competency, and fighting on the wrong issues, the party had apparently failed to recognize (or admit) that British society had changed, that it had become, in short, less concerned with traditional social values and practices. It fell to David Cameron, a politician from the 40-something generation, elected party leader in 2005 having only been in Parliament since 2001, to lead the modernization of the party – to make it once again electorally viable. A public process of 'decontamination' was the very necessary first step on the road back to power, if not to single-party government (Bale 2010; Kavanagh and Cowley 2010; Bale and Webb 2011). One dimension of Cameron's modernization, albeit one too often overlooked by mainstream political scientists, was feminization. At Westminster, women's enhanced descriptive and substantive representation had been, for more than a decade, to the Conservatives' detriment. Not only did Labour women MPs massively out-number Conservative women MPs in both absolute and percentage terms – indeed, they continue to do so even after the 2010 general election – the 1997–2010 Labour governments laid claim to having been the most feminist governments in British history (Childs 2008; Annesley et al 2007). Cameron was fully aware that British party politics had feminized under New Labour (Lovenduski 2005a; Childs 2008) and that his party had lost its historic support amongst women voters. In the five years since taking over as party leader, Cameron's Conservative party, has had, in respect of both dimensions of feminization (Lovenduski 2005a), to play the politics of catch up.

218

Sex, Gender and the Conservative Party set out to map, and make sense of, the gendered changes that we expected might take place as a consequence of the Conservative party's efforts to modernize. Preliminary though its conclusions have to be – the book only covers the time up to the 2010 general election – it hopefully contributes to conceptual understandings of women's representation and provides useful new qualitative and quantitative empirical data. Its ambition is to extend both the gender and politics scholarship, by bringing conservative women and conservative politics into the frame, and enhance mainstream political science understanding of political parties, party change and party systems, by bringing gender effects into play. It seeks to do this through identifying women's roles within the party, exploring the attitudes and behaviours of Conservative representatives in Parliament and its party members, examining the extent to which gendered analysis was present in particular policies, and how feminization played out within and without the party.

These overarching research questions begged many others. Addressing the gender and politics literature, *Sex, Gender and the Conservative Party* provides insights into how scholars might refine the concept of feminization. Evaluating efforts to deliver women's greater descriptive representation, the first dimension of feminization, are, at one level, straightforward. One needs merely to count the number of women elected to Westminster and compare this with previous elections. Even here, however, a secondary question arises, 'how many more women representatives count as *sufficient* an increase'? If parity of representation is the ultimate goal, and we see no reason why a lower arbitrary figure would be sufficient, then, as Lisa Young (2000) suggests, the standard should be, in the short to medium term, parity amongst a party's *newly elected* representatives. In 2010 the Conservative parliamentary party fell short of this. Moreover, as previously noted, documenting the number of women MPs tells us little of the process that might have given rise to these numbers. Recent reforms to the Conservative parliamentary selection processes need to be explained to provide both a case study of the first dimension of feminization and as part of the wider story of Conservative party change. Furthermore, given that feminization is neither a static concept nor an end state, analysis of women's descriptive representation in the Conservative party is an ongoing study. The welcome improvement in women's descriptive representation on the Conservative benches secured in 2010 has not resolved the issue of women's under-descriptive representation in the party. Not only do women MPs constitute less than one in five of all Tory MPs, there is no guarantee that the number of Conservative women MPs will improve again at the next general election. The evidence from comparative studies and the British Labour party, especially in 2001, suggests that women's descriptive representation at higher levels is unlikely to happen naturally. Hence, the Conservative party will need to ensure that parliamentary selection remains central to its efforts in this Parliament. Whether the party will finally accept the logic of equality guarantees (Campbell et al 2006) remains a critical and as yet unanswered question.

Applying the concept of descriptive representation beyond the Conservative *parliamentary* party the extant wider literature on party organization proved much less instructive. Comparative party research may note or speculate on sex differences in party membership, document whether particular parties provide for group representation for women on internal bodies, and sometimes refer to the existence of women's sections, factions or organizations. But only in a few is a more substantial analysis undertaken of the 'women's part' of a political party (Young 2000; Russell, M. 2005, for example). In setting out to document the role of the various 'women's parts' of the contemporary British Conservative party, this book moves beyond simplistic assessments of the Conservatives that construct it as the party *of* women because of women's historic force as party members and activists. Rather, it considers whether the representational institutions and forums for women within the party constitute sites for the substantive representation of women's issues. Here, the distinction drawn between inclusion and integration proves a useful starting point. The latter suggests something considerably more than just presence. Indeed, in researching the roles of the Conservative Women's Organization, the Shadow Minister for Women and the Women's Policy Group, amongst others, it became clear that this study spoke to mainstream debates about intra-party democracy (Childs 2010) – a lacuna in the extant gender and politics research, to which this research has hopefully begun to contribute.

Another assumption underpinning *Sex, Gender and the Conservative Party* is that if one is to accept that there is some kind of relationship between women's descriptive and substantive representation, then scholars are going to need to know much more about (small and big c) conservative representatives (Carroll and Liebowitz 2003: 2). It is now widely accepted that the link between women's descriptive and substantive representation, if ever conceived of as straightforward, can no longer be so considered. The assumptions of critical mass theory have long since been qualified: mediating factors are multiple; sites other than parliaments, and actors other than elected representatives, may be critical; and women's bodies are not the same thing as feminist minds. But taking conservative representatives seriously further complicates the story. Conservative women representatives count for descriptive representation but they might also claim and seek to act for women, and do so in ways that are implicitly or explicitly anti-feminist. Accordingly scholars need to examine how gender consciousness influences conservative representatives' political attitudes and behaviour. What kind of claims do they make, and what kind of actions do they undertake? Such questions are particularly pertinent given that much of the gender and politics literature has, until very recently, focused mostly on the attitudes and behaviour of leftist women (Celis and Childs 2011) and very often, adopted a feminist conceptualization of what constitutes substantive representation, presuming that when representatives act for women they must do so in a feminist direction. Subscribing to such a conceptualization might be normatively appealing for activists and gender and politics scholars who would prefer a feminist polity, but this would have to exclude any actions that representatives might take that do not fit with whatever definition of feminism is being used. When conservatives claim to represent women, engage in the constitutive representation of gender, and undertake activities towards substantive representation, and if we do not wish to dismiss their actions, *a priori*, as not constituting substantive representation, more sophisticated frameworks of analysis are necessary; ones that permit judgment between claims to act for women that do not presume that feminist substantive representation is the *only* kind of substantive representation (Celis and Childs 2011). Finally, substantive representation is not just about the attitudes and behaviour of individual representatives. Nor is it just about putting women's issues on the table. It is also about evaluating the extent to which legislation and public policy is changed. A party and a government's explicit policies 'for women' are, accordingly, central to any such assessment even as wider policy and legislative programmes reveal much of what it thinks about women and gender relations.

A long way from parity...descriptive representation in the Conservative parliamentary party

Counting women's bodies in parliaments and political parties, even as it cannot reveal anything much about women's integration in politics, establishes the fact of women's inclusion in, or exclusion from, our elected political institutions. And what we know is that inclusion has proven hard for many political parties to achieve, both in the UK and elsewhere. The British Conservative parliamentary party in 2010 is, clearly a more feminized body than previously. With 49 women MPs it has more than doubled its number compared with the 2005 Parliament. The party fell a little short of doubling the percentage of women MPs at the 2010 election, rising from 9 percent to 16 percent. Whilst a welcome improvement, these numbers and figures leave the Conservative party falling below the European average for women's legislative presence, which stands at 22 percent. It also continues to compare unfavourably to the Labour party which managed to return a parliamentary party that is one third female. The Conservatives also fare badly compared with many of its European 'sister' parties: it trails in 19th position. Of course, critics might argue that such evaluations are too harsh given that the Conservative party was starting from a very low base and that its supply pool was limited. There is something in this. Yet analysis of the selection data in 2010 (Campbell and Childs 2010; Ashe et al 2010) provide continuing evidence of the party's failure to select sufficient women for its vacant held and winnable seats; those seats that, all other things being equal, transform candidates into MPs. If we take the overall number of women candidates selected by the party, the Conservatives had the potential to return a parliamentary party that was 24 percent female, but they managed only 16 percent. As a percentage of the party's newly elected MPs, Conservative women constitute 22 percent, still a long way short of parity, albeit a figure that better reflects its overall percentage of women candidates. Looking to the future, the party clearly has ongoing problems with women's descriptive representation. Recall that Cameron himself has talked of the selection of women by his party as being too slow and has conceded the existence of selectorate discrimination. Recall too that the Labour party, at an election when it did very badly at the polls, efficiently turned 30 percent of candidates into more than 30 percent of its MPs. It did this by using an equality guarantee mechanism, All Women Shortlists (AWS).

Cameron's well publicized efforts to reform his party's parliamentary selection processes between 2005 and 2010 stopped short of AWS. Despite his apparent advocacy of them in his deposition to the Speaker's Conference in autumn 2009, there were none. Instead, the Conservatives relied on equality rhetoric and equality promotion measures. These look to have had some effect, but they are, by very definition, unable to guarantee substantial increases in the selection of women candidates for the seats the party will win. Certainly, they can guarantee that more women are seen by the selectorate, but they cannot force that selectorate to select women. Only a well designed and implemented equality guarantee can deliver that. Cameron's reluctance to lead the Conservatives any further on candidate selection finds some explanation in the antipathy of his party on the ground and in Parliament to embrace measures which they perceive offend against the principle of merit and constitute an unwelcome central intervention on local party autonomy. We do not wish to downplay the extent of grassroots feeling. Indeed, our focus group discussions and party membership survey throws additional light on members' attitudes towards efforts to enhance both the supply and demand of candidates, attitudes that will need to be tackled in the future. However, a direct consequence of the party's failure to make sufficient strides towards parity of representation in 2010 – which owes much to Cameron's failure to lead on this as strongly as he might have done – suggests that he has merely put off the day when the party has to revisit this issue.

Women's descriptive representation must be considered, then, an ongoing process for the Conservative party, as it is for the other parties at Westminster. Disconcertingly, at least for advocates of women's greater descriptive representation, the structural and political context in the current parliament may be considerably less favourable than in the 2005 one, when a new party leader faced Conservative MPs and members more disposed to the principle of modernization (Snowdon 2010: 212). Following three successive general election defeats, the grassroots party was supportive of Cameron and his modernizing agenda, in fact more so than the parliamentary party, although he had considerable support from among MPs, too (Childs 2005). Cameron had, as he would frequently reiterate, a 'mandate' for reform. When the mobilization of senior women in the parliamentary, voluntary and professional party, working alongside women's equality advocates in civil society and the media, are considered, the likelihood of significant moves on parliamentary candidate selection looked, at that time, greater than ever. Being now in government, the party leadership has much else to address than party reform: a coalition with the Liberal Democrats, who themselves have few women MPs and a history of antipathy towards equality guarantees (Evans 2011); an apparently (and increasingly) unhappy parliamentary right wing, who may make more demands of the party leadership as time goes on; similar disquiet amongst party members, who are already talking of party organizational reform, at least on the pages of www.conservativehome; and, finally, and dominating party political debate, an economic situation in which the government is advocating extensive spending cuts which need to be both implemented on the ground and defended to voters. If such an economic strategy were to impact most heavily upon women the Conservative party might find it harder to pursue a credible strategy regarding women's descriptive representation, as it, in the eyes of its critics, acts substantively not for but against women.

In the post-election period, membership discussion of candidate selection, if anything, has been preoccupied with the representation of class, which has been presented as a zero-sum game with women's descriptive representation.[2] Here the belief is, in essence, that women have had their turn. Other portents internal to the party do not look good at the time of writing, either. The first public comments on candidates by Baroness Warsi, the post-election Party co-Chairman, about whom some leading party gender equality activists have 'gender concerns', announced a 'wide ranging review' and spoke of the 'time for "quotas" for candidates from minority groups', having 'passed' (*Sunday Times* 13 June, 2010). Although it is not clear that she was talking about women – women are not a minority of the population – the article implied that she is less sympathetic to measures to enhance, if not guarantee, the selection of women than other leading women in the party.[3] Planned coalition reforms to Parliament may act as inhibiters of women's descriptive representation too. Reducing the size of the House is likely to limit the overall number of vacancies at the next general election as sitting MPs fight each other for selections. The new parliamentary expenses regime might differentially impact prospective MPs with young families who would wish to have 'proper' homes in both their constituency and Westminster, rather than a 'bedsit' in one location. These are likely to be disproportionately women.[4] Finally, leading Conservative Parliamentarian women activists may simply be too busy with government responsibilities to maintain their activism on this issue.

Against these seemingly unfavourable conditions, there remain some grounds for optimism. A consistent finding across the party member focus groups and our survey data is that some women and younger party members are more favourably disposed towards the case for women's greater descriptive representation. The same is true of Conservative Parliamentarians. And even more widely the principle of descriptive representation is largely supported. What is clearly required is for Cameron to move beyond his public acknowledgement of selectorate discrimination and to accept that, given a problem of party demand, the logic of equality guarantees is inescapable. In all this the party's leading equality activists, such as Theresa May, and other leading women, such as Anne Jenkin, Shireen Ritchie, Trish Morris, and Margot James, cannot afford to give up on this issue. If they previously believed that rule changes were necessary, even if they were mostly publicly hostile towards sex quotas, their voices should be louder from 2010. At this point we do not have systematic information about the support they might receive from the new intake of MPs, but some who should know, contend that many of the new women are favourably disposed on this issue. The activities of Women2win, and probably to a lesser extent the CWO, will likely be critical too. If it is the latter's job to seek out women members, the former must support and train those women who aspire to Parliament, and perhaps most importantly of all, both must act as a pressure group in the party, making demands and holding the party to account on this issue. The party's various gender equality activists might find additional succour from beyond their party. The Speaker of the House of Commons, John Bercow, has publicly made it clear that he remains committed to ensuring that the recommendations from the Speaker's Conference are implemented, although the precise manifestation of this is not as yet evident.[5] At the minimum, although not as yet in place, is the monitoring of party selection data, detailing the sex and other characteristics of prospective parliamentary candidates. Civil society organizations are also preparing to launch various public campaigns in 2011 on women's descriptive representation, although of course, their form and effect remains to be seen.

What of Cameron? It is our contention that intra-party hostility might be better contained, if not always dissipated, and turned into more positive feelings, if the party leadership were to engage in a continued and systematic process of changing attitudes. Significantly increasing women's descriptive representation at the next general election almost certainly requires further reforms to the Conservative parliamentary selection process. However unpalatable it may appear some form of equality guarantee looks to be necessary. Such a move requires political will that hitherto Cameron has not demonstrated. Nor is it obvious that Cameron considers women's descriptive representation to be something that requires his attention in the months ahead. Yet without some 'top-down' initiatives those in the party active on women's descriptive representation might well be left with the conclusion that the party's efforts to-date were (to paraphrase Kittilson 2006: 135) less about a 'fundamental shift' than a 'short-term symbolic' strategy to gain women's votes. This is because, logically, Cameron only needed to *signal* a transformation in his parliamentary party in advance of the 2010 election. The outcome, in terms of electoral appeal, stopped on Election Day because what mattered (at least for the outcome of the 2010 general election) was that he was *seen* to be acting. For these reasons if women's descriptive under-representation is pursued no further in the 2010 Parliament, one might reasonably infer that Cameron's motivation was instrumental rather than principled. If, on the other hand, efforts to change the parliamentary face of the Conservative party continues apace it would be harder to deny that his was an authentic desire to address the 'scandalous under-representation of women' in the Conservative party.

Moving from the legislative to the executive level confirms Conservative women politicians' limited presence. Overall, women constitute 15 percent of the coalition government and Cameron's first Cabinet had four women MPs, 17 percent, figures broadly in line with the numbers of women sitting on the Tory benches (16 percent). Theresa May is Home Secretary; Cheryl Gillan is Welsh Secretary; Caroline Spelman, Secretary of State for Environment Food and Rural Affairs, and Baroness Warsi, from the Lords, is Minister without Portfolio and Party Co-Chairman. May's appointment is clearly the highpoint, even if some in the media found it a surprising (read: critical) appointment.[6] In any case, in Cameron's Cabinet, the oft-observed pyramidal picture of women's descriptive representation appears then to hold – the nearer the apex of power the fewer the women (Lovenduski 2005a). No Rubicon has been passed either. Four women in the Cabinet appears to have become the minimum in British politics – the glass floor – below which administrations dare not go for fear of risking opprobrium. The figures leave the UK lagging behind other advanced democracies too.[7] It can be argued, of course, that some of the failure of Cabinet composition lies with the Liberal Democrats who apparently had no women that their party leader considered worthy of such status. Sarah Teather, Jo Swinson and Lynne Featherstone, that party's most high profile women MPs, only made it into the lower ranks of government. Cameron might well aspire to a Cabinet that is one third female by the end of 2010 parliament but this aspiration, one he stated on BBC Radio 4 Woman's Hour in 2007, is importantly and explicitly not a quota.[8]

The 'women's' part of the party: representation, institutionalization and accountability

If important strides are observable in women's parliamentary representation, what of women's participation in the 'women's' part of the Conservative party? Here there is again evidence of some positive moves. In brief, the party re-established a Vice Chairman for Women (albeit now lapsed), created a women's officer post, saw the Conservative Women's Organization experience a healthier few years, supported the establishment of the ginger group Women2win and, finally, the shadow Minister for Women, under the tutelage of May, brought women's issues much more to the party's fore. The Women's Policy Group Report, *Women in the World Today,* fed directly into the 2010 general election Manifesto. All of this is to the good, but the analysis of the 'women's part' of the contemporary Conservative party ultimately raised more questions than it answered, not least relating to questions of intra-party organizational relations, institutionalization, group representation and accountability.

The continued existence of the CWO suggests an ongoing commitment to the separate organization of women within the Conservative party, something that had previously been uncertain. Yet, this finding sits rather uneasily amongst claims in the comparative academic literature on parties which suggests that parties are moving away from representational towards plebiscitary forms, in which they refuse to differentiate members by group identity (Young and Cross 2002).[9] At the same time, and whilst the contemporary CWO clearly articulates gendered concerns and perspectives within the party, it cannot formally fulfil the criteria of a Quasi Women's Policy Agency – a concern of the gender and politics literature – because it does not articulate *women's movement* goals. Nevertheless, it constitutes an internal party body that, at the very least in terms of its leadership, seeks to act collectively for women by seeking to influence party policy, organization and party activities. In the middle years of the 2005 parliament, the CWO was much focused on 'big P' politics, in providing discursive forums for policy development, and working with the women's officer, the Vice-Chairman for Women and (then Shadow) Minister for Women in the Women's Policy Group. However, the extent to which the voice of women as articulated via the CWO is institutionalized within the party's structure, and even amongst the women's part of the Conservative party, has to be regarded as limited. Mostly it is informal and dependent upon good inter-personal relation, neither of which can be guaranteed. The CWO annual conference does not make resolutions; CWO forums and summits are attended by relevant Parliamentarians and ministers, but they are in no way bound by them; and there are no formal lines of accountability between the Minister for Women and the CWO. The post of women's officer has also shifted in terms of remit and location. There is much evidence to suggest, then, that relations between the CWO and the Shadow Minister in particular are asymmetric, in the latter's favour. This has the potential to create ill-feeling and border wars, as the CWO can feel less than fully integrated and included in policy decision making. Now it might be that direct accountability between women party members via the CWO to the Minister for

Women is undesirable. For an electoral-professional party this is probably most likely, as the Minister will prefer that responsibility lies with her, and not with the voluntary party organization. But it might still be better for the party to consider systematically the nature, remit and relations of its various women's structures. To address, in effect, the following questions: should the party re-establish a VC for Women? What relationship should the CWO have with the VC for Women if they were to do so? Is she their representative in the party and if so, does she act as a trustee or is she mandated? What of the Minister for Women? Should she articulate the views of the CWO to the Cabinet, vice versa, or some combination thereof? And what of women MPs, they apparently experience little representative relationship with the CWO or women party members? The answers to these questions might well, of course, be very different when a party is in office, compared with when it is in opposition.

In addition to these unanswered questions three further issues that emerge out of this analysis of the CWO warrant additional comment and future research. The first issue relates to resources. Given that the party seems to accept that women have group interests and perspectives and that these are to be represented, at least in part by the CWO, it is pertinent to raise issues of the organization's limited resources, as these currently constrain, according to its leadership, CWO activities and organization. And current party leadership support may well also be more symbolic than substantive. The second issue relates to the nature of the Conservative party woman member. As consequence of some of its new organizational forms, the CWO has recruited what looks to be a 'third' type of Tory woman. She is neither someone seeking political office, nor one content to play the traditional auxiliary role of sandwich-maker and envelope-stuffer. At this point in time, her number may be small, her future role in the party unclear, and her relations with the older more traditional women members uncertain. Anecdotally attitudinal differences seem apparent between them. There is, consequently, potential for tension between these different types of Conservative woman member. This is something the CWO leadership may well need to manage, both as an internal CWO issue and in respect of the wider party, if what constitutes women's issues and women's interests becomes subject to competing intra-party claims. Here, then are questions for the leadership for the CWO. Rather crudely, and in sum, does it wish to reflect its members' views or to lead them? Third, are concerns about future developments which relate especially to the continuation of precisely those activities that underpin our conclusion that the CWO constitutes something more than a traditional auxiliary organization. The establishment of CWO Forums and Summits were particularly associated with Fiona Hodgson's time as Chairman of the CWO. If these were to subsequently decline, or if the organization's input into policy development was downplayed, as the apparent shift to the party in government (embodied by the Minister for

Women) suggests, judgements about the CWO's nature would need to be revised.

Acting for women (in a liberally-feminist fashion)?

If one test of women's substantive representation by the Conservative party is what its 2010 general election manifesto set out for women, then the Tories had much more to say then than they had in the previous three or four elections (Childs et al 2010). More competitive on the 'women's terrain' this time around, the party was addressing women's issues, not least women's work/life balance, that previously it had mostly left to the two other main parties. Notwithstanding criticisms that can be levelled at judging a party by its manifesto – not least the lack of detail and small readership – the Conservatives presented a series of representations about, and number of pledges for, women. Many of these reflected directly the output of the Women's Policy Group report of 2008, even if the manifesto was less detailed. The representations within these two documents often reflect feminist analysis in so far as gender relations are recognized to be bifurcated, hierarchical and problematic. Differences between women are also noted. In much of *Women in the World Today (WIWT)* and the general election manifesto representations have the potential to be read in tension with more traditional views of conservatism, and conservative notions of gender. At the same time, other high profile policies, most notably Cameron's commitment to recognize marriage in the tax system, stood out as pledges that came not from the women's part of the party. They appeared, too, to reinforce, at least according to critics, the traditional single-earner family, even if it did also cover those in civil partnerships, and did not identify the sex of the stay-at-home parent, as Cameron and May were often keen to emphasize.

In the election campaign proper, many of the women's issues addressed in the party's manifesto did not feature heavily. Nor for that matter, did May, or any other leading Tory woman. Behind the scenes there was no one person 'running' a 'women's campaign'. Apparently the party had become relaxed about winning women's votes.[10] And whilst a miniwomen's manifesto had been considered it was not put out in hard copy. The dedicated women's web-pages on the party's website were, again, a poor imitation of *Women in the World Today*. Moreover, the one women's issue that did garner significant media coverage during the campaign was the marriage tax break which, recall, did not have its origins in the women's policy development process. Nor did it, for that matter, find much support either from leading women in the party or women MPs more widely,[11] despite Labour's Harriet Harman putting May publicly on the spot to support it – which she did.

After the general election, the coalition negotiations and government programme threw up some surprising women's policy commitments.[12] As might be expected, many Conservative pledges for women remained: on Sure Start, maternity units, and ending the couples' penalty, for example. Flexible working would also be extended 'to all employees, consulting with business on how best to do so'; there would be shared parental leave, 'from the earliest stages of pregnancy'; and in the face of the gender pay gap the coalition would 'promote equal pay and take a range of measures to end discrimination in the workplace'. These policies were complemented with commitments to 'look to promote gender equality on company boards'. However on sexual violence, the funding of new rape crisis centres looked less secure. There was a shift in language from delivery to consideration. But most disconcerting to many commentators was the inclusion of a pledge to 'extend anonymity' to defendants in rape cases. This pledge was in *neither* the Conservative *nor* the Liberal Democrat 2010 manifestos, although it is said to have been a Liberal Democrat policy in the past. But it still begged the question of from whence it came in the furtive hours of the coalition negotiations. Was the coalition's fraternity to be metaphorically sealed on women's bodies? In the face of media and Parliamentarian, including Conservative women MPs' criticism, the leadership ultimately implemented a 'U-Turn' and the coalition retreated from its commitment.[13] Finally, and despite the Liberal Democrats being allowed to abstain in any parliamentary vote, the coalition government retained the Conservative policy of recognizing marriage and civil partnerships in the tax system which the Tories could, had they wanted to, given up during the coalition negotiations (they clearly did not want to).

Some in the media saw in the outcome of the Coalition Agreement the absence of women from the coalition negotiation teams and, by, implication, the marginal role of May, who had yet to be appointed Home Secretary and Secretary of State for Women and Equality, and clearly some distance from the inner circle around Cameron. Soon afterwards the government found itself under renewed gendered attack. This time the accusation was that women would be disproportionately disadvantaged by the coalition's budgetary cuts. Drawing on House of Commons Library research, Yvette Cooper, then Labour's shadow Foreign Secretary and Minister for Women, suggested that this would be most likely, given women's greater dependency upon the public sector as both its employees and its beneficiaries. It was also reported that May had herself warned the government that in devising its emergency budget, a gender equality audit was necessary.[14] A High Court ruling in December 2010 subsequently found against the Fawcett Society, who had contended that the 'government had acted unlawfully in formulating the budget last June without paying due regard to gender equality laws'.[15] Be that as it may – and partisan debate is likely to continue – questions remain as to which of the Conservative 2010 pledges for women are implemented as a matter of urgency, which are kicked into the long grass, and whether the party's other policies (those not necessarily explicitly gendered) impact disproportionately and negatively on women. The role of May looks critical here as the post of a Women's Minister should institutionalize the substantive representation of women within government. It may be, as claimed by senior women, that there are other Conservative women MPs who are also happy to work on this brief, but it is unclear whether any of the new intake of Conservative women MPs will take up the mantle, providing a supply pool of women keen to carry on with the Conservatives new women's agenda.[16] In the meantime, and as both Home Secretary as well as Minister for Women and Equality, it is inevitable that May's focus will be disproportionately on the former, as events force her to fire fight.

Taking conservatism seriously...

At least in its current manifestation, and as articulated by its leading parliamentary women, a liberal-feminist position is that most associated with the contemporary British Conservative party. At this point there is little evidence, bar the odd MP, of socially conservative or anti-feminist conservative women representatives, akin to those evident in the US (see Dodsoon 2006: Reingold 2008a). The contemporary British Conservative party, broadly speaking, and at least at the top, supports women's equal opportunities in the public sphere, especially in respect of paid employment. The party currently offers policies for women that are in line with a liberal-feminist take on these issues. In some cases, such as gender pay audits, advocacy of statutory regulation might even be thought to stretch the limits of liberal arguments about state intervention, and might also be said to stretch conservative reluctance to admit that differences in the pay gap result not from individual actions but are more systemic. In this way today's Conservative party may well be offering a more substantial feminist critique than in the past when it was said to be unable to accept the systematic nature of gender relations (Campbell 1987). At the same time, the party maintains a firm commitment to more traditional family values. The Conservative leader's personal commitment to the family as an institution embodies this. For Cameron, the family is to be bolstered by government substantively (through financial recognition) as well as symbolically (via rhetorical support for the institution of marriage and civil partnerships). The reconciliation of the potentially oppositional goals of equal opportunities in the public sphere and more traditional roles in the private sphere (and the ideologies upon which they are premised) manifests itself within the contemporary Conservative party through the concept of choice. Deploying choice permits the party to formally 'sidestep' normative questions about what women (and men) *should* do. The role for government is, understood here, merely to enable choice, not to overtly favour one over another particular decision. It is, then, up to women to choose – a choice that is made within the private sphere, within their families – how to reconcile work and family life. Critics will contend, no doubt, that this choice is misleading, not least given the lack of resources to support particular choices that women may make.

What of party members and gender issues? Three tendencies within the party have been identified: the Traditional Conservatives, the Thatcherites and the Liberal Conservatives (Bryson and Heppell 2010). Importantly, whilst Liberal Conservatives appear the most feminist in the abstract when it comes to specific policies it is the Traditional Conservatives who are the most feminist. This tendency is more female and working class than the others; more than half of Traditional Conservatives, compared to less than one third of the Liberal Conservatives are women. On the issue of the economy, women members are more noticeably 'wet' than male members. They are also more centrist, less post-materialist and more 'One Nation'. This should be food for thought given the dominance of the economy in current political debate. The neo-liberal political economy of the coalition government's programme for 2010–2015 is unlikely to sit easily with many of the Conservative party women members. Indeed, the old conflicts between 'wets' and 'dries' of the 1980s may well re-emerge and reconstitute itself, at least in part, as a conflict between women and men in the party. Turning more specifically to the 'women's terrain', which also cuts across questions about the economy and the size and role of the state, Conservative women members are more predisposed to feminism than men – on issues such as equal opportunities, women's suitability for politics, and the impact of women's paid work on family life. More specifically still, there are sex differences in party member attitudes on childcare, and the issue of equal pay polarizes women and men members' views further.

The contemporary Conservative party: What kind of feminized party?

The Conservative party of 2010 is more feminized than the its predecessors: descriptive representation is higher in the parliamentary and wider party; parts of the party are 'for women' and the party programme, as evidenced at least by the 2010 manifesto, constitutes women as a group and offers them a series of specific pledges. Yet, the distinction drawn between a feminist and a feminized party, and the corresponding ideal typology that it generates (outlined in the introduction to this book), suggests that describing a political party as more feminized than before does not tell us very much about the way in which it is feminized, nor about how it might compare with other parties. By addressing a series of questions that should better illuminate both dimensions, the contemporary Conservative party looks to fit within the Responsive Party II model (see page 7), albeit with some qualification in respect of the second dimension of representation. This ideal party type has (1) low representation on the first dimension of feminization (the integration of women in parliamentary elites), lacking quotas or having only poorly designed and implemented ones; (2) fewer women members than men members, but with an integrated women's organization; and (3) positive and feminist responses on the second dimension (the integration of women's concerns).

The first question points to evaluating the level of women's participation in the parliamentary party and in the party more broadly. Given the critique of critical mass theory, and given the ratios of women to men in society, sex parity is to be the benchmark for descriptive representation. Without levels of descriptive representation nearing parity – or at least in the short-term, doing so amongst newly elected representatives and other newly elected or newly appointed party positions – the charge of token representation is liable to be made and hard to refute. The case for descriptive representation does not, admittedly, require that any subsequent claim is made about the effect or impact of women's political presence, but what it must signify is that the sex of the representative or other party actor matters, at least in some respect. In being underpinned in this way, descriptive representation accepts analysis that regards sex and gender as a politically salient group identity requiring political presence. In other words, women cannot be represented descriptively by those who are not female. For this reason, the failure to adopt one of the three equality strategies to deliver greater descriptive representation looks like an admission that gender is not being taken seriously by a particular party or political institution. In contrast, a party that adopts equality rhetoric, equality promotion and equality guarantees – and one should consider these as progressive strategies in both meanings of the word – would be judged superior to one that only adopts the first, or one that adopts the first and second but not the third. This would especially be true if the party also returned few women amongst its parliamentary representation or had few women in posts within its party structures. In line with this, the contemporary British Conservative party scores poorly. To be sure, improvements in its parliamentary representation were evident in 2010. But, as has been repeatedly stated, it falls far short of parity even amongst its newly elected MPs. In terms of women's participation in the wider party, there is too often a lack of information to draw strong conclusions. It is said that party membership is 40 percent female, that women constitute nearly one third of the National Convention, just under one quarter of regional officers and 40 percent of regional chairman. Women's presence on other committees is not forthcoming.

The second and third questions look to whether women's participation is substantive or symbolic, and integrated or segregated; whether the 'women's part' of the party is formally integrated into the wider party structure and policy making bodies.[17] Here, the pre-Cameron history was one of marginalization in the late 1990s amid rumour of abolition. Since then the CWO looks to have experienced a revival and has been more active, not least in respect of the development of women's policy in the middle years of the 2000s. Engagement between the CWO and other parts of the party with responsibility for women – most importantly the Shadow Minister for Women, via the Women's Policy Group – are suggestive of the fact that the Conservative party recognizes, or at least did so in the period under study, that women constitute a group within the party that warrant institutional support for group representation. Here, then, is acknowledgment of the existence of women's issues that should be addressed as part of the formal policy making procedures of the party. Of course, there are criticisms to be leveled at the party's structures for the substantive representation of women. The women's policy review was not part of, nor central to, the party's six independent policy reviews, but rather bolted on. The women's parts of the party are hardly well resourced. And as time progressed, it became clear that the driver of policy was the Shadow Minister for women and much less the Women's Policy Group *per se*. The lines of accountability between the different women's part of the party were never clarified but increasingly seem top-down from the Shadow Minister, a state of play not necessarily appreciated by other women within the party and women party members. It also begs questions once again of intra-party democracy (Childs 2010). Nevertheless, during the party's modernization under Cameron, women's issues were articulated to the party leadership, and the policy proposals for women that emerged drew on debates that had been had within the CWO leadership, and via CWO annual conferences, AGMs, and Forums, with women party members.

The fourth guiding question asks whether a party regards women as a corporate entity capable of being represented (both descriptively and substantively) and if so, whether the party is susceptible to feminist arguments for this. The answers to the first three questions just outlined suggest affirmative answers in both respects. But there is a secondary dimension to this question, namely, about how the party makes the case for these. Here the conclusion is less straightforward. The case for women's group representation within the Conservative party structure is underpinned by recognition that women have issues that are particular to them, and perspectives that derive from women's gendered experiences and concerns. Women party members, at least of the older, more traditional type, may well reject any notion that such an appreciation reflects, or indeed has to reflect, a feminist consciousness, although the party member survey indicates that women are more likely to score highly on the feminist index and to support feminist policies. Those in posts 'for women' within the party are more likely to openly acknowledge a liberal-feminist conservative feminism. It is probably the case that the party leaders were driven by more base instincts – electoral instrumentalism in advance of the 2010 general election.

The fifth question addresses the Conservative party's and coalition government's policies and whether, irrespective of motive, the Tories tactical use of 'choice' offers the potential to reconcile any latent or actual tension between the party's explicit policies for women and its wider policies on the economy (which are neo-liberal), together with Cameron's emphasis on marriage and the family (which, whilst tempered by also covering civil partnerships, would be more easily classified as traditionally or socially conservative). Subsequent government decisions might yet invite greater critical comment from feminists in wider society and from some women within the party. These may well see the impact of budgetary cuts as disproportionately and negatively falling on women, and see the emphasis on marriage as old-fashioned and misjudged, and symbolic rather than substantive. Ultimately, and as clichéd as it is, only time will tell whether the feminization of the Conservative party between 2005–2010 contributes to a feminization of government over the 2010 Parliament and whether it gives rise to a further feminization of the Conservative party, voluntary, professional and parliamentary, before and after the next election.

Methods Appendix

Sex, Gender and the Conservative Party draws on eight research components, combining qualitative and quantitative research methods. (i) A survey of party members; (ii) in-depth, semi-structured interviews with Conservative MPs, Peers and party professionals; (iii) focus groups of party members; (iv) focus groups of non-partisan and floating voters; (v) analysis of parliamentary behaviour on 'women's legislation'; (vi) qualitative analysis of Conservative policy over time; (vii) secondary data analysis of the British Election Study (BES) 2010; and (viii) secondary analysis of comparative literature on women's representation in European centre-right political parties. In this appendix, we discuss the implementation of the first four. The others are, for ease of reading, addressed in the main body of the book.

(i) Party Member Survey

A specially commissioned survey of Conservative party members was conducted in July 2009. The survey was conducted by YouGov using an internet panel of Conservative party members. A sample of 1690 respondents was recruited, and the results reported here are not weighted in any way. We decided to work with the raw data for two reasons: first, there are no known population parameters that could be used for the Conservative party membership's current demographic profile; second, a previous YouGov survey of the party's members conducted at the time of the last leadership election (December 2005) produced an extremely accurate prediction of that election on the basis of raw data (i.e., to within one percentage point of the actual result). Attempts to weight that data on that occasion made no appreciable difference to the outcome. The fieldwork was conducted July 24–27, 2009.

The main demographic characteristics of the sample are reported in Table A.1. These show differences from previous surveys of the party's membership; Seyd and Whiteley's well-known study of the party in the early 1990s (1994: 50) revealed a membership which was more evenly divided between men and women (51/49), was even more middle class (86 percent coming from the salariat, routine non-manual or petit bourgeoisie), and older (67 percent being more than 55 years of age) than our sample. Even so, as might be expected, our sample has a distinctly middle class, middle aged and southern profile. This is broadly consistent with previous findings about the party's support base. In addition, we note that nearly three-quarters of the sample regarded themselves as middle class (though only half thought their parents had been), and only a fifth were regular religious observants (in that they attended religious ceremonies at least once a month). The average Conservative member has been a party member for 26 years, reflecting the relatively aged profile of the sample (55); 31 percent consider themselves either very or fairly active, with 17 percent feeling they are more active than five years earlier and 30 percent less active.

Table A.1 Demographic Profile of Conservative Party Members, 2009

Male	Female	18–34	35–54	55	ABC1	C2DE	London	Rest of South	Midlands/ Wales	North	Scotland
60	40	16	21	62	73	27	14	47	18	16	4

Note: All figures and percentages.

(ii)   MP and Peers Interviews

Interviews with MPs and Peers were undertaken between June 2008 and January 2009, with the majority taking place between September and November 2008.[1]

We sought to interview *all* Conservative women MPs and Peers (the total population) alongside a matched sample of male MPs and Peers. Interviewing both women and men was designed to meet criticisms levelled at research that relies upon interview data from only women (for example, Childs 2004). Our matching strategy for MPs looked to pair men with women on the following bases: cohort (year of entry to the House of Commons); date of birth; size of parliamentary majority; second party competitor; urban/rural seat; and the percentage of professional, social renters and non-white populations in the constituency (Waller and Criddle 2007). For the Lords, our criteria were: date of creation of peerage and date of birth. These approaches often identified more than one suitable man per woman, as would be likely given the greater numbers of Conservative men MPs and Peers relative to women.

As we expected we did not secure interviews with all Conservative women Parliamentarians. However, overall we interviewed a total of 21 women and 24 men. Out of the total number of 17 Conservative women MPs we interviewed ten (nearly 60 percent). We also interviewed nine male MPs, who 'in the round' appeared more reluctant to participate in the research. The matching, again as expected, was not perfect, although in eight out of the ten cases the women MPs were well-matched; only in one of these was the match somewhat less than perfect. In terms of age, the sample of women MPs included younger and older women MPs, those born in the 1940s, 1950s and 1960s, although the sample included more women born in the latter two decades, with a couple of the older (and retiring) cohort not participating. It also included women from the 1992, 1997 and 2001 and 2005 intakes but not those from 1983 or 1987. There was also a good representation of front bench women MPs. In terms of the size of electoral majority in their constituencies, the participating and non-participating women were very similar, albeit it with participating MPs more likely to be facing Liberal Democrat opponents as the second placed party. There were very few differences in terms of urban/rural distinctions and the other demographic differences, as might be expected given that these were all Conservative seats.

From the Lords 11 out of a total of 35 Conservative women Peers were interviewed – just under one-third – alongside 15 male Peers. In contrast to the lower chamber where women MPs were apparently keen to participate, in the Lords it was much harder to confirm interviews with women. One-third is, even so, a fair sample size for qualitative interviews. In terms of matching, eight women were closely matched; three were not; and there were four 'extra' men.

The interviews were undertaken by Childs, Webb and Marthaler, the project's research officer. Interviews were, for the most part, conducted in the Palace of Westminster, with a handful taking place either in MPs and Peers' homes or their offices outside of the parliamentary estate. Most interviews were digitally recorded, with one (of a female Peer) conducted by telephone. Of those that were recorded all were fully transcribed. The interviews were based on an interview schedule (see below), although given the nature of semi-structured interviews the schedule guided, rather than determined, the order of the topics covered. It was felt that all interviewees' responses, noting the handful more male than female participants, should be included in the analysis on the grounds that the differences in number were not sufficient to unbalance our analysis, and that their insights would be useful. This is in part, of course, also a reflection of the fact that qualitative analysis does not seek to provide representative accounts, generalizable beyond the sample.

Interview Schedule MPs & Peers

Conservative Ideology
- what does being Consv mean to you?
  o prompts : economic/social sphere; suggest social morality (ie, liberty/authority) green issues
  o role of state

Party Direction
- where do you think party is?
- where is party going?
- where should party be going?

Modernization
- what understanding of – personal and party's own
- prompts: policy, organization, communications
  o what drivers of
  o with whom associated – prompt Cameron

Policy-making
- reflections on – prompt – democratic, transparent, fair,
  o indivs key to this –
  o role of MPs in this
  o role of party members
  o party organizations Board, Consv future, CWO, etc
  o special advisors around DC

Women's policy
- DC said party more family friendly – understanding
- DC said party more women friendly – understanding
- are there women's issues – what are they?
  o prompt views on:
    ▪ tax policy re: marriage
    ▪ right request flexible working for those children under age 18
    ▪ parental cf maternity leave
    ▪ compulsory pay audits
    ▪ human trafficking
    ▪ abortion
- is party becoming feminist? what their understanding
- Do you think that the loss of support from women voters was significant in explaining the general election outcomes since 1997?
- If so, what could be done to attract more women voters to the party once again?
  o prompt – policies
  o prompt – communication – separate women's manifesto

Party Representation

Political recruitment
- *MPs ONLY* – reflections on own selection –
- selectorates' criteria

ALL
- reflections on way which MPs selected – prompt – democratic, transparent, fair
- what role being local candidates plays in selection
- comment on reforms parlia selection
  o prompt: support primary list candidates
  o prompt: primaries
  o prompt: sex quotas at shortlisting stages
  o prompt: AWS
- Reflections on intra-party conflict – prompt – leader too much say?
- who in party favour/who is against

Women's under-repre
- under-repre women in Parliament – thoughts no.s Consv women MPs/Peers ie, does this matter? If so, why? If not why not?
- explanations for women's under-repre
- what should be done? why?
  o prompts – justice, symbolic, substantive

SRW
- claim women more likely act for women – views on this –
- can you give an examples of this?
- views on NL women – MPs and Ministers
  o prompt – feminized agenda?
  o feminized style?

Party Organization:
- what most important parts of Consv Party
- garner views on:
  o CWO
  o VC women – Margot James
  o Shadow Minister for Women – Theresa May
  o WPG – have read Report Women in the Today's World

(iii)   Party Member Focus Groups[2]

Six focus groups were conducted by Ipsos-MORI in June 2008. Three focus groups each were held in London and Bristol. Tables A.1 and A.2 show the constituencies from which the sample for the focus groups was recruited, along with the appropriate local Conservative Associations. Although Bristol is the largest city in the west of England, the constituencies in the surrounding areas are mainly semi-rural or rural, providing us with a suitable comparative split.

Table A.2   London Constituencies

Parliamentary Constituency	Local Conservative Association
Orpington	Orpington
Hammersmith	Hammersmith
Putney	Putney (Wandsworth)
Wimbledon	Wimbledon
Kensington	Kensington, Chelsea & Fulham
Southwark	Bermondsey & Old Southwark
Vauxhall	Vauxhall
Battersea	Battersea (Wandsworth)

Table A.3   Bristol Constituencies

Parliamentary Constituency	Local Conservative Association
Weston Super Mare	Weston Super Mare
Woodspring	Woodspring
Wells	Wells
Forest of Dean	Forest of Dean
Bristol West	Bristol & South Gloucestershire*
Bristol South West	Bristol & South Gloucestershire*
Bristol North West	Bristol & South Gloucestershire*

*Bristol and South Gloucestershire constituency association covers three separate Bristol parliamentary constituencies.

As the Conservative party Central Office could not disclose the contact details of constituency party members without their explicit permission, a revision of the proposed methodology was required in order to recruit the focus groups. Party officers were contacted at each of the local associations and asked to circulate an 'opt-in' form to their registered members. In seeking support for this, a letter from the Party Chairman Caroline Spelman and Liz St Clair, the Woman's Officer, was sent to show that Central Office officially recognized the research. Constituency party members who were interested in taking part in the focus groups then filled in the form and returned it directly to Ipsos MORI. Upon receipt of this form their details were logged in a spreadsheet which was used to recruit for the focus groups.

In order to ensure the focus groups contained participants from a range of backgrounds, quotas were set on sex, age, ethnicity, constituency and level of activism. The sex quota was particularly important; one male, one female and one mixed group would take place in both London and Bristol. By organizing the groups in this way we could identify whether attitudes and perceptions towards the subject of descriptive representation would change across different group environments. Due to difficulties in recruitment (particularly the low number of 'opt-ins' from the

Table A.4   Target and Actual Quotas for London and Bristol Focus Groups

Group 1	10 people recruited according to the following quota: **8 attendees** Age – younger Sex – mix Constituency – at least three Ethnicity – at least 1 BME Activism – at least 1 constituency officer
Group 2	10 people recruited according to the following quota: **9 attendees** Age – younger Sex – male Constituency – at least three Ethnicity – at least 1 BME Activism – at least 1 constituency officer
Group 3	10 people recruited according to the following quota: **6 attendees** Age – older Sex – female Constituency – at least three Ethnicity – at least 1 BME Activism – at least 1 constituency officer
Group 4	10 people recruited according to the following quota: **7 attendees** Age – older Sex – mix Constituency – at least three Ethnicity – at least 1 BME Activism – at least 1 constituency officer
Group 5	10 people recruited according to the following quota: **8 attendees** Age – younger Sex – male Constituency – at least three Ethnicity – at least 1 BME Activism – at least 1 constituency officer
Group 6	10 people recruited according to the following quota: **5 attendees** Age – older Sex – female Constituency – at least three Ethnicity – at least 1 BME Activism – at least 1 constituency officer

Table A.5 Focus Group Breakdown, Pre- and Post-Questionnaire Data

		Group 1 London mixed	Group 2 London all male	Group 3 London all female	Group 4 Bristol mixed	Group 5 Bristol all male	Group 6 Bristol all female
Sex	Male	5	7	–	5	8	–
	Female	4	–	6	4	–	5
	Not stated	–	1	2	–	–	–
Age	Under 55	8	6	1	1	1	2
	Over 55	1	2	7	7	7	1
	Not stated	–	–	–	1	–	2
Officer/Activist	Yes	4	4	6	5	7	3
Regularly attend party meetings	Yes	–	1	–	1	–	1
	No	4	3	3	2	1	–
	Not stated	5	4	5	6	7	4
Ethnic minority	Yes	–	1	1	1	–	–
	Total	9	8	8	9	8	5
	Total (attendees)	9	8	6	7	8	5

Bristol constituencies), the quotas on all but sex had to be relaxed somewhat. However, where possible they were maintained, and the focus groups still contained a good range of participants. Table A.4 outlines the target and actual quotas and Table A.5 presents attendee data based on the pre-post-questionnaire returns.

In designing the focus groups, we anticipated three possible sources of variation among our participants:

1) Sex
2) Gender-generation
3) Metropolitan/Provincial

The first expectation reflects existing research on women's and men's attitudes, where sex differences, though rarely absolute and often quite small, are found in survey data of mass public opinion (Campbell et al 2010; Campbell 2006: 103). The second expectation reflects findings from the voting behaviour literature (Campbell 2006; Norris 2001) which suggests both that younger women have a greater propensity to vote for the Labour party than both younger men, and older women and men, and that ideological gender-generation gaps underpin these, with younger women more left-wing and more feminist (Campbell 2006). Consequently, we might expect younger Conservative women party members to be relatively more left wing and more feminist than older Conservative women, as well as male Conservative party members both young and old. This second expectation also reflects the characterization of Conservative party women members in the 1990s of being of two distinct types (Maguire 1998): first, the traditional woman party member and secondly, the 'career' woman who was seeking political office. We would expect these two types to be from distinct generations, with the latter being younger than the former. The final expectation reflects a concern that a focus on the changes undertaken at the elite level regarding gender may reflect a metropolitan bias which lack support elsewhere in the country. Previous observations (Childs 2008) suggest that many gender equality activists in the party, and the manifestations of these, such as Women2win and the CWO Women's Forums, might be considered London-centric and predominantly attract atypical members – most notably, younger and more business-oriented women.

The first two expectations underpinned the decision to hold single-sex and mixed groups. These would permit comparisons between the responses of women and men when they are discussing the issues in single and mixed settings. The moderators were of the opposite sex, so the all-male groups had female moderators and vice versa. This was a deliberate strategy advocated by Ipsos-MORI based on the view (and contra some feminist research methods) that in single-sex groups moderators of the opposite sex are more likely to receive more sophisticated responses than moderators of the same sex. This is because focus group participants do not assume that the moderator knows or understands what a particular focus group member means when they speak.

It is important to note that, as with all qualitative research, the focus groups were designed to be illustrative rather than statistically valid. It therefore provides insight but does not allow strong conclusions to be drawn about the extent to which views are held in any quantitative sense among Conservative party members overall. A major reason for using focus groups at the early stage of the research was that we intended the group discussions to help formulate and refine the hypotheses that we would subsequently test in the quantitative stage of work. The survey of party members and elites would be shaped in part by the findings of the focus groups.

When the focus groups were conducted, all the national opinion polls were showing the Conservatives with an ample lead over Labour (ranging from 13 to 22 points), enough to ensure a substantial Commons majority at a general election. Conservative confidence was reinforced by having seen the poll leads recently translated into substantive electoral victories, with the best local election results for decades and a first by-election gain for 26 years at Crewe & Nantwich. This may have had a particularly pronounced effect on party morale in the London groups: Boris Johnson's election as London Mayor being perhaps the highest profile success with continuing news stories from the new regime at City Hall a constant reminder of this victory.

Focus Group Schedule

Key Questions	Notes	Time
1. Introduction		5 mins
Thank attendees for taking part. Introduce self, and client/note taker if present, Ipsos MORI and explain the aim of the discussion (i.e. discussion on the future of the Conservative Party – do not mention gender at this stage). Role of Ipsos MORI – research organisation, all opinions valid etc. Confidentiality: Remind respondents how they were recruited for the Group, (i.e. List of Party members provided by the Conservative Party, should have been contacted by telephone and invited to take part). Reassure them that all responses are anonymous and that information about individual cases will not be passed on to any third party. Ask permission to record/video and check that everyone has signed the video permission form.	**Welcome**: orientates interviewees, gets them prepared to take part in the discussion. Outlines the 'rules' of the interview (including those we are required to tell them about under MRS and Data Protection Act guidelines).	
2. Icebreaker		10 mins
What are your views on the Conservative Party in general at the moment? Talking about the Conservative Party in general, if the Party was a car, what would it be? Why? **(WRITE ON FLIP CHART)** What do you think of David Cameron as Party Leader? What are the important issues for the party? And what are the important issues for the country as a whole? What does the Party need to do, or to change, in order to win votes? In your opinion, how is the party changing? **PROBE: ARE THESE GOOD OR BAD CHANGES?** How would you define 'modernisation'? Are you aware of what the Party and David Cameron are looking to do to modernise? PROBE. What do you know about it? What are some of the goals of modernisation?	General questions allow interviewees to ease into the discussion and should give some interesting background information on their attitude towards the Conservative Party in general. Should also give a good impression of satisfaction/dissatisfaction with the current leadership and the direction of the Conservative Party. Do not probe specifically for gender here but note any spontaneous references to it.	

Focus Group Schedule – *continued*

Key Questions	Notes	Time
3. Gender Roles and Equality		10 mins
Just to start out, when you hear the word 'equality' what comes to mind? What contexts do you associate with 'equality'? PROBE: social, political, work, etc. What sorts of groups does this apply to? (**PROBE: ETHNICITY, AGE, RELIGION, DISABILITY, GENDER. LOOK FOR SPONTANEOUS GENDER MENTIONS)** I'd now like to discuss equality between men and women. To what extent do you think that this is an issue in society at the moment? In politics? **PROBE ON:** – Importance – Gender roles – Barriers to equality (if any) – Work – Home (In family, looking after children etc.) – Politics	This section will focus the discussion around the gender issue and will gauge the group's general views on the matter on a traditional feminist spectrum. Discussion should highlight opinions on the impact of gender across all areas. From work and politics, to the home. Gauge groups views on a traditional feminist spectrum. (Key Question)	
4. Women's Issues/Substantive Representation of Women		30 mins
What issues, if any, do you think are specific to women, i.e. are 'women's issues'? **PROBE ON ISSUES: WRITE ON FLIPCHART** PROBES: Health, education, security, as well as more explicit women's issues like domestic violence and the 'Glass ceiling etc', and ask which they associate with men or women. (**LOOK FOR MENTIONS OF RECENT ABORTION/IVF DEBATES)**	The order from here onwards is interchangeable. It is important that the discussion flows naturally. This is so we get an idea of relative importance by seeing which issues are raised spontaneously. Each section needs to be discussed equally thoroughly though.	

Focus Group Schedule – *continued*

Key Questions	Notes	Time
CAN INTRODUCE IPSOS MORI POLITICAL MONITOR DATA (BY GENDER) ON IMPT ISSUES HERE AS EVIDENCE In your view, how important are women's rights/equality generally? How about in today's society? How would you compare issues around women's rights with other issues such as age, social class, race and religion? What are the differences? Similarities? How do you think the Conservative Party should go about trying to win women's votes? Should the Conservative Party try to appeal to women separately to men? Why/Why Not? PROBE *If **necessary** read out statistics on Conservative's declining share of women's vote in 2005 General Election: They had 33% turnout of women's votes in 2001 – this dropped to 32% turnout in 2005. Labour got 38% of women's votes, more than the 34% among men (first time in our polling history that Labour had won a higher proportion of women's votes than men's). Within this, Conservatives' share of the female vote between the ages 18–24 dropped by 2%, 25–34 by 4%, and 35–54 by 4%. Women over 55 increased their support by 1%.* PROBE whether taking these statistics into account; the Conservatives do need to appeal to women separately? QUOTE (will have on handout as well): *"I am proud that the Conservative Party is taking the lead on the issue of sexual violence against women. But I want us to do more. I want to make sure that when we come into government, we have an integrated strategy to tackle all violence against women. Over the weeks and months ahead, the Conservative Party will be developing an integrated strategy to tackle violence against women – and we will be consulting leading experts as we do so. This is an issue that is vitally important to me. It's about public attitudes towards women. It's about making people responsible for their actions. Ultimately, it's about the sort of society I want Britain to be."* – **David Cameron**	This also follows on well from the more general gender issues, shaping, and adding more detail and focus to the discussion and helping it to flow freely. Also, will find out whether gender is as important to people as current 'hot' issues such as race and religion. This section covers Substantive Representation of Women. i.e. the effect that female representation has on the issues etc being focused on. Quotes will be available on a handout Read out quotes (and pass out printouts of quotes) during discussion so to illustrate male and female views on 'women's issues' i.e. whether male/female representation alters issues debated/legislated on	

Focus Group Schedule – *continued*

Key Questions	Notes	Time
QUOTE (will have on handout as well): "*I want to make this country more family-friendly…The world is changing, men want to be more involved in bringing up their children…Yesterday, Theresa May set out our plans to offer all parents twelve months' parental leave, to be shared by mother and father as they choose…More flexible working. Extending parental leave. Corporate responsibility. More NHS health visitors. I know what some of you might be thinking. All this family-friendly stuff he's going on about: it's not really very Conservative, is it? Let me tell you why I think it's not just Conservative, but it's seriously Conservative.*" – **David Cameron**		
QUOTE (will have on handout as well): What are your initial thoughts on these statements? How important will the Conservative Party's focus on women's issues be in winning elections? Would this make the party seem more electable and 'moderate', or not? PROBE: Why/why not? Why do you say that? Do you think the party should be working at being seen as 'moderate' or not? **KEY ISSUE.** IF NO: What do you think WOULD make the party more electable? How do the Conservatives compare on this issue to other Parties (especially Labour)? How does this fit in with 'traditional Conservative values'? What impact will it have on party unity? **IF NOT MENTIONED BEFORE** Do you think the Conservative MPs are right/not right to want to reduce the upper limit for abortions from 24 weeks? Why? **IF NOT MENTIONED BEFORE** What do you think about Iain Duncan Smith's comment that IVF clinics should consider 'need for a father' before allowing women to begin fertility treatment? Why?	Particular emphasis here will be given to the potential impact women's issues could have on how electable the Conservative Party appears to the electorate, and whether focusing on women will damage or improve Party unity.	
BREAK		10 mins

Focus Group Schedule – *continued*

Key Questions	Notes	Time
5. Substantive Representation of Women and Direct Representation of Women Combined		5 mins
Do you think that male/female MPs have different perspectives on the same issues? Which issues? KEY ISSUE. IF IT HELPS, YOU CAN PROMPT USING THE LIST OF ISSUES FROM BEFORE.	This section links SRW and DRW. It will help the discussion to flow naturally.	
6. Women's Representation/Direct Representation of Women		30 mins
Are women under-represented at Westminster? Why/why not? Does this matter to you? To the party? 9% of Conservative Party MPs are female – does this matter to you? To the party? KEY ISSUE. Why, in your view, are women under-represented (IF AGREE THEY ARE), overall and among Conservative MPs? PROBE; Do you think it is an issue of 'supply-side' or 'demand-side'?	The significance of representation needs to be pushed. Having previously discussed the general role of women in society the Group can now look in greater detail at the Conservative Party itself.	
QUOTE (will have on handout as well): *Far too few MPs are women.* *And nowhere is it more urgent that the process start than in the Conservative Party. Looking at its elected representatives, you will see a predominantly white, male party.* *Given that we now see an ethnically diverse society, where women increasingly play a major role, the Conservative Party just doesn't look like the people that it is claiming to represent.* **Theresa May**	Supply side: Not enough women putting themselves forward. Demand Side: Party not selecting those women who do put themselves forward. Quote will be available on a handout.	
QUOTE (will have on handout as well): *I don't think it matters if you're a man, woman, young or old – all that matters is that whoever is in charge has got there on their own merit.* – **Ann Widdecombe** PROBE for thoughts on these statements. Does the level of women's representation make a difference to debates and issues that are prioritized in the Conservative Party and Government? Why/why not? KEY ISSUE.	Use quotes to illustrate range of views in the Party. Could be read earlier depending on how the moderator feels the discussion is flowing.	

Focus Group Schedule – *continued*

Key Questions	Notes	Time
IF NOT COVERED AT THE START: What are you aware of the Conservative Party doing to achieve more of a gender balance, if anything? **PROBE**: rhetoric, Primaries, A lists etc. **WRITE ON FLIPCHART** Also, what do you think of these measures, and will they work?	At the last election 128 out of 644 MPs were women, 17 Conservative MPs were women, only three more on the previous election.	
Bearing this in mind:	Whether the Party, and Parliament, should be statistically representative of society is a vitally important question. We need to find out why people feel women are under represented and whether it is something that could, and should, be improved. We also need to establish the extent to which this is a priority.	
What do you think should the Conservative Party be doing in future? PROBE: Rhetoric/promotion/guarantees? What will work? Is it a matter for centre or local parties? What about in local government/European Parliament?	Examples – Rhetoric: speeches, platforms, writings etc. Exhort female candidates to come forward etc. – Promotion: Set targets; give training/ financial help to female candidates etc. – Guarantees: Quotas on Party candidates (either Party or legislative), reserved seats etc.	
How does this fit in with 'traditional Conservative values'?		
How will this impact on party unity, if at all? How? PROBE.		
What about what other parties are doing (especially Labour)?		
IF TIME: What is the role of the electoral system? I.e. Is achieving equality 'easier' in proportional systems?	Again, it is important to establish the impact that this could have on Party values and unity and whether the Conservative's need to change to progress.	

Focus Group Schedule – *continued*

Key Questions	Notes	Time
7. Wrap Up		15 mins
Is gender balance and equality something appropriate for the Conservative Party to prioritise? Why/why not? PROBE What would the effect be on electoral appeal? PROBE whether this would mean the Party was turning towards the centre ground, and whether this is seen as a good or bad thing.	Should probe whether feminisation would help the party to convince the electorate that it is turning towards the political centre.	
What would be your ideal Conservative Party? What would the role of women/focus on women's issues be in it? How realistic is this?	If so, whether this is likely to gain them more electoral support.	
	Finally, it will be interesting to see how the debate has shaped interviewee's ideas on their ideal Conservative Party.	
Distribute post-group questionnaires		
Thank participants and hand out £30 incentives.		

Party Members Opt-in Form

Research on the future direction of the Conservative Party

The Universities of Bristol and Sussex are undertaking a series of focus groups among Conservative Party members, looking into their views on a range of important issues about the future direction of the Conservative Party. Ipsos MORI, the independent market research company, have been commissioned by the Universities to carry out these focus groups. The groups will provide constituency members with an opportunity to voice their opinions on the party and should be very interesting to participate in. There is a £30 'thank you' for everyone who takes part in a group.

The focus groups on the future direction of the Conservative Party will take place in the next few weeks at a location convenient to you.

If you are interested in taking part then please **forward this email to** [...] filling in the requested details below. It is very important that you fill in this information as Ipsos MORI does not have access to your details otherwise.

Alternatively you can print off a copy of this form, complete it, and return it to the freepost address: ..... You will not need a stamp.

It can also be faxed to...

If you wish to contact...directly with any queries or to confirm your participation by telephone then he can be reached directly on...

If you do volunteer to take part, an Ipsos MORI recruiter may be in touch in the next few weeks to arrange your attendance at one of the focus groups. Please note that not everyone who returns this form will necessarily be contacted to take part.

Please reply by returning this form by **Wednesday 16th July**. Once again, on behalf of the Conservative Party, Bristol & Sussex Universities and Ipsos MORI, thank you for your interest.

Your details

Title:
First name:
Surname:
Name of local party:
Home address:
Primary telephone number (important):
Alternative telephone number:
Email address:

Please forward this to...by **16th July**.

Alternatively, if completed by hand then please fill in and return to the following address:

....

(iv) Voter Focus Groups

Seven discussion groups in total were organized and conducted by Ipsos-MORI in December 2008, involving 'floating voters' and members of the public that have voted for the Conservative party but were not actually party members. Three were held in Harrow and four in Borough (sites of Ipsos-MORI). The purpose of splitting the groups over two different venues was to ensure that we could recruit members of the public from outside of London as well inner city residents. Some effort was also made to recruit participants from marginal constituencies (where the margin between the 1st and 2nd place in the 2005 election was less than 15 percent) such as: Hemel Hempstead; St. Albans; Watford; Croydon Central; Battersea; Harrow West; Hendon; and Eltham.

In order to ensure the discussion groups contained participants from a range of backgrounds, quotas were set on sex, age, ethnicity, and social grades. The sex quota was particularly important; one male, one female and one mixed group would take place in both locations as well as an extra mixed group in Borough. By organizing the groups in this way we could identify whether attitudes and perceptions towards the subject of gender representation would change across different group environments.

Table A.6 Borough Voter Focus Groups

	GROUP 1	GROUP 2	GROUP 3	GROUP 7
DATE	Thursday 4th December	Thursday 4th December	Wednesday 3rd December	Monday 15th December
GROUP DESCRIPTION	10 people recruited to the following quotas 9 attendees	10 people recruited to the following quotas 9 attendees	10 people recruited to the following quotas 8 attendees	10 people recruited to the following quotas 7 attendees
	Age – mix	Age – mix	Age – mix	Age – mix
	Sex – mix	Sex – male	Sex – female	Sex – mix
	Ethnicity – at least 1 BME	Ethnicity – at least 1 BME	Ethnicity – at least 1 BME	Ethnicity – at least 1 BME
	Social Grade: ABC1	Social Grade: ABC1	Social Grade: C2DE	Social Grade: ABC1
	Voter: Floating	Voter: Conservative	Voter: Floating	Voter: Floating

Table A.7 Harrow Voter Focus Groups

	GROUP 4	GROUP 5	GROUP 6
DATE	Monday 8th December	Monday 8th December	Thursday 11th December
GROUP DESCRIPTION	10 people recruited to the following quotas	10 people recruited to the following quotas	10 people recruited to the following quotas
	9 attendees	6 attendees	9 attendees
	Age – mix	Age – mix	Age – mix
	Sex – male	Sex – mix	Sex – female
	Ethnicity – at least 1 BME	Ethnicity – at least 1 BME	Ethnicity – at least 1 BME
	Social Grade: C2DE	Social Grade: C2DE	Social Grade: ABC1
	Voter: Floating	Voter: Conservative	Voter: Conservative

Focus Group Schedule

Key Questions	Notes	Time
1. Introduction		5 mins
Thank attendees for taking part.	**Welcome**: orientates interviewees, gets them prepared to take part in the discussion.	
Introduce self, and client/note taker if present, Ipsos MORI and explain the aim of the discussion (i.e. discussion on politics in Britain – do <u>not</u> mention gender at this stage).		
Role of Ipsos MORI – research organisation, all opinions valid etc.		
Confidentiality: Reassure them that all responses are anonymous and that information about individual cases will not be passed on to any third party.	Outlines the 'rules' of the interview (including those we are required to tell them about under MRS and Data Protection Act guidelines).	
Ask permission to record/video and check that everyone has signed the video permission form.		
2. Icebreaker		10 mins
What are your views on the Conservative Party in general at the moment?	General questions allow interviewees to ease into the discussion and should give some interesting background information on their attitude towards the Conservative Party in general.	
Talking about the Conservative Party in general, if the Party was a car (or could be adapted e.g. drink, animal, person at a party etc) what would it be? Why? (**WRITE ON FLIP CHART**) LOOK FOR GENDER REFERENCES BUT DON'T PROBE YET		
What about the Labour Party?		
Have you noticed any changes in the Conservative Party over the past couple of years? PROBE What have you noticed?		
Does the Conservative Party seem less extreme/more in touch than it has been previously?	Should also give a good impression of satisfaction/dissatisfaction with the current leadership and the direction of the Conservative Party.	
Do you think the Conservatives have succeeded in shaking off the 'nasty party image'? IF NOT MENTIONED ALREADY		
What do you think of David Cameron as Conservative Party leader?	Do not probe specifically for gender here but note any spontaneous references to it.	
What kind of policies do you associate with the Conservative Party under David Cameron? PROBE Are these different than under previous Conservative leaders?		
What kind of policies influence your choice of what party to vote for?		
Which party do you think is currently the most competent to manage the economy? SKIP IF SHORT OF TIME	Try not to spend too much time here. This section is for context purposes only.	
Do you agree with the Conservatives' claim that Britain is a 'broken society'? IF YES, PROBE: what do the Conservatives mean by this?		
Which party has the best approach for solving this problem? SKIP IF SHORT OF TIME		

Focus Group Schedule – *continued*

Key Questions	Notes	Time
3. Gender Roles and Equality		10 mins
Moving on, when you hear the word 'equality' what comes to mind? What contexts do you associate with 'equality'? PROBE: social, political, work, etc. What sorts of groups does this apply to? (**PROBE: ETHNICITY, AGE, RELIGION, DISABILITY, GENDER. LOOK FOR SPONTANEOUS GENDER MENTIONS**) I'd now like to discuss equality between men and women. To what extent do you think that this is an issue in society at the moment? In politics? **PROBE ON:** – Importance – Gender roles – Barriers to equality (if any) – Work – Home (In family, looking after children etc.) – Politics	This section will focus the discussion around the gender issue and will gauge the group's general views on the matter on a traditional feminist spectrum. Discussion should highlight opinions on the impact of gender across all areas. From work and politics, to the home. Gauge groups views on a traditional feminist spectrum.	
4. Women's Issues/Substantive Representation of Women		30 mins
What issues, if any, do you think are specific to women, i.e. are 'women's issues'? **PROBE ON ISSUES: WRITE ON FLIPCHART** PROBES: Health, education, security, as well as more explicit women's issues like domestic violence, abortion and the 'glass ceiling', gender pay gap etc, and ask which they associate with men or women.	This follows on well from the more general gender issues, shaping, and adding more detail and focus to the discussion and helping it to flow freely. Also, will find out whether gender is as important to people as current 'hot' issues such as race and religion.	

Focus Group Schedule – *continued*

Key Questions	Notes	Time
In your view, how important are women's rights/equality generally? How about in today's society? How would you compare issues around women's rights with other issues such as age, social class, race and religion? What are the differences? Similarities?	This section covers Substantive Representation of Women. i.e. the effect that female representation has on the issues etc being focused on.	
Do you think women and men prioritise different issues?		
What do you think would make you more likely to vote Conservative? What about other people?	Particular emphasis here will be given to the potential impact	
The Conservative Party has lost women's votes since 1997 So should the Conservative Party try to specifically target women's votes? Why/Why Not? PROBE If yes, how? LOOK FOR REFERENCES TO POLICIES, LANGUAGE, RHETORIC, PHILOSOPHY ETC.	women's issues could have on how electable the Conservative Party appears to the electorate.	
What, if anything, should they change?		
Would this make the Party seem more moderate? Why/Why not?	KEY QUESTIONS	
Would doing this make you more likely to vote Conservative or not? PROBE: Why/why not? Why do you say that?		
What about other people?		
Who would it attract? Who would it repel?		
BREAK		10 mins

Focus Group Schedule – *continued*

Key Questions	Notes	Time
5. Substantive Representation of Women and Direct Representation of Women Combined		20 mins
Are the Conservatives a more or less 'women friendly' party than: 1. they have been previously? PROBE HOW, IF AT ALL, THIS HAS AFFECTED THEIR VIEW OF THE PARTY 2. other parties? PROBE ESPECIALLY LABOUR PROBE IF CHANGES NOTICED, What would be the impact of abandoning or reversing these changes? Are the Conservatives a more or less 'family friendly' party than: 1. they were before 2. other parties Who do you think are the most prominent Conservative Party politicians at the moment? PROBE Do these people have positive or negative images? Who are the most prominent Conservative Party female politicians? PROBE Do they have positive or negative images? PROBE What are your recollections of female Conservative politicians?	This section links SRW and DRW. It will help the discussion to flow naturally. KEY QUESTIONS	

Focus Group Schedule – *continued*

Key Questions	Notes	Time
MODERATOR SHOW GROUP PICTURES OF CONSERVATIVE POLITICIANS AND SEE IF THEY RECOGNISE THEM WITHOUT PROMPTING PROBE ON: RECOGNITION; WHAT THEY THINK OF THE POLITICIANS; HOW THIS COMPARES TO RECOGNITION/VIEWS OF MALE CONSERVATIVE POLITICIANS Do you think that male/female MPs have different perspectives on the same issues? Which issues? IF IT HELPS, YOU CAN PROMPT USING THE LIST OF ISSUES FROM BEFORE.	NOTE FOR HANDOUT: 1. **Caroline Spelman** – Conservative Party Chairman 2. **Ann Widdecombe** – Conservative MP and former Shadow Home Secretary 3. **Maria Miller** – Shadow Minister, Children, Schools and Families 4. **Theresa May** – Shadow Minister for Women 5. **Theresa Villiers** – Shadow Transport Secretary 6. **George Osborne** – Shadow Chancellor of the Exchequer 7. **David Davis** – Conservative MP and former Shadow Home Secretary	

Focus Group Schedule – *continued*

Key Questions	Notes	Time
6. Women's Representation/Direct Representation of Women		20 mins
Are women under-represented at Westminster? PROBE Why/why not? Does this matter to you? What proportion of the Conservative Parliamentary Party do you think are women? **WRITE ON FLIPCHART** (9% of Conservative MPs are women.) PROBE does this lack of female Conservative MPs matter to you? If so why? How do you think the Conservative Party compares with other parties on this? (Especially Labour)	The significance of representation needs to be pushed. Having previously discussed the general role of women in society the Group can now look in greater detail at the Conservative Party itself.	
Does the level of women's representation make a difference to debates and issues that are prioritised in the Conservative Party and Government? Why/why not? Should the Conservative Party actively be seeking to recruit a greater number of women MPs?	At the last election 128 out of 644 MPs were women, 17 Conservative MPs were women, only 3 more on the previous election thus 9% of Conservative MPs are female. Labour has 98 female MPs which equates to 28% their MPs, whilst the Lib Dems have 16% female MPs.	
PROBE IF YES, which would be the best methods? LOOK FOR WHETHER THEY SUPPORT RHETORIC, PROMOTION OR GUARANTEES. COULD RANK IDEAS IN ORDER OF EFFECTIVENESS. (Using post-it notes) ○ All women shortlists ○ quotas for women (e.g. at the shortlisting stage for candidates, in overall number of candidates?) ○ better training/encouragement for women candidates ○ something else? What would be the effect of such measures on ordinary voters? Would these measures make you more likely to vote for the Conservative Party? Why/why not? Will it make the Conservative Party more electable/moderate? Why/why not?	Whether the Party, and Parliament, should be statistically representative of society is a vitally important question. We need to find out why people feel women are under represented and whether it is something that could, and should, be improved. We also need to establish the extent to which this is a priority. E.g. Rhetoric is encouraging etc., promotion is non-sexist selection and training etc, guarantees is All Women Shortlists etc.	

Focus Group Schedule – *continued*

Key Questions	Notes	Time
7. Wrap Up		15 mins
Is gender balance and equality something appropriate for the Conservative Party to prioritise? Why/why not? PROBE What would the effect be on electoral appeal? PROBE whether this would mean the Party was turning towards the centre ground, and whether this is seen as a good or bad thing.	Should probe whether feminisation would help the party to convince the electorate that it is turning towards the political centre. If so, whether this is likely to gain them more electoral support.	
Distribute post-group questionnaires		
Thank participants and hand out £30 incentives.		

Notes

Introduction

1 David Cameron, 2005. http://www.timesonline.co.uk/tol/news/politics/article-757902.ece, accessed February 28, 2011.

2 Subsequent research also suggested that men and women prioritize different issues, with younger women most concerned about education and older women prioritizing healthcare (Campbell 2006).

3 Auto/biographies of women MPs in the House during the 1980s routinely include at least a line or two recounting examples of prejudice when seeking selection as Conservative parliamentary candidates: Edwina Currie (2002, 2002); Theresa Gorman (2001: 114, 117); Kochan (2000: xi, 78) writing the biography of Ann Widdecombe; Gillian Shephard (2000: 271–2); Emma Nicholson (1996: 54, 57, 106–8); and Jill Knight (1995: 13, 44–5).

4 Bryson and Heppell (2010: 32) cite contributions by Bale (2010), Denham and O'Hara (2007), Evans (2008), and Quinn (2008). This is true too of Snowdon (2010: 222) who makes, for example, no reference to the women's policy report as part of the modernization of Tory party policy.

5 See the individual chapters by Denver (2010), Green (2010), and Curtice (2010) in Geddes and Tonge (ed).

6 This is not to say that there were no discussions to this effect. Imminent tax cuts were, for example, much wanted by the right of the Conservative party.

7 See also Bryson and Heppell (2010) who are in agreement with our analysis. In any case, there was never any reason to exclude gender from mainstream analytic frameworks of conservatism. As feminist political theorists have long reminded us, representations of gender and gender relations are fundamental to political ideas (Coole 1993). The same is also true for previous Conservative administrations. It is, for example, notable that Cameron's efforts to feminize in order to modernize (or at least symbolize modernization) mirror efforts by Edward Heath in the 1970s (Maguire 1998: 137).

8 See for example Cameron's speech at the Conservative Women's Conference in November 2008.

9 See Chapter 5 for discussions of manifesto analysis and the party's policies.

10 See newspaper coverage of Cameron's 2008 Party Conference speech: *Daily Mail; Daily Telegraph; Guardian;* and *Independent* (October 2, 2008). Note that Cameron is very much in Hague's shoes when seeking to promote marriage (Bale 2010; Garnett 2003a; Dorey 2003).

11 Snowdon (2010); Bale (2010); Jones (2010).

12 Feminization is considered a process rather than an end point. What is at issue is the relative integration of women and their concerns and perspectives into parties, political institutions and policy (Lovenduski 2005a).

13 See Chapter 2.

14 http://www.parliament.uk/business/news/2009/10/gordon-brown-david-cameron-and-nick-clegg-appear-before-mps/, accessed November 5, 2010. Public opinion is more mixed. A recent survey finds that sex is the least important of a range of identities that a prospective MP might have when the public is asked to choose between various candidate attributes (Childs and Cowley 2011).

Chapter 1   Conservatism, Representation and Feminization

1   Adapted from Campbell (1987: 264).
2   Those advocating the integration of presence theory with theories of institutional change include Lovenduski (2005a); Mackay (2004); Dodson (2006); Reingold (2008a,b).
3   This book admittedly addresses symbolic representation only marginally.
4   Dovi (2008, see also Celis 2004) maintains that assessments need determine which women are not being adequately represented in respect of each of these, and that women's 'multiple' concerns be present.
5   Sections of this chapter draw on Celis and Childs (2011).
6   The Conservative party's efforts in this respect are examined in the following two chapters.
7   The following draws extensively on work undertaken with Mona Lena Krook (Childs and Krook 2008 in Childs 2008).
8   The role of gender in Kanter's account is also limited. Hers is more a theory of minority status, even though implicitly she relies upon gender differences. It is also not clear whether there are discrete 'tipping points' or whether performance pressures change continuously as their relative proportions change (Childs and Krook 2008: 110, in Childs 2008).
9   Some studies focus only on what women representatives do, and elide women's bodies with feminist minds – expecting and judging actions in terms of feminist change – whereas 'gender consciousness' representatives, of either sex may, be critical to achieve women's substantive representation (Reingold 2000).
10   Hawkesworth (2003); Kathlene (1995); Carroll (2001); Trimble and Arscott (2003); Gotell and Brodie (1991); Dodson (2001); Chaney (2006); Thomas (1994); Weldon (2002); Reingold (2000); Swers (2002); Childs and Withey (2006); Bratton and Ray (2002); Reingold (2008a,b); Dodson (2006).
11   In this way, the new approach resonates with talk of 'feminist advocacy coalitions' (Mazur 2002) and 'strategic alliances' (Waylen 2004) that can be key to the feminist substantive representation of women (Mazur 2002: 177), even if sympathetic non-feminist allies in key decision making positions are sometimes necessary. Importantly, critical actors may not even be women.
12   This concept resonates with much in the original formulations of both Kanter and Dahlerup.
13   This is not to say that people and groups do not exist 'prior to evocation...there is always a referent' (Saward 2006: 313).
14   The qualification regarding essentialism in this quotation suggests that whilst the substantive representation of women might be considered to work with a concept of sex and the constitutive representation of gender with a concept of gender, this may not be so clear cut. Scholars of the former are often pointed in maintaining that their assumptions are not underpinned by unproblematic notions of sex (see Childs and Krook 2006a,b,c for a rejection of critical mass theory which is reliant upon the presence of women to deliver substantive representation, for example). Increasingly too, scholars acknowledge that examining empirically women's substantive representation involves investigations of assumptions about women and men, and gender relations (Celis et al 2008).
15   Though Squires (2008) suggests examination of this relationship she does not state how this might be operationalized. This is discussed in the final section of this chapter.

16 For example, Dovi (2008); Dodson (2006); Schreiber (2008); Duerst-Lahti (2008); Wolbrecht et al (2008); Beckwith (2008); Reingold (2000); Swers (2002); Childs (2004); Dovi (2008); Lovenduski (2005a).

17 Can we say there really is a connection between descriptive and substantive representation if female self-proclaimed representatives of women 'make a difference' by *being more conservative and less feminist* than their male colleagues even as they attribute it to gender? (Dodson 2006: 27)

18 Note, that it is also claimed that Democrats too like to use women to garner legitimacy. Dillard (2005: 27) in a neat turn of phrase, talks of the right 'hiding behind the A line skirts of the women'. See also Reingold (2008b: 144), citing Swers. These observations beg questions of symbolic representation, not answered here. Namely, if parties use women as tokens or symbols of moral authority does this undermine feminist conceptions of symbolic representation?

19 Democrats reference middle aged, older, Latinas, African American, poor, rural and women workers, feminists, military, veterans whereas Republican women reference traditional role women, single mothers, victims of crime, and women small business owners. Republicans 'touted' all issues as women's issues and focus on subset of women's issues whilst Democrat women talk of particular groups of women.

20 Conservative women's groups attract support from, and mobilize women by, mediating conservative values through feminist language and mediate feminist concerns through conservative language. 'Women's issues' are made more palatable to conservatives and what constitutes conservative issues is broadened, re-gendering conservative movements (Schreiber 2008: 11).

21 It is said to be harder to be accused of being anti-woman, if the conservative voice articulating the said view is female. The example provided is Phyllis Shaffly's opposition to the Equal Rights Amendment in the US.

22 Dovi's (2008: 160) 'tokens'.

23 Note here that in Saward's (2006) conceptualization representatives are not limited to elected ones, or only to women representatives.

24 Note here that we are not suggesting that only women can act for women.

25 Duerst-Lahti (2008) advocates the concept of feminalism as gender ideology that can incorporate both feminist and non- and anti-feminist perspectives. However this concept, whilst offering benefits to scholars, has as yet to widely taken up. See Dovi (2008: 154). According to Reingold (2008b: 137) Dodson (2006) suggests that both feminist and anti-feminist initiatives are 'acts' of representation '*if*' they 'reflect a conscious effort to forge responsive connections with women and women's groups'.

26 This is not, of course, to say that women cannot be attracted to conservative politics for non-gendered reasons.

27 Gains achieved by the British women's movement in the preceding decades were not universally overthrown by the Conservative Premierships of Margaret Thatcher and John Major in the 1980s and 1990s (Bashevkin 1998; Bryson and Heppell 2010).

28 Bryson and Heppell (2010) argue that whilst conservatives and (some feminists) might agree that pornography is harmful to women, the reasons for this will likely differ. The latter are likely to identify systems of male power and see women as exploited whereas the former are likely to see this as an individual problem associated with deviant men and as a threat to family values and conventional morality (see also Schreiber 2008).

29 It is also claimed that feminism and conservatism meet on the terrain of 'fear' (Campbell 1987: 67, 148): fear of crime in general, and fear of gendered crime in particular.

30 I would like to thank Joni Lovenduski for crystallizing this view.

31 Note, this typology does not negate the claim made above that Approach 2 offers the best means to conceptualize conservative representatives claims of representation but is rather a means by which conservative claims might be judged on a feminist basis. Given Schreiber's depiction of her two groups as anti-feminist it may be that this distinction is less real in practice in the US.

32 A similar point was made by Jeffries (1996: 49).

33 This contention will be returned to in Chapters 5 and 6. See Dodson (2006) and Childs (2006) cited in Bryson and Heppell (2010).

34 Conservative claims and actions can be regarded as constituting the substantive representation of women when they meet at least one of the following criteria (Celis et al 2009): (1) are directly *constructed* as being of importance to women, (2) *presented* as only affecting women, (3) *discussed* in terms of gender difference, (4) *spoken* of in terms of gendered effects, and/or (5) *framed* in terms of equality between women and men.

35 Lovenduski and Norris (2003); Swers (2002: 10); Reingold (2000: 50); Tremblay (1998); Dodson (2006).

36 Dodson argues that variance theory that relies on regression analysis of roll call data should be replaced by a process approach that examines the 'deliberative process' that precedes acting for women. Such a shift in research method is also advocated by Celis et al (2008).

37 Acknowledging the likely multiple sites and actors suggests that research must investigate, *inter alia*, the actions of male as well as women representatives, members of legislative executives, women's policy agencies (WPA) and femo-crats, as well as civil society groups (Mackay 2004; Lovenduski 2005b).

38 See also Dodson (2006) who talks of the 'deliberative process' that precedes acting for women.

39 As stated above, this book does not consider in any comprehensive or systematic way symbolic representation.

40 'Magari' as the Italians would put it, as Joni Lovenduski told me.

41 I would like to thank Philip Cowley and Richard Heffernan for both putting their thoughts on this to me.

Chapter 2   Women Members and the Party's Women's Organizations

1 As one ex-CWO Chairman put it.

2 This chapter focuses on the post-2005 period. Developments in earlier years are only very briefly noted for purposes of context.

3 The concept of QWPA was first developed in RNGs research to discuss women's commissions in political parties in parliamentary systems in post-industrial societies (Lovenduski 2005b: 3) According to Campbell (1987: 34) the Primrose League is an example of a Ladies auxillary. 'The League's function was to organize women for the Conservative cause; it was *not* to organize for the cause of women. See also Maguire (1998) on the Primrose League and Kittilson (2006) on the Conservative National Women's Committee.

4   The reasoning here is that the women, whilst gendering the party's law and order debates, nonetheless left the relationship between the women and the party leadership unaltered.

5   This occurred under the Chairmanship of Don Porter.

6   CWO complaints following the 2005 general election again ape previous women's criticism of marginalization from manifesto writing in the mid-1960s (Maguire 1998: 174).

7   *The Route to Downing Street.*

8   Chairman of the women's organization, Pam Parker in a private letter and report sent to Michael Howard. This was passed to one of the authors by a non-Conservative male member of the House of Lords.

9   http://www.conservatives.com/tile.do?def=party.useful.link.page&ref=cwnc

10 Whiteley (2009: 246) also find this distribution of party membership by sex. In the early 1990s the predecessor organization of CWO was said to have some 250,000 members (CWNC 'Route to Downing Street', March 2004). http://one-nationtory.com/2010/10/conservative-party-membership-drop-an-analysis.html accessed October 1, 2010. Conservative party membership shows a decline from 400,000 in the mid-1990s, and 290,000 in mid-2000s. A loss of member is shared by other major political parties in the UK and other western democracies (Mair and Van Biezen 2001). Note that the Conservative party does not publicly disclose its overall level of membership, and that there is no legal requirement for it, or any UK registered political party, to do so. The distribution of women and men throughout the party structures suggests asymmetry of representation, as outlined in Table 2.6 in the Appendix to this chapter. An internal report into the party's youth organization, Conservative Future (CF) found near parity of membership. Women constituted in 2005/6 just under half of its 18 000 members. But this does not translate into equality of participation at the officer level of the organization. Women were about 40 percent of the National Executive; just over 10 percent of Association Branch Chairman and Area Chairman; less than 5 percent of University Branch Chairman; and there were no women Area Deputy Chairman. This distribution was felt by CF to reflect a combination of a failure by women to stand for office; a perception that women are put off by the aggressive style of many university branches; and because women are pushed into 'lesser' roles like social secretary', from which it is claimed to more difficult to run for Chairman from. Keen to 'to dispel the "Tory Boy" stereotype', efforts to increase women's participation would include, mentoring targeting and training alongside the co-option of women 'place in senior roles'. Contemporary figures were not available at the time of writing to evaluate whether any or all of these efforts came to fruition. The current CWO leadership claim that many more women are involved in CF and that there are good relations between CWO and CF. Future research might look into the progression of younger women through the party.

11 http://www.parliament.uk/documents/commons/lib/research/briefings/snsg-05125.pdf, http://onenationtory.com/2010/10/conservative-party-membership-drop-an-analysis.html accessed October 11, 2010.

12 This figure comes from the CWO leadership.

13 Attempts under Fiona Hodgson to establish this information were unsuccessful.

14 It is responsible for all operational matters including: fundraising, membership and candidates. It is made up of representatives from each section of the party – the voluntary, political and professional. http://www.conservatives.com/People/Members_of_the_Board.aspx accessed August 10, 2010.

15 The current CWO leadership maintain, however, that it is important that 'the women's voice is not just invested in one person nor only in the women on the Board'.

16 CWO entry to 2007 National Excellence Awards, Membership and Affiliation. Conservative Future is funded by the centre.

17 CWO entry to 2007 National Excellence Awards, Membership and Affiliation.

18 According to Tessa Keswick (2000: 13) the CWNC did not have a desk at Central Office.

19 The previous chairman benefitted from her husband being in the House of Lords, which provided her with a parliamentary pass and informal contacts with Parliamentarians. Note, that the CF chairman does not have a pass, either.

20 The CWO Chairman, Hodgson, also participated in the party's social action activities in Rwanda.

21 CWO entry to 2007 National Excellence Awards, Membership and Affiliation.

22 CWO entry to 2007 National Excellence Awards, Membership and Affiliation.

23 CWO entry to 2007 National Excellence Awards, Membership and Affiliation. Note other sections of the voluntary party, other than the Conservative Policy Forum, do not address policy issues.

24 Ratios of men to women speakers may be less meaningful at other CWO events, although one observable pattern is where the issue is to do with women's bodily integrity and/or the family/children the number of women speakers is, overall, higher than for other topics.

25 CWO entry to 2007 National Excellence Awards, Membership and Affiliation.

26 CWO entry to 2007 National Excellence Awards, Membership and Affiliation.

27 Autumn 2008 CWO Newsletter. Audience seems smaller, less diverse, fewer younger women than previous year.

28 Alistair Burt; Anna Soubry PPC; Edward Gardiner; Helen Grant, PPC; Iain Dale in conversation with Eric Pickles; Theresa May.

29 Observation. One of the authors was sitting in the balcony of the Hall. All of the women in the audience appeared to be over 50 and many over 60. There were only a handful of men, three of whom were younger and two older. All appeared white, bar one. The audience also appeared smaller than in the previous two years.

30 Figures from the CWO.

31 Figures from CWO.

32 CWO entry to 2007 National Excellence Awards, Membership and Affiliation.

33 According to the CWO leadership.

34 Whist attendee figures are not a relevant criterion of a successful Summit, given that they are about relevant organizations, it is worth noting that the Sixth Form event in 2007 attracted some 150 young women.

35 CWO entry to 2007 National Excellence Awards, Membership and Affiliation.

36 CWO entry to 2007 National Excellence Awards, Membership and Affiliation.

37 Interview 2010.

38 Observation.

39 Observation.

40 Observation.

41 Observation.

42 Observation.

43 Observation.

44 It also encourages views amongst Muslim women which are 'open and expansive, spreading core Conservative values of equality and democracy and aspiration, achievement and change'. CWO autumn 2007 newsletter.

45 CWO entry to 2007 National Excellence Awards, Membership and Affiliation.
46 Interview 2010.
47 CWO entry to 2007 National Excellence Awards, Membership and affiliation. Ovaisi, a medical doctor, attended the first meeting having been invited via a member of the House of Lords who knew her father.
48 The Group did not see itself as a 'recruiting' site for Muslim support for the Conservative party, either in terms of voters or prospective parliamentary candidates. It was critical of the way in which certain leaders of the 'Muslim Community' are taken to be representative of all Muslims. Hence, it was adamant that it would not be affiliated to, nor captured by, other groups.
49 Unless otherwise indicated, figures are from the CWO.
50 Observation.
51 Observation.
52 Observation.
53 Observation.
54 Interview 2010.
55 Interview 2010.
56 This view draws on observations of the Women's Conferences by one of the authors.
57 Overheard discussion, in the toilets at the Conference.
58 Recognition of marriage in the tax system, celebrated by Cameron, did not come out of the women's party of the Conservative party, nor does it receive fulsome support from interviewed women MPs (see Chapter 5).
59 She also, in one of the author's view, patronizingly praised a black woman for having asked a 'clear' question and bemoans the African 'history lesson'. This conference was, in the CWO leadership's view, explicitly international in focus, and it was recognized that subsequent conferences would need to address issues that were 'closer to home'. According to the CWO leadership, more recent conferences topics such as international development (2009) and women in the justice system (2010) have gained considerable empathy with the audience.
60 CWO entry to 2007 National Excellence Awards, Membership and Affiliation. In 2006, CWO champions included: William Hague MP, Don Porter (Chairman of the Conservative Convention and Deputy Chairman of the Conservative Party) and Cllr Shireen Ritchie (Chairman of the Candidates Committee).
61 CWO entry to 2007 National Excellence Awards, Membership and Affiliation. The list of MPs, MEPs, and Peers shows that 18 women and 24 men were invited to speak at CWO events.
62 New research might establish this in the future, but see below and Chapter 5 for discussions of gendered policy and the 2010 general election manifesto.
63 I would like to thank Elizabeth Evans for sharing this observation with me.
64 Two women Peers are a little less sure that the CWO has fared better in recent years, and for one, more critical, older, male MP the CWO has become tainted by its association with May and 'people like her' who 'compartmentalize' women.
65 Its continuation after the 2010 general election was rather unclear.
66 CWNC (2004) 'Route to Downing St'.
67 CWO Leadership.
68 Note our rejection of Bale's (2010: 132) criticism of manifesto analysis for failing 'to factor in the extent to which, in the real, world, parties are defined by what

they talk (and by what they are forced to talk) about, not what they write in documents that only a tiny minority of even their own members bother to read'.

69 *Guardian* April 29, 2010.
70 Marmite is a savoury spread of which it is said – and its marketing makes much of – that it is either loved or hated. May is long remembered, and criticized by Conservatives for what has become infamous as her 'nasty party' speech at the 2002 Conference. At the same time, women in the party, even those who are sometimes critical of her inter-personal skills, rate her as a (shadow) Minister and recognize that she has the highest profile of Tory women, bar Ann Widdecombe, who became something of a media 'darling', not least through her participation in the BBC 1, TV show, 'Strictly Come Dancing'.
71 This view is held by supporters and critics of May.
72 Interview, woman MP.
73 May, whilst widely praised by many senior women in the parliamentary and voluntary party, is not always considered such a 'team' player, although, as noted above, criticisms have been leveled at Chairmen of the CWO too.
74 The party does not collate these figures. National Convention 239/849; 4/10 Regional Chairmen; 7/30 Regional Officers.

Chapter 3 Conservative Legislative Recruitment

1 *Telegraph* 10 May, 2010. The delayed vote in Thirsk and Malton constituency some three weeks, which returned Anne McIntosh MP, took the total number of Conservative women MPs to 49.
2 This figure was used, for example, by Cameron on Woman's Hour in February 2010 and at the Party's Spring Conference in 2010.
3 In Cameron's December 12, 2005 speech he claimed that his plans for 'positive action' would 'guarantee' more women and ethnic Conservative MPs. As is discussed in greater detail later in this Chapter, none of his reforms were designed to guarantee this. At best they enhanced the *chances* of greater diversity amongst Conservative parliamentary candidates.
4 Bale (2010: 382) agrees with this interpretation.
5 http://www.ipu.org/wmn-e/classif.htm accessed 27 June 2010.
6 Given popular perceptions of Anglo-US and French relations (inferiority and superiority respectively), some will no doubt find this comforting.
7 This drop is too often, and too easily, unremarked as percentages are rounded to 18 percent. Table 3.1 also reveals more clearly that the drop in 2001 reflects the loss of Labour women MPs, whose numbers declined from 101 to 95 – a pattern that matches the Labour party's failure to employ AWS in 2001 unlike 1997, 2005 and 2010.
8 101/120; 95/118; 98/128; 81/143, 1997, 2001, 2005 and 2010 respectively.
9 This figure includes Sylvia Heal, First Deputy Chairman of Ways and Means and Rachel Squire (Labour) who since died.
10 This excludes Anne McIntosh, whose election was delayed by the death of one of the candidates during the General Election. She was elected some three weeks after the election.
11 Updated following the 2003 by-election.
12 This figure includes the late Patsy Calton.

13 This figure does not include the constituency of South Staffordshire where the election was suspended due to the death of the male Liberal Democrat candidate.

14 Cf *Sunday Times* (26 July 2009) which reports that, the 'team promoting female candidates' are focused on the selection of more women as replacements for expenses scandal retirees.

15 Winnable seats are where the party came second in 2001 and the majority was less than 5 percent and 10 percent.

16 This excludes ex-Conservative Andrew Pelling MP who re-stood as an Independent. Labour's Clare Short and Bob Waring are included; Conservatives Quentin Davies, Derek Conway and Bob Spink are included.

17 Four Labour seats were abolished.

18 This reinforces the importance of good quota design and implementation. For example in Slovenia, the legislative quotas refer to candidates not elected members. The role of quotas is returned to later in the chapter.

19 There are party quotas at the European level.

20 According to the 'Quota project' the Romanian Democratic party has party quotas.

21 Ditto, the higher levels of representation in the Scottish Parliament and National Assembly for Wales, (where women constitute some 33 and 45 percent respectively), were achieved without changes in the wider cultural and socio-economic environments. Importantly, the women MSPs and AMs were disproportionately returned from the plurality parts of the electoral system, and not as many think, from the PR side of the mixed electoral systems (Childs 2008).

22 Hence the downplaying of other factors. The UK is broadly egalitarian and secular, even if it is not a strongly social-democratic; and women's equal enfranchisement dates from 1928, and for some women, notably wealthier ones, since 1918. The presence of a plurality electoral system at Westminster and the partisan use of quotas are more limiting. In the UK's single member, 'first past the post system', political parties tend to select the 'safe' candidate in an individual constituency – the candidate who looks most like existing (male) representatives. Plus, in the absence of prescriptive quotas, selectorates are not forced to select women over men.

23 The following sections form the basis for parts of Ashe et al (2010).

24 Kenny (2009: 24–5) contends that Norris and Lovenduski (1995) downplay both the 'extent to which the eligibility pool is already shaped and distorted by gender norms' and the possibility of selectorate discrimination.

25 See for example, Lawless and Fox's (2005) study of supply which reveals that women are likely to overestimate their qualifications to run for office and are less likely to receive encouragement to stand by political office, itself an important determinant of supply (and cited in Krook 2010b).

26 Lawless and Fox (2005) have shifted scholarship back to supply, but do so in ways that complement the reconceptualization of political recruitment advanced by Krook: traditional gender socialization explains the gender gap in levels of political ambition through (1) traditional family role orientation, namely women's family responsibilities which would make politics a 'third' job; (2) masculinized political institutions which impact on concepts of candidate quality, electability and background – the preferred candidate remains male; and (3) gender psyche, which propels men into politics but relegates women to the electoral arena's periphery. In sum: 'politics often exists as a reasonable career possibility for men, but does not even appear on the radar screen for many women' (2005: 11). This study, moreover, impresses the importance of political gatekeepers seeking out women and suggesting

they stand for political office, for it is both more important to women, and yet less likely to happen (2005: 89).

27 The narrowing of the political class to graduate, professional politicians has been widely noted.

28 See Lawless and Fox (2005: 144): 'as long as women must meet higher standards, both self-imposed and external, then the apparent absence of voter bias against women candidates must reflect the higher average quality of women candidates, as compared to men.

29 In November 2009 Cameron announced that the candidate list would be reopened. Jeremy Middleton, Chairman of the National Conservative Convention, responded to concerns about the reforms on www.conservativehome (accessed 7 August 2009), arguing these are 'exceptional times leading to exceptional pressures on candidate selection'. The post-expenses scandal resignations mean that new selections must take place 'as soon as possible' and, hence, the new rules constitute a 'pragmatic' solution to a 'difficult problem'. Importantly he stresses that Local Association picks the shortlist, holds the interviews and runs the selection process. He also stresses that the rules were agreed 'collectively' by 'all members of the Board, which includes representatives from both Houses of Parliament, the Chairman's office and the Voluntary Party' – presumably to preempt accusations that representatives of the voluntary party were excluded.

30 The Party Chairman's preference was for sitting MPs to announce their retirement pre-Christmas (www.conservativehome.com accessed 30 July 2009). Jonathon Isaby, of Conservativehome, makes the same appeal on the grounds of avoiding 'the scenario where the members who have loyally worked for them over the years have that restrictive shortlist foisted upon them (*Times* on line, November 19, 2009).

31 The *Telegraph* (February 15, 2009) reports that Cameron is seeking women with 'experience of demanding jobs especially in the public sector' to see off accusations that the party has selected 'lightweight' women. See Lawless and Fox (2005: 79–81) for discussions of the larger women's supply pool for the US Democratic party relative to Republicans, something accountable by the more liberal attitudes of US women.

32 *Sunday Times* July 26, 2009.

33 So too did the Liberal Democrats, thereby, leaving Labour as the only party, once again, to employ all three equality strategies (Ashe et al 2010).

34 The Speaker's Conference was established in 2008 and reported in 2010 (Speakers Conference 2010; Ashe et al 2010). One author, Sarah Childs, was one of the special advisers to the Speaker's Conference.

35 Interviews not identified for reasons of anonymity. Note that some women in the party had been calling for AWS (Keswick 2000). The by-election rules had themselves generated some dispute. Constituency chairman were reportedly 'very, very unhappy'.

36 *Observer* May 24, 2009. Francis Maude – a key modernizer – would also have settled for one third women candidates (Snowdon 2010: 247).

37 Of course, it may be that the review was symbolic rather than substantive, part of signposting the party's efforts on legislative recruitment rather than designed to have a practical impact, as discussed later.

38 Deputy and Vice Chairman Minutes, October 28, 2008.

39 *Observer* May 3, 2009.

40 Subsequent research will need to be undertaken to establish this.

41 The sex of one Priority List candidate is unknown. This brings the total to 101.

42   Sex aside, and at least until the expenses scandal caused them to be widely consti-
     tuted as a possible panacea for all the ills of Parliament, local constituencies were
     fearful of the cost of primaries and unhappy about giving the power to select candi-
     dates to non-party members, and in open primaries, to non-Conservative voters.
     The mood music, since then, suggests that they are the party's preferred mode of
     selection. Note however, that the Totnes primary cost some 40,000 pounds to the
     Party centrally (*Guardian* August 5, 2009).
43   *London Review of Books*, 2007.
44   See Kenny (2009) for a discussion of 'localness' in the selection of Labour candi-
     dates in Scotland. One interviewed Peer questions whether local candidates are
     of sufficient parliamentary material.
45   Interview not revealed for reasons of anonymity.
46   Lansley (Garnett and Lynch 2003) talks of the need for a new system of selection
     so that the party has a larger number of women and BME MPs: adopting equal
     opportunities policies inside the Conservative party and in each Association. See
     also Snowdon (2010).
47   Although John Bercow does not name May, she is the obvious candidate for his
     musings (*Guardian* January 30, 2009): 'it is a project that needs to be taken on by
     someone with the passion and influence to translate a representative parliament
     from a vision to a fact'. A successful 2010 PPC agrees that under Cameron May
     has been able to 'put the pressure on', not least because she is 'prepared to fight
     her corner'.
48   In his December 12, 2005 speech Cameron states: 'some say there's no need for
     positive action...that, over time, the number of women...will inevitably
     rise...there's no need to take steps to accelerate the process. I completely
     disagree.'
49   At the 2008 CWO conference, Cameron declared: 'We didn't transform the
     number of women candidates because it might make our party look good....[but]
     so that in government we have people with ideas and experience to help make
     Britain a fairer and more family-friendly place'. See also his December 12, 2005
     speech: 'nothing to do with crude calculation, or crazed political correctness. It's
     about political effectiveness' (see Section III for discussions of the relationship
     between the descriptive and substantive representation of women). The Speaker
     concurs that the descriptive representation of women not only makes use of
     women's talent but engenders the substantive representation of women: 'the
     Commons is a far better placed to address domestic violence, equal pay, child-
     care, the work-life balance and the fight against racism in a way that the white
     male monopoly never did or could' (*Guardian* January 30, 2009).
50   As Kittilson (2006: 32) suggests, 'in certain contests, increases in women's parlia-
     mentary representation occurred after party leaders anticipated that women's votes
     could be won by selecting more women candidates'.
51   See also Taylor (2003) and Ashcroft (2005).
52   Bale (2010: 348, 382) agrees with this interpretation.

Chapter 4   Reforming Parliamentary Selection: Party Change, Parliamentarian and Party Member Attitudes

 1   Focus Group Member.
 2   Labour's AWS imposed a centralized selection process on the party (Childs 2004,
     2008; M. Russell 2005). Note that increasing the numbers of Conservative women

MPs might also bring parliamentary benefits to a leader – that MPs so selected would feel a personal loyalty.

3   Sex quotas are used in more than 100 countries (Krook 2006).

4   The *Spectator* (February 13, 2010) reports that her agent made 'deeply insensitive remarks about pregnant women'. Cash tendered her resignation when the association chairman was elected as President. See Conservative home for grassroots views: http://conservativehome.blogs.com/goldlist/2010/02/joanne-cash-resigns-as-tory-candidate-for westminster-north.html, accessed February 9, 2010.

5   February 2010. The *Times* (November 16, 2009) maintains that it was Truss' 'lack of candour about her marital indiscretion that ignited this local revolt'. In the *Sunday Times* (July 26, 2009) Cash's friendship with Michael Gove MP and Cameron's then Director of Communications, Andy Coulson, and the fact that she lives in Notting Hill, 'yards' from the Chancellor, George Osborne, is noted.

6   In June 2005, predating Cameron's leadership, May claimed that the 'local involvement' might not be maintained if 'our best and most saleable candidates are left on the shelf or only selected for seats where they have little or no chance of winning'.

7   As Cameron acknowledged on BBC Radio 4's Woman's Hour.

8   He made a very similar comment at the 2010 Spring Conference: 'And it was you, it wasn't me, it was you who selected those brilliant women candidates...'

9   *Spectator* February 20, 2010. The column was written by Melissa Kite, deputy political editor of the *Sunday Telegraph*. Whilst not necessarily representative of Conservative party members, Conservativehome is the 'institutionalized forum for complaints' , and one importantly that informs wider media coverage of the party (Bale 2010: 291)

10 *Spectator* February 13, 2010.

11 *Times* November 16, 2009.

12 See also Jonathon Isaby *Times* on line, November 17, 2009.

13 *Times* November 16, 2009.

14 BBC October 27, 2009. http://news.bbc.co.uk/go/pr/fr/-/uk_politics/8327362.stm; *Guardian* November 17, 2009; *Times* November 16, 2009.

15 *Guardian* November 17, 2009.

16 Conservativehome October 29, 2009. Indeed, Montgomerie called for Maples not to be involved in the drawing up of any AWS (which he was not). Instead John Middleton, representing the voluntary party, would be involved. Conservativehome January 15, 2010. http://conservativehome.blogs.com/goldlist/2010/01/john-maples-will-play-no-role-in-the-shortlisting-of-candidates-under-the-byelection-rules.html. There was still concern about the size of the shortlist, with critics arguing for six or eight, and concern over whether Pickles and Patrick McLoughlin (then opposition chief whip) would 'impose Cameron's wishes' on Middleton.

17 Conservativehome, http://conservativehome.blogs.com/goldlist/2010/01/john-maples-mp-to-retire.html. Accessed January 10, 2010.

18 The consequent selection 'assumed the air of class war: the young, upstart techno-savvy generation versus the older established names' (*Observer* February 21, 2010). In the event Nadhim Zahawi, a BME outsider candidate won. One woman's under-stated personality may have been mistaken for an 'uncommitted one' (*Spectator* February 27, 2010).

19 Where we refer to the findings from pre and post questionnaires completed by focus group participants, please note that these findings are indicative only, and are included to help determine the extent to which views are widely shared, or contested, across the focus groups. They should not be viewed as representative of the views of all floating voters and/or Conservative Party members in Britain.

20 See Methods Appendix for details.
21 This section draws heavily on Childs, Webb and Marthaler (2008).
22 A general supply side factor not discussed in gendered terms is identified as the cost of selection. There are also concerns about the parachuting in of favoured sons although this is not discussed in gendered terms.
23 Bailey ultimately failed to be elected for Hammersmith in May 2010.
24 In the US Melody Crowder-Meyer (2009), finds that the sex of the party chair affects the selection of women candidates: higher numbers of women in the party organization yields more women candidates for the Democratic Party but fewer for the Republicans. This may be accounted for either because women are recruited into the party organization as back-room staff and officers, but not as candidates, or because women holding party positions are less likely to promote women as candidates on the basis of traditional assumptions about a woman's 'place'. Either way, though, this research is unable to prove definite bias on the part women selectors.
25 Ditto Baroness Verma who was elevated in 2006 having failed in both 2001 and 2005 to be elected to the lower House. The 'appointment route' to Parliament is also noticeable for a number of senior Conservative women active in the voluntary and professional party who fail to get elected to the Commons. These include: Peta Buscombe (CWO) and Trish Morris (Candidates) (see Taylor 2003).
26 If many of the party members were not keen on equality promotion measures to begin with it seems as though the focus group discussion itself engendered greater antipathy, at least in respect of the stronger forms of equality promotion. Of course, the focus groups were not designed to shift opinion.
27 Note that we cross-tabulated these split-sample questions against sex in order to see if women showed more evidence of bias against female candidates, or vice versa. In fact, we could find no such evidence; these bivariate relationships all proved to be statistically non-significant. There is some evidence of bias against BME candidates given the relative unpopularity of 'Leslie Green', who has links with Black and Asian groups. Cf Kavanagh and Cowley (2010), who report voter discrimination against BME candidates at the 2010 General Election.
28 *January* 2009. David Davis, Peter Lilley, John Whittingdale, David Heathcote Amory, Greg Knight, Graham Brady, Ann Winterton, Christopher Chope, and Sir Nicholas Winterton.
29 See May (2004: 200–5) for an early public denunciation of selectorate discrimination by a leading Conservative woman MP.
30 One PPC spoke of wearing a skirt in an attempt to limit the extent to which the 'the old ladies' on the selection committee found her 'scary'. But the 'short skirt defence' was questioned by another MP who considered it a 'face-saving' exercise; the association did not wish to tell her she was not good enough. Nonetheless, having cried and drowned her sorrows in half a bottle of sherry on that occasion, at subsequent selections she wore a longer 'frumpy' skirt – actions that imply she was not absolutely sure that she had not been selected because her skirt was too short.
31 It also risks leaving the executive and senior positions within parliamentary parties to men, as older women entering Parliament will lack the expected parliamentary experience for promotion into government.
32 See also *Sunday Telegraph* February 15, 2009.
33 For one woman Peer, new Labour's women would be better off 'with a shopping trolley'.
34 One critical male MP did concede that a named woman Priority List candidate was 'good', albeit on the basis of her husband's and father's credentials.

35 He is also highly critical of party organization *per se*.

36 One male Peer recounted his local association having given their selected woman candidate 'an easy ride' because they had decided – though he talks of Cameron's method of generalized 'persuasion' – that 'it was about time' to have a woman MP. He added that given that one no longer got 'two for the price of one' (the MP and his wife), local associations might as well select women candidates. However, recognizing the importance of parties seeking out women, on the basis of her own experience, one woman Peer advocates more talent spotting.

37 'I say to them, 70 percent of candidates are still white male and so you really are not an endangered species and that usually ends the conversation'. One woman Peer, a former MP, contended that debates over parliamentary selection had moderated opposition to Conservative selection measures for the European Parliament.

38 Note that the interviews were conducted prior to Cameron's October 2009 announcement in favour of AWS.

39 Snowdon (2010) argues that Steve Hilton advised Cameron to hold out.

40 In their view, most of the party's winnable and vacant held seats had already selected, so relaxing the use of the Priority List would have little or no practical effect on the number of women MPs, even if it reduced the percentage of women selected as PPCs. In the event, the unexpected vacancies following the expenses scandal, suggests this was, albeit with hindsight, an erroneous judgement – a view supported by two individuals key to the party's recruitment efforts. When the party announced the reopening of the candidates list, it was the most read news story on the Conservative party website (according to the party website, January 5, 2010). Note that readers of Conservativehome were interested in what was perceived as a defeat for Cameron's efforts to increase the selection of women parliamentary candidates than 'the' story of 2009 – the parliamentary expenses scandal, which was the second most looked at item.

41 There is little evidence of net growth in party membership at the time of writing but we cannot rule out the prospect of a gradual change in the balance of attitudes which reflects generational turnover.

42 The impact of the new intake of MPs in 2010 remains to be seen. The 2010 British Representation Study will provide data on this.

Chapter 5   Party Member Attitudes and Women's Policy (by and for women?)

1 Senior Conservative woman, private interview.

2 See Childs et al (2010). In the February 1974 manifesto, there had been nothing on women or the family; the 1979 one was silent about women, although it did address 'helping' the family (Campbell 1987: 161).

3 All quotes, unless otherwise indicated, are from *WIWT*.

4 In the Report proper, women's body image and the issue of eating disorders are included in this section.

5 These are 'simple counts' which do not distinguish between substantive comments and others.

6 The inclusion of a statement that 'false allegations' of rape are no higher than for other crimes suggests that Report's authors felt the need to qualify their analysis in this area.

7 This allows women 'who enter as spouses to apply for residency if they can prove the relationship broke down due to domestic violence'.

8 This statement is oddly placed in the opening sentence to the section 'The Role of Women in International Development'.

9 The Fawcett Society sought the parties' positions on: the economy; work/family life; crime and justice; democracy and political reform; attitudes; media and culture; equality and human rights.

10 Labour would maintain the DNA database and expand services. The Liberal Democrats advocated more diverse elected police authorities, and would permit buses to drop off mid-stop. Labour also had unique policies on teenage pregnancy, lap-dancing clubs (albeit stated in terms of the impact on neighborhoods not women), political representation at Westminster, the ending of male primacy in the Royal Family, and equal opportunities. The Liberal Democrats advocated citizen's pensions and confirmed their support for the Human Rights Act (Campbell and Childs 2010).

11 Conservative MPs are less pro-choice (Cowley and Stuart 2010).

12 Recall, this is a policy that did not come out of the women's part of the party.

13 Interview, Spring 2008. It is harder for the party to maintain the language of choice if a future Conservative government privileges one particular family form through providing for recognition of marriage and civil partnerships in the tax system.

14 These scales offer robust measures of two-dimensional respondent ideology, which is reflected in Cronbach's Alpha high reliability coefficients of 0.87 for the left-right scale and 0.71 for the libertarianism-authoritarianism scale in our dataset.

15 Note that each item was coded so that 1 represented the most of left-wing or libertarian response, while 5 represented the most right-wing or authoritarian response. Confirmatory factor analysis reveals that these scales are orthogonal to each other. The confirmatory factor analysis uses the maximum likelihood method to produce two factors which cumulatively explain 45 percent of the variance in attitudes. The factors are unambiguously the classic left-right and liberty-authority dimensions of belief. For reasons of space we are not reporting the full details of this analysis here, but they are available from the authors on request.

16 Compared with a sample of Conservative MPs and parliamentary candidates at the time of the 2005 election Conservative party members would currently seem to be significantly less right-wing than, but at least as socially authoritarian, as their (would be) parliamentary elites. This produced scores of 3.97 (n = 229) on the same left-right scale, and 3.80 (n = 112) on the liberty-authority scale. The data for Parliamentarians comes from the British Representation Survey, 2005, directed by Joni Lovenduski, Sarah Childs and Rosie Campbell. It is possible, of course, that the very different economic contexts in which the 2005 BRS and the Conservative Membership Survey of 2009 took place explains why the latter's respondents were less inclined than the former's to adopt radical right-wing postures on issues of redistribution and social justice.

17 Note that this is actually 'fighting rising prices' in the original formulation by Inglehart, but it would make little sense to have asked respondents such a question in the summer of 2009, when there was virtually no – or indeed, by some calculations, negative – inflation. Hence we substituted 'fighting unemployment' as a contextually more appropriate materialist objective.

18 These figures are similar to those for Conservative voters in the electorate as a whole (Webb 2000: 65).

19 Widely recognized to have been an extremely vexed issue for British Conservatives since the 1980s, having provoked serious intra-party conflict in the 1990s, recent analysis suggests Europe has largely been assimilated at the level of the parliamentary party, with Tory MPs now holding a clearly Eurosceptic profile (Webb 2008).

20 This is even more radical than Conservative MPs, whose mean score was 7.6 in 2005 (Webb 2008, Table 5). Note that the mean score on this scale is unchanged for all Conservative candidates in 2005, irrespective of whether they were actually returned to Parliament or not (mean = 7.56, n = 219).

21 Together, these five items constitute a very reliable summary attitudinal scale through which we can measure respondents' overall orientation towards feminism (Cronbach's Alpha = 0.741).

22 See note to Table 5.9 for an explanation of how this is constructed.

23 This attitudinal scale ('Genderscale') is constructed from the 12 items reported in Table 5.10 and is coded so that it runs from 1 (high support for reform) to 5 (low support for reform).

24 We used the backward stepwise method to enter the independent variables in order to maximize the parsimony in our model.

25 Analysis of residual diagnostics confirms that none of the key assumptions of OLS (linearity, homoscedasticity, no multicollinearity or autcorrelation) are violated in our data. Specifically, none of the independent variables are highly correlated with one another (even social grade and left-right position only share a correlation coefficient value of −0.323). The Durbin-Watson statistic of 2.041 indicates no autocorrelation; Variance Inflation Factors (VIF) scores are all low (average = 1.08), and tolerance statistics relatively high (average = 0.927), thus confirming that multicollinearity is not a problem; and visual examination of scatterplots reveals the linearity and homoscedasticity of standardized residuals. These findings hold equally for the models summarized in Table 5.12 and 5.13. The variables were coded as follows: selectreform – scale running from 1 (high support for reform) to 5 (low support for reform); Left-Right scale – scale running from 1 (left) to 5 (right); Liberty-Authority scale – scale running from 1 (libertarian) to 5 (authoritarian); feminism – scale running from 1 (antifeminist-traditionalist) to 5 (feminist-progressive); Postmaterialism – dummy variable where 1 = postmaterialist and 0 = other; Materialism – dummy variable where 1 = materialist and 0 = other; sex – 0 = male, 1 = female; Age: Interval scale running from 18–83; Social grade – 1 = A, 2 = B, 3 = C1, 4 = C2, 5 = D, 6 = E; Age finished full-time education = 1 = 15 or under, 2 = 16, 3 = 17/18, 4 = 19, 5 = 20 or over, 6 = still in full-time education; sexageinteraction = 'centred' interaction term for gender and age; i.e., each individual score for gender and age has the sample mean for the same variable subtracted from it, before these two centred variable values are multiplied together. The variables are centred in order to minimize the risk of multicollinearity between them and the new interaction term that is created (see Jaccard and Turrisi 2003). Note that Tables 5.11, 5.12 and 5.13 only reports details of the final model after all non-significant independent variables had been eliminated by backward stepwise procedure whereby those terms which do not make a statistically significant contribution to prediction of the dependent variable are dropped. Full details of all models reported in this paper are available on request from the authors.

26 See also Keswick (2000: 16).

Chapter 6   Sex, Gender and Parliamentary Behaviour in the 2005 Parliament

1 Theresa May, Second Reading WFA 2008.

2 A 'Bill' becomes an 'Act' with 'Royal Assent', the final legislative stage in the UK Parliament.

3   A PMB is a public bill sponsored by a member of either House who is not a Minister (H of L 2001). PMBs are introduced by four means: ballot, the ten-minute rule procedure, presentation, and those brought from the Lords, of which the EPFW is an example. The ballot is 'a sort of legislative prize draw' – some 400 members will participate of whom 20 will have their names drawn and receive priority in introducing their bills (Rogers and Walters 2006: 225). Ten minute rule bills refer to the process 'beginning in the 7th week of the session…[where] one MP [on a first come first serve basis] is called to make a speech of not more than ten minutes setting out the case for a bill and seeking the leave of the House to introduce it.' Ten minute rule bills occur on Tuesday and Wednesdays before the main business of the day and are therefore likely to attract attention. In presentation the MP does not seek the leave of the House.

4   The Conservatives contested 41 percent of all government Bills at Second or Third Reading in the 1997 Parliament, 32 percent in the 2001 Parliament, but only 21 percent between 2005–7 (Cowley and Stuart undated).

5   First, the causes of unequal pay are disputed; secondly, the principle of flexible working is treated with caution by those who advocate the 'business interest'; and thirdly, the Labour government had been for some time, planning to introduce an Equality Bill, that it claimed would address the concerns raised in the EPFW Bill.

6   Most importantly for this analysis, Lords' PMBs reach the Commons late in the parliamentary session. If a PMB passes its Lords' stages it must be taken up by an MP (H of L 2001: 4). Only 13 Fridays are set aside for PMBs although governments may provide more time for those it supports.

7   As Cowley (1998: 3) writes, 'it is easier to list' issues of conscience that it is to 'define what links' them.

8   There may have been whipping of Labour members to ensure a high turnout and there are suggestions that Gordon Brown had made his views known to increase Labour MPs' support for 24 weeks (*Daily Mail* May 21, 2008).

9   The subjective judgment and expertise of the researcher becomes central to the qualitative analysis of the data for constitutive representation (Burnham et al 2004: 236; Harrison 2001). Qualitative content analysis is considered by some (Burnham et al 2004: 249) to be 'very similar' to discourse analysis in that both involve the 'analysis of the dominant discourses or political languages that frame our social and political world and our understanding of it'. It is acknowledged that what constitutes discourse analysis, and variants thereof, are widely debated.

10   The limited nature of any conclusions is accordingly acknowledged.

11   Parliamentary voting data is transparent, extensive, and mostly correct hard data that can be easily analyzed quantitatively (Cowley 2002).

12   Peter Luff MP (Con), Commons Second Reading.

13   Labour women were slightly over-represented at 30 percent, when they constitute 28 percent of the PLP (86 out of 291). Conservative women constituted 15 out of 149 voting MPs (10 percent when they constitute 9 percent of the parliamentary Conservative Party. The Liberal Democrats saw seven women vote out of 46, 15 percent, when their percentage of the parliamentary party is 16 percent).

14   http://www.dailymail.co.uk/news/article-513264/Sir-Alan-Sugar-Why-I-think-twice-employing-woman.html

15   See for example, the Conservative MPs, Tobias Ellwood and Stewart Jackson.

16   Baroness Walmsley (LD) and the Bishop of Southwell contend that the level of payment for APL and Additional Maternity Leave (AML) is too low. Lord Razzell

(LD) favours higher pay over a shorter period of time and the enhancement of OPL, while Lord Northbourne (CB) is critical of the dependent nature of father's rights to APL.

17   This is despite the argument that APL goes to the heart of the debate about gender equality. If extending maternity leave can be understood in terms of traditional gender roles – helping women to care for children – APL challenges traditional notions of who cares for children and who goes out to work. The Government's pro-fatherhood position did not go unchallenged. Norman Lamb (LD), in the Commons pointedly asked whether it was really in favour of paternity leave, given that the low pay meant that very few men would be able to take up APL. In the Lords there was concern about the inflexibility and inadequacy of ordinary paternity leave (OPL), raised by Baroness Walmsely (LD).

18   Baroness Morris (Con) Lords Second Reading.

19   Baroness Morris (Con) makes this clear in her opening statement in Parliament.

20   This might also be a rhetorical inter-party competition strategy to undermine the Conservative position.

21   Not least, Baronesses Prosser (Lab) and Gould (Lab), and Howe (CB), although note that Lord Hunt (Con) talks of women being 'given every opportunity to fulfil their potential'.

22   Clare Curtis-Thomas (Lab) contends for this proposition; Dawn Primarolo (Lab) against.

23   The full case study also makes reference to the Committee's Minority Report.

24   The first six months post-childbirth is one difference arguably presented as natural.

25   These percentages are based on an n of 10.

26   Once again these are on very small numbers (n = 7).

27   Explaining this requires additional research.

28   Note that the women do not claim to be owners of Small and medium enterprises (SME) – Baroness Morris (Con) recounts her family's small cake shop.

29   Eleanor Laing (Con), Julie Kirkbride (Con) and Kitty Ussher (Lab).

30   In the EPFW debate Baroness Morris (Con) implies she is a mother, which she is.

31   The legislation did not directly address abortion so no comparison with its representations and those made in the STC report can be made. The abortion amendments that were voted on in the House of Commons and Lords came from critics of the STC Report and therefore are unsurprisingly strongly out of kilter with its representations, both constitutive and substantive.

32   See Endnote 17 above. See also Ussher (Lab).

33   *Choice and Flexibility Regulatory Impact Assessment.*

34   The fourth pledge 'to help women into work and up the careers ladder, through for example, improved careers advice to young women so that they can make informed choices with knowledge about 'the financial and professional consequences of their decisions', and focuses on the difficulties women, highly and less qualified, face on returning to the paid employment market post child-birth/ caring. The third pledge is (as in the Lords' Second Reading) enhanced by an aspiration to extend flexible working as widely as possible. This will be achieved by ensuring regulations are simple and easy to implement and ensuring that the public sector 'becomes a world leader' in flexible working.

35   Nine male MPs (Eric Forth, Mike Weir, Peter Bone, Jim Devine, Sadiq Khan, John Redwood, Mark Tami, Keith Vaz and Rob Marris) were not identified as having any interests related to the legislation.

36   Source: http://www.parliament.uk/mpslordsandoffices/mps_and_lords/alphabetical_list_of_members.cfm#P, accessed 21 July 2009.

37   Source: http://www.parliament.uk/mpslordsandoffices/mps_and_lords/alphabet-
     ical_list_of_members.cfm#P, accessed 21 July 2009.
38   Source: http://www.parliament.uk/mpslordsandoffices/mps_and_lords/alphabet-
     ical_list_of_members.cfm#P, accessed 21 July 2009.
39   For those MPs who spoke on abortion.
40   For those MPs who spoke on abortion. http://www.parliament.uk/mpslordsand-
     offices/mps_and_lords/alms.cfm accessed on 28/05/09.

Chapter 7   Feminization and Party Cohesion: Conservative Ideological Tendencies and Gender Politics

1   Note that this chapter draws on Webb and Childs (2011).
2   Party Member focus group participant.
3   Note, however, that David Hine (1982) has argued the term 'tendency' must
    imply some degree of stability of personnel if it is to be identifiable at all. For if a
    tendency has no identifiable group of personnel, then how is it to be different-
    iated from the non-aligned members of a party? Hine's preferred definition of
    a tendency is therefore: '...a group which displays a broad position upon some
    ideological or value-based continuum (e.g., left, centrist, right) but which lacks
    clearly defined membership, leadership or discipline, makes few attempts to coor-
    dinate activities or extend itself throughout all levels of party organization'. In
    our view this represents a modest but helpful improvement on Rose's original
    definition.
4   Our data set only measures attitudes and not organization or behaviour, there-
    fore, we cannot claim to be able to identify factions.
5   In brief, the first statistical criterion is the *mean score on each of the two attitudinal
    scales* referred to above (Left-Right and Libertarian-Authoritarian) of the various
    clusters generated by a particular model. Cluster means inform us on average pre-
    cisely how left-wing, right-wing, libertarian or authoritarian each of the clusters is,
    and thus identify the nature of each in a substantive sense. Clearly, this needs
    to produce a model that is *substantively interpretable*. Beyond this, two further sta-
    tistical criteria are employed: The *F-ratios* generated by analysis of variance
    whether the differences between cluster means are statistically significant; *no model
    is accepted unless cluster means are significantly and substantively different on either the
    Left-Right or Liberty-Authority scales*. In addition, we refer to the *eta²* coefficient
    which measures the strength of these cluster models (or more exactly, the ratio of
    variation explained by cluster group differences to that which is unexplained by
    them); we feel that a cluster model should not been considered acceptable unless
    eta^2 indicates that it explains at least 50 percent of the variation in each of the atti-
    tudinal scales. The final criterion which is applied is the principle of *parsimony*. As a
    general rule, it makes sense to opt for the simplest meaningful model which con-
    forms to the statistical criteria and provides a substantively interpretation of intra-
    party attitudinal differences. For further detail on our approach to cluster analysis,
    see Webb (2008: 433–434).
6   See Webb (2008) Table 4.
7   To some observers there might appear to be a case for describing this outlook
    as 'One Nation'. However, we are mindful of the argument that it is a myth to
    regard the One Nation approach as characterized by a clear preference for an
    extended state. Rather, while the welfare of the poorer members of society has

been a frequent refrain of One Nation adherents, there has also been a perennial tension among them as to the appropriate level of state intervention needed to achieve this end. Although there has been a tendency for intra-party critics of Thatcherism to invoke the One Nation brand in opposition to it, a cursory examination of the membership of the One Nation Group since its inception in 1950 quickly reveals that it has always included both those renowned for their limited state, free market preferences (e.g., Powell, Joseph) and those associated with a willingness to entertain dirigiste interventionism (Heath, Gilmour). Consequently, we feel that the label Traditional Conservative better captures this blend social conservatism and interventionism. For a detailed consideration of this issue see Seawright (2010).

8 Note, however, that the relatively left-wing orientation of many Conservative party members is not so surprising when viewed in the light of the very similar findings reported by Whiteley and his colleagues (1994: 198–9) nearly two decades ago: 'Perhaps most significantly, while the average grassroots members think of themselves as being on the centre-right of the ideological spectrum within the party, some 41 percent of them can be found in categories 1 to 5 of the left-right party scale, i.e. in the left-wing to centrist positions'.

9 Note, however, that we also considered the alternative of a four-cluster model of intra-party tendencies. This would have retained the three clusters shown in Table 7.1/Figure 7.1, and added of a further small cluster in the left-libertarian quadrant. After some reflection, we rejected this possibility for a number of reasons: first, such individuals only constitute 5 percent of our sample; second, previous work on the probably more politically sophisticated parliamentary elites only reveals three Conservative clusters, which raises the question of whether some of our respondents have clearly defined attitudinal structures at all; and finally, the four-cluster solution falls by one of the key statistical criteria that we established, which was that to be acceptable, a cluster model must explain at least 50 percent of the variance in both the left-right and liberty-authority scales. While the eta-squared coefficients reported in Table 7.1 clearly show that this is true for the three-cluster model, the four-cluster model produces an unacceptably low eta-squared of 0.47 for the liberty-authority scale. For all of these reasons, it seems to us that the more parsimonious model is to be preferred.

10 *Observer* February 14, 2010.

11 See http://www.fawcettsociety.org.uk/, accessed 20 October 2010.

12 http://www.wbg.org.uk/

13 http://www.yvettecooper.com/women-bear-brunt-of-budget-cuts

Chapter 8   The Feminization Strategy and the Electorate

1 http://aberconwyconservatives.co.uk/ive-never-voted-tory-before-but-julies-story/, accessed February 8, 2011.

2 The data come from a weighted sample of voters interviewed as part of the British Election Study. The dependent variable is dichotomously coded, with 1 representing a Conservative vote and 0 representing any other choice. This is the therefore a model which assesses the probability of an individual voting for the party given a score on a specific variable from the model, while holding all other effects in the model constant. The logistic regression coefficients b show the change in the predicted logged odds of a respondent voting Conservative for a one-unit change in the independent variable; a positive figure indicates an increase in the odds

on voting Conservative, while a negative coefficient indicates a reduction in the odds of a Conservative vote for a one unit change in the predictor. *Exp(b)* is interpretively similar, except that it does not require logarithmic transformation in the way that *b* does (Field 2005: 225). The key point to bear in mind here is that if an *Exp(b)* coefficient has a value greater than 1, then it indicates that as the predictor increases in value by one unit, the odds on a Conservative vote increase, while a value of less than 1 indicates a decrease in the odds on support for the Tories.

3 The 2 log likelihood figure and the omnibus significance test confirm this, but the various R^2 figures are very low, which is not surprising for a model which only takes into account demographic factors.

4 The model shows the following things: Compared to manual employees, all other occupational grades (especially senior white collar and small business owners) are more likely to vote Conservative; private sector employees are significantly more likely to vote Tory than voluntary sector employees are, but public sector workers are not; but graduates are significantly more likely to support the party than non-graduates are; Black and Asian Britons are significantly less likely to vote Conservative than other ethnic groups; men are significantly less likely to support the party than women; all age groups up to the age of 60 are significantly less likely to favour the Conservatives than those over 65; and the gender-generation term reveals that young men under 24 years of age are significantly more likely to vote Tory than women over the age of 65. This last point confirms that the gender-generation interaction has some explanatory utility, although it does not capture all of the nuances that we have explored through the three-way crosstabulation in Table 8.4.

5 www.centreforsocialjustice.org.uk

6 Respondents were surveyed during the campaign before Election Day.

7 All results reported here are only intended to complement the foregoing quantitative analysis of BES data; as with all qualitative research, this work is designed to be illustrative rather than statistically valid. Thirty two individuals constitute our sample. See Methods Appendix for more detail.

8 On the basis of what we know about the preferences of younger generations of women voters regarding the level and quality of public services, questions of cuts to public services and tax rises are likely to become increasingly pertinent as the Conservative/Liberal Democrat coalition address the economic legacy inherited from the Labour government. As discussed in the previous Chapter, various feminist civil society groups alongside Labour Shadow Ministers have offered gendered criticism of the Government's cuts, contending that they disproportionately impact on women: (1) because more women work in the public sector; (2) because women are more likely to use the public services; and (3) because women are disproportionately dependent upon state benefits.

9 Of course, and as stated in Chapter 5, policy pledges for women outlined in opposition and even in a party's manifesto are not the same thing as the implementation of these once in government. It is not clear as yet which of the party's policies explicitly for women will be enacted in the 2010 Parliament.

Conclusion

1 Theresa May MP, June 2005 'Speech to the Adelaide Group'.

2 *Guardian* November 6, 2009.

3 Publicly, Warsi is known for her antipathy towards minority pressure groups and the politics of identity in general (*Observer* March 29, 2009): [she prefers to] be judged as an individual rather than 'as a Muslim or woman'. Note that she stood unsuccessfully for election in 2005 before Cameron appointed her to the Lords two years later, apparently impatient for the election of a Muslim woman.

4 Private comments by Labour women MPs told to one of the authors.

5 Bercow's personal advocacy of AWS is in the public domain (*Guardian* January 30, 2009). Having noted the 'global evidence' of the effectiveness of AWS, he decries: 'It's time the Conservative party went in for a bit of shameless plagiarism. Central Office can impose all-women or all-BME shortlists, or both...'

6 Apparently she was not considered 'good enough' for this job. Following Labour's much derided, first female Home Secretary, Jacqui Smith, the implicit question seemed to be, could any woman be Home Secretary? (*Times* April 28, 2009).

7 http://www.guardian.co.uk/politics/2010/may/13/cabinet-women-diversity, accessed February 21, 2011.

8 http://www.bbc.co.uk/radio4/womanshour/01/2008_11_mon.shtml

9 Lisa Young (2000; undated) notes that the Canadian Reform party refuses to recognize women as a group suggesting a shift away from 'measures ensuring the representation of women in party affairs'.

10 Private information, party worker close to Cameron.

11 For reasons of anonymity, the identity of these women MPs is not revealed.

12 HM Government, *The Coalition: Our Programme for Government,* 2010.

13 *Evening Standard* July 19, 2010. Cf analysis of the 1990s and 2000 Conservative party manifestos. In the former, gendered crime is acknowledged whilst in the latter, there are no such crime pledges for women.

14 http://www.guardian.co.uk/politics/interactive/2010/aug/03/theresa-may-letter-chancellor-cuts, accessed August 4, 2010.

15 http://www.guardian.co.uk/world/2010/dec/06/fawcett-society-loses-court-challenge-budget, accessed December 6, 2010.

16 The BRS 2010 should enable analysis of this.

17 Observations made in the intra-party democracy literature (Young and Cross 2002) suggesting that the plebiscitary party rejects group representation warrants subsequent research to explore the extent to which political parties are rejecting women's organizations. If this pattern is widely observable the typology of feminized political parties might require some revision.

Methods Appendix

1 Interviews with 'informant' Parliamentarians and party officials were ongoing throughout the project. These interviews – which need to remain anonymous – were designed to pick up on developments within the party and the wider political environment and took place both at regular intervals and in response to particular events and initial findings from other components of the research design. The data from these interviews, most of which were digitally recorded, informed the overall analysis of the project, but do not themselves constitute a distinct set of data to be analysed discretely.

2 This and the following section draw on reports provided to us by Ipsos-MORI.

References

Annesley, C. (2010) 'Gender, Politics and Policy Change: The Case of Welfare Reform under New Labour', *Government and Opposition*, 45(1): 50–72.

Annesley, C. and Gains, F. (2010) 'The Core Executive: Gender Power and Change', *Political Studies*, 58, 5.

Annesley, C., Gains, F. and Rummery, K. (2007) *Women and New Labour: Engendering Politics* (Bristol: Policy Press).

Ashcroft, M. (2005) *Smell the Coffee: A Wake Up Call for the Conservative Party* (UK: CGI).

Ashe, J., Campbell, R., Childs, S. and Evans, E. (2010) 'Stand by your Man', *British Politics*, 5.

Baker, G. (2005) 'Revisiting the Concept of Representation', *Parliamentary Affairs*, 59, 1.

Baldez, L. (2004) 'Elected Bodies', *Legislative Studies Quarterly*, XXIX, 2.

Baldez, L. (2007) 'Primaries vs. Quotas: Gender and Candidate Nominations in Mexico, 2003', *Latin American Politics and Society*, 49, 3.

Bale, T. (2010) *The Conservative Party* (Cambridge: Polity).

Bale, T. (2007) 'And with One Bound He was Free? David Cameron and the Problem of Party Change', paper given to authors.

Bale, T. and Webb, P. (2011) 'The Conservative Party', in N. Allen and J. Bartle (eds) *Britain at the Polls 2010* (London: Sage).

Ball, S. (2003) 'The Conservatives in Opposition, 1906–79: A Comparative Analysis', in M. Garnett and P. Lynch (eds) *The Conservatives in Crisis* (Manchester: Manchester University Press).

Bara, J. (2005a) 'A Question of Trust: Implementing Party Manifestos', *Parliamentary Affairs*, 58, 3.

Bara, J. and Budge, I. (2001) 'Party Policy and Ideology: Still New Labour?', *Parliamentary Affairs*, 54, 4.

Barbour, R. S. and Kitzinger, J. (1999) *Developing Focus Group Research* (London: Sage).

Bartle, J. (2005) 'Homogenous Models and Heterogeneous Voters', *Political Studies*, 53, 4.

Bashevkin, S. (2000) 'From Tough Times to Better Times', *International Political Science Review*, 21, 4.

Bashevkin, S. (1998) *Women on the Defensive* (Chicago: CUP).

Beckwith, K. (2008) 'Conclusion: Between Participation and Representation', in C. Wolbrecht, K. Beckwith and L. Baldez (eds) *Political Women and American Democracy* (Cambridge: Cambridge University Press).

Beckwith, K. and Cowell-Myers, K. (2007) 'Sheer Numbers: Critical Representation Thresholds and Women's Political Representation', *Perspectives on Politics*, 5, 3.

Beckwith, K. and Cowell-Myers, K. (2003) 'Sheer Numbers', paper presented at Annual Meeting of the American Political Science Association, Philadelphia.

Beckwith, K. (2003) 'Number and Newness', paper given to the author.

Beech, M. (2009) 'Cameron and Conservative Ideology', in M. Beech and S. Lee (eds) *The Conservatives under David Cameron* (Basingstoke: Palgrave).

Berrington, H. (1973) *Backbench Opinion in the House of Commons 1945–55* (Oxford: Pergamon).

Berrington, H. and Hague, R. (1998) 'Europe, Thatcherism and Traditionalism', in H. Berrington (ed.) *Britain in the 1990s* (London: Frank Cass).

Bhavnani, R. R. (2009) 'Do Electoral Quotas Work after they are Withdrawn?', *APSR*, 103, 1.

Birch, A. H. (1993) *The Concepts and Theories of Modern Democracy* (London: Routledge).

Birch, A. H. (1971) *Representation* (Basingstoke: Macmillan).

Bochel, C. and Briggs, J. (2000) 'Do Women Make a Difference', *Politics*, 20, 2.

Bolleyer, N. (2009) 'Inside the Cartel Party: Party Organization in Government and Opposition', *Political Studies*, 57, 3.

Boucek, F. (2009) 'Rethinking factionalism', *Party Politics*, 15, 4.

Bratton, K. A. and Ray, L. P. (2002) 'Descriptive Representation, Policy Outcomes, and Municipal Day-Care Coverage in Norway', *American Journal of Political Science*, 46, 2.

Bryson, V. and Heppell, T. (2010) 'Conservatism and Feminism: The Case of the British Conservative Party', *Journal of Political Ideologies*, 15, 1.

Budge, I. (1999) 'Party Policy and Ideology: Reversing the 1950s?', in G. Evans and P. Norris (eds) *Critical Elections* (London: Sage).

Burnham, P., Gilland, K., Grant, W. and Layton-Henry, Z. (2004) *Research Methods in Politics* (Basingstoke: Palgrave).

Campbell, B. (1987) *Iron Ladies* (London: Virago).

Campbell, R. (2006) *Gender and the Vote in Britain* (Colchester, Essex: ECPR Press).

Campbell, R. (2004) 'Gender, Ideology and Issue Preference: Is There Such a Thing as a Political Women's Interest in Britain?', *British Journal of Politics and International Relations*, 6, 1.

Campbell, R. and Childs, S. (2010) 'Wives, Wags and Mothers....But What about Women MPs, Sex and Gender at the 2010 General Election', in A. Geddes and J. Tonge (eds) *Britain Votes: The 2010 General Election*, Special Edition of *Parliamentary Affairs* (Oxford: Oxford University Press).

Campbell, R., Childs, S. and Lovenduski, J. (2007) 'Descriptive and Substantive Representation: The Difference between Wanting and Needing Women Representatives', paper prepared for ECPR Joint Sessions of Workshops, Helsinki.

Campbell, R., Childs, S. and Lovenduski, J. (2006) 'Equality Guarantees and the Conservative Party', *Political Quarterly*, 7, 1.

Campbell, R., Lovenduski, J. and Childs, S. (2010) 'Do Women Need Women MPs? A Comparison of Mass and Elite Attitudes', *British Journal of Political Science*, 40, 1.

Campbell, R. and Winters, K. (2006a) 'The 2005 British General Election', in R. Campbell, *Gender and the Vote in Britain* (Colchester, Essex: ECPR Press).

Carroll, S. J. (2003) *Women and American Politics* (Oxford: Oxford University Press).

Carroll, S. J. (2002) 'Representing Women: Congresswomen's Perceptions of Their Representational Roles', in C. Rosenthal (ed.) *Women Transforming Congress* (Norman: University of Oklahoma Press).

Carroll, S. J. (2001) *The Impact of Women in Public Office* (Bloomington: Indiana University Press).

Carroll, S. J. (1999) 'The Disempowerment of the Gender Gap: Soccer Moms and the 1996 Elections', *PS*, 32, 1.

Carroll, S. J. (1994) *Women as Candidates in American Politics* (Bloomington and Indianapolis: Indiana University Press).

Carroll, S. J. (1988) 'Women's Autonomy and the Gender Gap: 1980 and 1982', in C. Mueller (ed.) *The Politics of the Gender Gap* (California: Sage).

Carroll, S. J. (1984) 'Woman Candidates and Support for Feminist Concerns: The Closet Feminist Syndrome', *Western Political Quarterly*, 37.

Carroll, S. J. and Liebowitz, D. J. (2003) 'New Challenges, New Questions, New Directions', in S. J. Carroll (ed.) *Women and American Politics* (Oxford: Oxford University Press).

Carroll, S. J. and Schreiber, R. (1997) 'Media Coverage of Women in the 103rd Congress', in P. Norris (ed.) *Women, Media and Politics* (Oxford: Oxford University Press).

Carver, T. (1996) *Gender is Not a Synonym for Woman* (Boulder: Lynne Reinner).

Celis, K. (2008) 'Gendering Representation', in Gary Goertz and Amy Mazur (eds) *Politics, Gender, and Concepts* (Cambridge: CUP).

Celis, K. (2006a) 'Substantive Representation of Women and the Impact of Descriptive Representation. Case: The Belgian Lower House 1900–1979', *Journal of Women, Politics and Policy*, 28, 2.

Celis, K. (2006b) 'Gendering Political Representation. Theory and Empirical Research', Paper presented at the Political Studies Association Annual Conference, Reading.

Celis, K. (2005) 'Reconciling Theory and Empirical Research. Methodological Reflections on 'Women MP's representing Women('s Interests)', Paper presented at the Annual Meeting of the American Political Science Association, Washington DC.

Celis, K. (2004) 'Substantive and Descriptive Representation: Investigating the Impact of the Voting Right and of Descriptive Representation on the Substantive Representation of Women in the Belgian Lower House (1900–1979)', Paper presented at the Annual Meeting of the American Political Science Association, Chicago, IL.

Celis, K. and Childs, S. (2011) 'The Substantive Representation of Women: What to Do with Conservative Claims?', *Political Studies*, forthcoming.

Celis, K., Childs, S., Kantola, J. and Krook, M. L (2010) 'Constituting Women's Interests through Representative Claims', Paper prepared for APSA Annual Meeting, 2009, Toronto.

Celis, K., Childs, S., Kantola, J. and Krook, M. L. (2008) 'Rethinking Women's Substantive Representation', *Representation*, 44, 2.

Celis, K., Childs, S., Kantola, J. and Krook, M. L. (2007) 'Rethinking Women's Substantive Representation', Paper prepared for the ECPR Joint Sessions of Workshops, University of Helsinki.

Chaney, P. (2006) 'Critical Mass, Deliberation and the Substantive Representation of Women', *Political Studies*, 54, 4.

Childs, S. (2010) 'Engendering Intra Party Democracy: Lessons from the United Kingdom', unpublished paper prepared for Intra Party Democracy Workshop, Carleton University, Ottawa, 30–31st August.

Childs, S. (2008) *Women and British Party Politics* (London: Routledge).

Childs, S. (2006) 'Political Parties', in P. Dunleavy et al (eds) *Developments in British Politics 8* (Basingstoke: Palgrave).

Childs, S. (2005) 'Feminizing British Politics: Sex and Gender in the 2005 General Election', in A. Geddes and J. Tonge (eds) *Britain Decides: The UK General Election 2005* (Basingstoke: Palgrave).

Childs, S. (2004) *New Labour's Women MPs: Women Representing Women* (London: Routledge).

Childs, S. (2003) 'The Sex Discrimination (Election Candidates) Act and its Implications', *Representation*, 39, 2.

Childs, S. (2002) 'Competing Conceptions of Representation and the Passage of the Sex Discrimination (Election Candidates) Bill', *Journal of Legislative Studies*, 8, 3.

Childs, S. (2001a) 'In Their Own Words: New Labour Women MPs and the Substantive Representation of Women', *British Journal of Politics and International Relations*, 3, 1.

Childs, S. (2001b) 'Attitudinally Feminist'? The New Labour Women MPs and the Substantive Representation of Women', *Politics*, 21, 3.

Childs, S. and Cowley, P. (2011) 'The Politics of Local Presence: Is there a Case for Descriptive Representation?', *Political Studies*, 59, 1.

Childs, S. and Krook, M. L. (2009) 'Analyzing Women's Substantive Representation: From Critical Mass to Critical Actors', *Government and Opposition*, 44, 2.

Childs, S. and Krook, M. L. (2008) 'Critical Mass Theory and Women's Political Representation', *Political Studies*, 56, 3.

Childs, S. and Krook. M. L. (2006a) 'Gender and Politics: The State of the Art', *Politics*, 26, 1.

Childs, S. and Krook, M. L. (2006b) 'Gender, Politics, and Political Science: A Reply to Michael Moran', *Politics*, 26, 3.

Childs, S. and Krook, M. L. (2006c) 'Should Feminists Give up on Critical Mass? A Contingent Yes', *Politics and Gender*, 2, 4.

Childs, S. and Lovenduski, J. (2012) 'Political Representation', in Celis, K. et al (eds) *Oxford Handbook on Gender and Politics*, forthcoming (Oxford: Blackwells).

Childs, S., Lovenduski, J. and Campbell, R. (2005) *Women on Top* (London: Hansard Society).

Childs, S., Webb, P. and Marthaler, S. (2010) 'Constituting and Substantively Representing Women: Applying New Approaches to a UK Case Study', *Politics and Gender*, 6, 2.

Childs, S., Webb, P. and Marthaler, S. (2008) 'The Feminization of the Conservative Parliamentary Party', *The Political Quarterly*, 80, 2.

Childs, S. and Withey, J. (2006) 'The Substantive Representation of Women: Reducing the VAT on Sanitary Products in the UK', *Parliamentary Affairs*, 59, 1.

Childs, S. and Withey, J. (2004) 'Do Women Sign for Women? Sex and the Signing of Early Day Motions in the 1997 Parliament', *Political Studies* 52, 4.

Clark, G. and Kelly, S. (2004) 'Echoes of Butler? The Conservative Research Department and the Making of Conservative Policy', *Political Quarterly*, 75, 4.

Clarke, H. D., Sanders, D., Stewart, M. C. and Whiteley, P. F. (2004) *Political Choice in Britain* (Oxford: Oxford University Press).

Conservative Party (undated) *Human Trafficking One Year On* (London).

Conway, M. M. (2001) 'Women and Political Participation', *PS*, 34, 2, June.

Coole, D. (1993) *Women in Political Theory* (Hemel Hempstead: Harvester-Wheatsheaf & Colorado, Lynne Rienner).

Cowley, P. (2005) *The Rebels* (London: Politicos).

Cowley, P. (2002) *Revolts and Rebellions: Parliamentary Voting Under Blair* (London: Politicos).

Cowley, P. (1998) *Conscience and Parliament* (London: Frank Cass).

Cowley, P. and Childs, S. (2003) 'Too Spineless Too Rebel', *British Journal of Political Science*, 33, 3.

Cowley, P. and Green, J. (2005) 'New Leaders, Same Problems', in A. Geddes and J. Tonge (eds) *Britain Decides: The UK General Election 2005* (Basingstoke: Palgrave).

Cowley, P. and Stuart, M. (2010) 'Party Rules OK', *Parliamentary Affairs*, 63, 1.

Cowley, P. and Stuart, M. (2003) 'The Conservative Parliamentary Party', in M. Garnett and P. Lynch (eds) *The Conservatives in Crisis* (Manchester: Manchester University Press).

Cowell-Myers, K. (2003) *Women Legislators in Northern Ireland: Gender and Politics in the New Legislative Assembly* (Centre for Advancement of Women in Politics School of Politics, Queens University Belfast, Occasional paper # 3).

Cowell-Meyers, K. (2001) 'Gender, Power, and Peace: A Preliminary Look at Women in the Northern Ireland Assembly', *Women & Politics*, 23, 3.

Cowell-Meyers, K. and Langbein (2009) 'Linking Women's Descriptive and Substantive Representation in the United States', *Politics and Gender*, 5, 4.

Criddle, B. (2005) 'MPs and Candidates', in D. Kavanagh and D. Butler (eds) *The British General Election of 2005* (Basingstoke: Palgrave).

Criddle, B. (2002) 'MPs and Candidates', in D. Butler and D. Kavanagh (eds) *The British General Election of 2001* (Basingstoke: Palgrave).

Criddle, B. (1997) 'MPs and Candidates', in D. Butler and D. Kavanagh (eds) *The British General Election of 1997* (Basingstoke: Macmillan).

Criddle, B. (1992) 'MPs and Candidates', in D. Butler and D. Kavanagh (eds) *The British General Election of 1992* (Basingstoke: Macmillan).

Crompton, R. and Lyonette, C. (2005) 'The New Gender Essentialism – Domestic and Family "Choices" and their Relation to Attitudes', *The British Journal of Sociology*, 56, 4.

Crowder-Meyer, M. (2009) 'Party Strength and Activity and Women's Political Representation at the Local Level', paper presented to APSA Annual meeting, Toronto, September.

Crowley, J. E. (2004) 'When Tokens Matter', *Legislative Studies Quarterly*, 29, 1.

Currell, M. (1974) *Political Woman* (London: Croom Helm).

Currie, E. (2002) *Diaries 1987–1992* (London: Little Brown).

Curtice, J. (2010) 'So What Went Wrong with the Electoral System', in A. Geddes and J. Tonge (eds) *Britain Votes: The 2010 General Election*, Special Edition Of *Parliamentary Affairs* (Oxford: Oxford University Press).

Cutts, D., Childs, S. and Fieldhouse, E. (2008) 'This Is What You Get When You Don't Listen', *Party Politics*, 14, 5.

Dahlerup, D. (2006) *Women, Quotas and Politics* (London: Routledge).

Dahlerup, D. (2002) *Gender Quotas in a Comparative Perspective* (Geneva: ECPR Research Session Report).

Dahlerup, D. (1998) 'Using Quotas to Increase Women's Political Representation', in A. Karam, *Women In Parliament Beyond Numbers* (Stockholm: IDEA).

Dahlerup, D. (1988) 'From a Small to a Large Minority: Women in Scandinavian Politics', *Scandinavian Political Studies*, 11, 4.

Dahlerup, D. (1984) 'Overcoming the Barriers: An Approach to how Women's Issues are kept from the Political Agenda', in J. H. Stiehm (ed.) *Women's Views of the Political World of Men* (New York: Transnational Publishers).

Dahlerup, D. and Freidenvall, L. (2005) 'Quotas as a Fast Track to Equal Political Representation for Women: Why Scandinavia is No Longer the Model', *International Feminist Journal of Politics*, 7, 1.

Dahlerup, D. and Freidenvall, L. (2003) 'Quotas as a Fast Track to Equal Political Representation for Women: Why Scandinavia is No Longer the Model', Paper presented to the 19th International Political Science Association World Congress. Durban, South Africa, June 29–July 4.

Darcy, R., Welch, S. and Clark, J. (1994) *Women, Elections and Representation* (Lincoln and London: University of Nebraska Press).

Deacon, D., Wring, D. and Golding, P. (2007) 'The "Take a Break Campaign?": National Print Media Reporting of the Election', in D. Wring, J. Green, R. Mortimore and S. Atkinson (eds) *Political Communication: The General Election Campaign of 2005* (Basingstoke: Palgrave Macmillan).

Deacon, D., Wring, D. and Golding, P. (2006) 'Same Campaign, Differing Agendas', *British Politics*, 1, 2.

Denham, A. and O'Hara, K. (2007) *Democratizing Conservative Party Leadership* (Manchester: Manchester University Press).

Denver, D. (2010) 'The Results: How Britain Voted', in A. Geddes and J. Tonge (eds) *Britain Votes: The 2010 General Election*, Special Edition of *Parliamentary Affairs* (Oxford: Oxford University Press).

Deutchman, I. A. and Ellison, A. (2004) 'When Feminists Don't Fit: The Case of Pauline Hanson', *International Feminist Journal of Politics*, 6, 1.

Deutchman, I. A. and Ellison, A. (1999) 'A Star is Born: The Roller Coaster Ride of Pauline Hanson in the News', *Media, Culture & Society*, 21, 1.

Diamond, I. and Hartsock, N. (1998) 'Beyond Interests in Politics', in A. Phillips (ed.) *Feminism and Politics* (Oxford: Oxford University Press).

Dillard, A. D. (2005) 'Adventures in Conservative Feminism', *Society*, March/April.

Dobrowolsky, A. and Hart, V. (2003) *Women Making Constitutions* (Basingstoke: Palgrave).

Dodson, D. L. (2006) *The Impact of Women in Congress* (Oxford: Oxford University Press).

Dodson, D. L. (2001) 'The Impact of Women in Congress: Re-thinking Ideas about Difference', paper presented to APSA, Women and Politics Special Session, San Francisco, August.

Dodson, D. L. (1998) 'Representing Women's Interests in the US House of Representatives', in S. Thomas and C. Wilcox (eds) *Women and Elective Office* (Oxford: Oxford University Press).

Dodson, D. L. and Carroll, S. J. (1991) *Reshaping the Agenda: Women in State Legislatures* (New Brunswick: Center for American Women and Politics).

Dolan, K. (2001) 'Electoral Context, Issues, and Voting for Women in the 1990s', in K. O'Conner (eds) *Women and Congress: Running, Winning and Ruling* (Binghamton: The Haworth Press).

Dolan, K. and Ford, L. E. (1998) 'Are All Women State Legislators Alike', in S. Thomas and C. Wilcox (eds) *Women and Elective Office* (Oxford: Oxford University Press).

Dolan, K. and Ford, L. E. (1995) 'Women in State Legislatures: Feminist Identity and Legislative Behaviours', *APQ*, 23.

Dorey, P. (2003) 'Conservative Policy under Hague', in M. Garnett and P. Lynch (eds) *The Conservatives in Crisis* (Manchester: Manchester University Press).

Dovi, S. (2008) 'Theorizing Women's Representation in the United States', in C. Wolbrecht, K. Beckwith and L. Baldez (eds) *Political Women and American Democracy* (Cambridge: Cambridge University Press).

Dovi, S. (2002) 'Preferable Descriptive Representatives: Will Just Any Woman, Black or Latino Do?', *APSR*, 96, 4.

Downs, A. (1957) *An Economic Theory of Democracy* (New York: Harper Row).

Dryzek, J. S. and Niemeyer, S. (2008) 'Discursive Representation', *APSR*, 102, 4.

Duerst-Lahti, G. (2008) 'Gender Ideology: Masculinism and Feminalism', in G. Goertz and A. Mazur (eds) *Politics, Gender and Concepts* (NY: Cambridge University Press).

Dunleavy, P. and Husbands, C. (1985) *British Democracy at the Crossroads: Voting and Party Competition in the 1980s* (London: Allen and Unwin).

Duverger, M. (1955) *The Political Role of Women* (Paris: UNESCO).

The Electoral Commission (2002) 'Candidates at a General Election Factsheet' (www.electoralcommission.org.uk).

Elgood, J., Vinter, L. and Williams, R. (2002) *Man Enough for the Job? A Study of Parliamentary Candidates* (Manchester: EOC).

Elliot, F. and Hanning, J. (2007) *Cameron, the Rise of the New Conservative* (London: Fourth Estate).

Erickson, L. (1997) 'Might More Women Make a Difference?', *Canadian Journal of Political Science*, 30, 4.

Evans, E. (2011) *Gender and the Liberal Democrats: Representing Women?* (Manchester: MUP).

Evans, E. (2007) 'Grassroots Influence: Pressure Groups within the Liberal Democrats', *Political Quarterly*, 78, 1.

Evans, S. (2008) 'Consigning its Past to History? David Cameron and the Conservative Party', *Parliamentary Affairs*, 61, 2.

Field, A. P. (2005). *Discovering Statistics Using SPSS: and Sex and Drugs and Rock 'n' Roll* (2nd edition). London: Sage.

Franceshet (2008) 'Gendered Institutions and Women's Substantive Representation', paper presented to ECPR Joint Sessions, Rennes.

Freidenvall, L. (2005) 'A Discursive Struggle – The Swedish National Federation of Social Democratic Women and Gender Qutoas', *Nordic Journal of Women's Studies*, 13, 3.

Freidenvall, L. (2003) 'Women's Political Representation and Gender Quotas – the Swedish Case', *The Research Program on Gender Quotas Working Paper Series 2003*, 2. Department of Political Science, Stockholm University.

Friedman, E. J. (2009) 'Re(gion)alizing Women's Human Rights in Latin America', *Politics and Gender*, 5, 3.

Gamble, A. (1994) *The Free Economy and the Strong State* (Basingstoke: Macmillan).

Garnett, M. and Lynch, P. (2003) *The Conservatives in Crisis* (Manchester: Manchester University Press).

Garnett, M. (2003a) 'The Leadership Gamble of William Hague', in M. Garnett and P. Lynch (eds) *The Conservatives in Crisis* (Manchester: Manchester University Press).

Garnett, M. (2003b) 'A Question of Definition? Ideology and the Conservative Party 1997–2001', in M. Garnett and P. Lynch (eds) *The Conservatives in Crisis* (Manchester: Manchester University Press).

Goot, M. and Reid, E. (1975) 'Women and Voting Studies', in Rose, R. (ed.) *Contemporary Political Sociology Series* (London: Sage).

Gotell, L. and Brodie, J. (1991) 'Women and Parties: More Than an Issue of Numbers', in H. G. Thorburn (ed.) *Party Politics in Canada* (Scarborough: Prentice-Hall Canada).

Green, J. (2010) 'Strategic Recovery? The Conservatives under David Cameron', in A. Geddes and J. Tonge (eds) *Britain Votes: The 2010 General Election*, Special Edition Of *Parliamentary Affairs* (Oxford: Oxford University Press).

Greenbaum, T. L. (1998) *The Handbook for Focus Group Research* (Thousand Oaks: Sage).

Gorman, T. (2001) *No, Prime Minister* (London: John Blake).

Hajnal, Z. L. (2009) 'Who loses in American Democracy', *APSR*, 103.

Hansard Society (2000) *Women at the Top 2000: Cracking the Public Sector Glass Ceiling* (London: Hansard Society and Fawcett Society).

Hansard Society (1990) *The Report of The Hansard Society Commission on Women At The Top* (London: Hansard Society).

Harrison, L. (2001) *Political Research* (London: Routledge).

Hawkesworth, M. (2003) 'Congressional Enactments of Race-Gender', *APSR* 97, 4.

Heffernan, R. (2003) 'Political Parties and the Party System', in P. Dunleavy et al (ed.) *Developments in British Politics 7* (Basingstoke: Macmillan).

Heffernan, R. (2010) 'British Political Leadership: The Authoritative Party Leader and the Predominant Prime Minister', paper prepared for the APSA Annual meeting, Washington.

Hindmoor, A. (2005) *New Labour at the Centre* (Oxford: Oxford University Press).

Hine, D. (1982) 'Factionalism in West European Parties', *West European Politics*, 5, 1.

Hinojosa, M. (2009) 'Whatever the Party Asks of Me', *Politics and Gender*, 5, 3.

House of Commons (2009) 'Membership of UK Political Parties. SN/SG/5125.

House of Commons (undated) *Women in the House of Commons*, Fact Sheet.

House of Lords (2001) *Promoting a Private Members Bill in the House of Lords* http://www.publications.parliament.uk/pa/ld/ldpmbill.pdf

Inglehart, R. and Norris, P. (2000) 'The Development Theory of the Gender Gap', *International Political Science Review*, 21, 4.

Jaccard, J. and Turrisi, R. (2003) *Interaction Effects in Multiple Regression* (London: Sage Publications).

Jeffries, A. (1996) 'British Conservatism: Individualism and Gender', *Journal of Political Ideologies*, 1, 1.

Jones, D. (2010) *Cameron on Cameron* (London: Fourth Estate).

Kanter, R. M. (1977a) 'Some Effects of Proportions on Group Life', *American Journal of Sociology*, 82, 5.

Kanter, R. M. (1977b) *Men and Women of the Corporation* (New York: Basic Books).

Kantola, J. and Squires, J. (undated) 'From State Feminism to Market Feminism?', paper given to authors.

Kathlene, L. (1995) 'Position Power Versus Gender Power', in G. Duerst-Lahti, G. and R. M. Kelly (eds) *Gender Power, Leadership and Governance* (Ann Arbor: University of Michigan Press).

Katz, R. and Mair, P. (1995) 'Changing Models of Party Organization and Party Democracy', *Party Politics*, 1, 1.

Kavangh, D. and Cowley, P. (2010) *The British General Election of 2010* (Basingstoke: Palgrave).

Kelly, R. (2008) 'Conservatism Under Cameron', *Politics Review* 17, 3.

Kelly, R. (2003) 'Organizational Reform and the Extra Parliamentary Party', in M. Garnett and P. Lynch (eds) *The Conservatives in Crisis* (Manchester: Manchester University Press).

Kelly, R. (1989) *Conservative Party Conferences* (MUP: Manchester).

Kenney, S. (1996) 'New Research on Gendered Political Institutions', *Political Research Quarterly*, 49, 2.

Kenny, M. (2009) 'Gendering Institutions: The Political Recruitment of Women in Post Devolution Scotland', PhD, University of Edinburgh.

Kenny, M. (2009) 'Taking the Temperature of the UK's Political Elite', *Parliamentary Affairs*, 62, 1.

Keswick, T. (2000) *Second Amongst Equals* (London: Centre for Policy Studies).

Kingdon, J. W. (1984) *Agendas, Alternatives, and Public Policies* (Boston: Little, Brown).

Kittilison, M. C. (2006) *Challenging Parties, Changing Parliaments* (Columbus: Ohio State Univ. Press).

Knight, J. (1995) *About the House* (London: Churchill Press).

Kochan, N. (2000) *Ann Widdecombe, Right From the Beginning* (London: Politicos).

Krook, M. L. (2010a) 'Women's Representation in Parliament', *Political Studies*, 58, 5.

Krook, M. L. (2010b) 'Why are Fewer Women than Men Elected?', *Political Studies Review*, 8, 2.

Krook, M. L. (2009a) *Quotas for Women in Politics: Gender and Candidate Selection Reform Worldwide* (Oxford University Press: USA).

Krook, M. L. (2009b) 'Beyond Supply and Demand', *Political Research Quarterly*, 63, 4.

Krook, M. L. (2006) 'Reforming Representation: The Diffusion of Candidate Gender Quotas Worldwide', *Politics and Gender*, 2, 3.

Krook, M. L. (2005) *Politicizing Representation: Campaigns for Candidate Gender Quotas Worldwide*, Ph.D. Diss., Columbia University.

Krook, M. L. (2003) 'Gender Quotas: A Framework for Analysis', paper presented to the General Conference of the ECPR, Marburg, Germany, September 18–21.

Krook, M. L., Lovenduski, J. and Squires, J. (2006) 'Western Europe, North America, Australia and New Zealand', in D. Dahlerup (ed.) *Women Quotas and Politics* (London: Routledge).

Krook, M. L. and Mackay, F. (2011) *Gender, Politics and Institutions* (Basingstoke: Palgrave).

Krook, M. L. and Squires, J. (2006) 'Gender Quotas in British Politics', *British Politics*, 1, 1.

Krueger, R. A. and Casey, M. A. (2000) *Focus Groups, A Practical Guide for Applied Research* (California: Sage).

Lansley, A. (2003) 'The Conservative Challenge', in M. Garnett and P. Lynch (eds) *The Conservatives in Crisis* (Manchester: Manchester University Press).

Lawless, J. L. and Fox, R. L. (2005) *It Takes a Candidate: Why Women Don't Run for Office* (New York: Cambridge University Press).

Lovenduski, J. (2005a) *Feminizing Politics* (Cambridge: Polity).

Lovenduski, J. (2005b) *State Feminism and the Political Representation of Women* (Cambridge: Cambridge University Press).

Lovenduski, J. (2001) 'Women and Politics: Minority Representation or Critical Mass', in P. Norris (ed.) *Britain Votes 2001* (Oxford: Oxford University Press).

Lovenduski, J. (1998) Gendering Research in Political Science', *Annual Review of Political Science*, 1.

Lovenduski, J. (1997) 'Gender Politics: A Breakthrough for Women?', *Parliamentary Affairs*, 50, 4.

Lovenduski, J. (1996) 'Sex, Gender and British Politics', in J. Lovenduski and P. Norris (eds) *Women in Politics* (Oxford: Oxford University Press).

Lovenduski, J. (1994) 'Will Quotas Make Women More Women-Friendly?', *Renewal*, 2, 1.

Lovenduski, J. (1993) 'Introduction: The Dynamics of Gender and Party', in J. Lovenduski and P. Norris (eds) *Gender and Party Politics* (London: Sage).

Lovenduski, J. (1990) 'Feminism and West European Politics: An Overview', in D. W. Urwin and W. E. Paterson (eds) *Politics in Western Europe Today* (London: Longman).

Lovenduski, J. and Guadagnini, M. (2010) Political Representation', in D. McBride and A. Mazur (2010) *The Politics of State Feminism* (Philadelphia: Temple University Press).

Lovenduski, J. and Norris, P. (2003) 'Westminster Women: The Politics of Presence', *Political Studies*, 51, 1.

Lovenduski, J. and Norris, P. (1996) *Women in Politics* (Oxford: Oxford University Press).

Lovenduski, J. and Norris, P. (1994a) 'The Recruitment of Parliamentary Candidates', in L. Robins, H., Blackmore and R. Pyper (eds) *Britain's Changing Party System* (London: Leicester University Press).

Lovenduski, J. and Norris, P. (1994b) 'Labour and the Unions: After the Brighton Conference', *Government and Opposition*, 29, 2.

Lovenduski, J. and Norris, P. (1993) *Gender and Party Politics* (London: Sage).

Lovenduski, J. and Norris, P. (1991) 'Party Rules and Women's Representation: Reforming the British Labour Party', in I. Crewe et al (eds) *British Elections and Parties Yearbook* (Hemel Hempstead: Harvester Wheatsheaf).

Lovenduski, J. and Norris, P. (1989) 'Selecting Women Candidates: Obstacles to the Feminisation of the House of Commons', *European Journal of Political Research*, 17.

Lovenduski, J., Norris, P. and Burness, C. (1994) 'The Party and Women', in A. Seldon and S. Ball (eds) *Conservative Century, The Conservative Party Since 1900* (Oxford: Oxford University Press).

Lovenduski, J. and Randall, V. (1993) *Contemporary Feminist Politics* (Oxford: Oxford University Press).

Lynch, P. and Garnett, M. (2003b) 'Conclusions', in M. Garnett and P. Lynch (eds) *The Conservatives in Crisis* (Manchester: Manchester University Press).

Lynch, P. and Garnett, M. (2003a) 'Introduction', in M. Garnett and P. Lynch (eds) *The Conservatives in Crisis* (Manchester: Manchester University Press).

Mackay, F. (2008) '"Thick" Conceptions of Substantive Representation: Women, Gender and Political Institutions', *Representation*, 44, 2.

Mackay, F. (2004) 'Gender and Political Representation in the UK', *British Journal of Politics and International Relations*, 6, 1.

McKenzie, R. T. (1955) *Political Parties* (London: Heinemann).

Maguire, G. E. (1998) *Conservative Woman* (Oxford: Macmillan and St Anthony's).

Mair, P. and Van Biezen, I. (2001) 'Party Membership in 20 European Democracies 1980–2000', *Party Politics*, 7, 1.

Manheim, J. B. and Rich, R. C. (1995) *Empirical Political Analysis* (NY: Longman).

Mansbridge, J. (2005) 'Quota Problems: Combating the Dangers of Essentialism', *Politics and Gender* 1, 4.

Mansbridge, J. (2003) 'Rethinking Representation', *American Political Science Review*, 97, 4.

Mansbridge, J. (1999) 'Should Blacks Represent Blacks and Women Represent Women? A Contingent "Yes", *The Journal of Politics*, 61, 3.

Marthaler, S., Childs, S. and Webb, P. (2008) 'Gender Representation and Centre-Right Political Parties', paper presented at 2008 Women and Politics Annual Conference, University of Surrey.

Mateo Diaz, M. (2005) *Representing Women: Female Legislators in West European Parliaments* (Essex: ECPR).

Matland, R. E. (2006) 'Electoral Quotas', in D. Dahlerup (ed.) *Women, Quotas and Politics* (London: Routledge).

Matland, R. E. and Studlar, D. T. (1996) 'The Contagion Effect of Women Candidates in Single-Member District and Proportional Representation Electoral Systems: Canada and Norway', *The Journal of Politics*, 58, 3.

May, T. (2005) 'Speech' presented at the launch of the Hansard Society's *Women at the Top 2005 Report, Changing Numbers, Changing Politics?* (Portcullis House, London).

May, T. (2004) 'Women in the House', *Parliamentary Affairs*, 57, 4.

Mazur, A. G. (2002) *Theorising Feminist Policy* (Oxford: Oxford University Press).

Mazur, A. G. (2003) 'The Impact of Women's Participation and Leadership on Policy Outcome', paper pared for UN, DESA, DAW, ECA and IPU Expert Group Meeting on Equal participation of women and men in decision-making processes, with particular emphasis on political participation and leadership, October 2005.

Morgan, D. L. (1988) *Focus Groups as Qualitative Research* (Newbury Park: Sage).

Mullin, C. (2010) 'A Few Words of Friendly Advice for Aspiring MPs', in the *Times Guide to the House of Commons* (London: HarperCollins).

Nicholson, E. (1996) *Secret Society* (London: Indigo).

Norman, J. and Ganesh, J. (2006) *Compassionate Conservatism* (London: Policy Exchange).

Norris, P. (2004) *Electoral Engineering* (Cambridge: Cambridge University Press).

Norris, P. (2001) 'The Gender Gap: Old Challenges, New Approaches', in S. Carroll (ed.) *Women and American Politics* (Oxford: OUP).

Norris, P. (2000a) 'Gender and Cotemporary British Politics', in C. Hay (ed.) *British Politics Today* (Cambridge: Polity).

Norris, P. (2000b) 'Women's Representation and Electoral Systems', in R. Rose (ed.) *Encyclopaedia of Electoral Systems* (Washington DC: CQ Press).

Norris, P. (1999a) 'New Politicians? Changes in Party Competition at Westminster', in P. Norris and G. Evans (eds) *Critical Elections* (London: Sage).

Norris, P. (1999b) 'Gender: A Gender-Generation Gap?', in P. Norris and G. Evans (eds) *Critical Elections* (London: Sage).

Norris, P. (1998) 'A Gender-Generation Gap' http://www.ksg.harvard.edu/people/pnorris/Gendergap.htm

Norris, P. (1997a) *Passages to Power* (Cambridge: Cambridge University Press).

Norris, P. (1997b) *Women, Media, and Politics* (Oxford: Oxford University Press).

Norris, P. (1997c) 'The Puzzle of Constituency Service', *Journal of Legislative Studies*, 3, 2.

Norris, P. (1996) 'Women Politicians: Transforming Westminster?', in J. Lovenduski and P. Norris (eds) *Women in Politics* (Oxford: Oxford University Press).

Norris, P. (1995) 'May's Law of Curvilinear Disparity Revisited: Leaders, Officers, Members and Voters in British Political Parties', *Party Politics*, January, 1.

Norris, P. (1993) 'Conclusions: Comparing Legislative Recruitment', in J. Lovenduski and P. Norris (eds) *Gender and Party Politics* (London: Sage).

Norris, P. and Lovenduski, J. (1995) *Political Recruitment* (Cambridge: Cambridge University Press).

Norris, P. and Lovenduski, J. (1993a) 'Gender and Party Politics in Britain', in J. Lovenduski and P. Norris (eds) *Gender and Party Politics* (London: Sage).

Norris, P. and Lovenduski, J. (1993b) 'If Only More Candidates Came Forward: Supply-side Explanations of Candidate Selection in Britain', *British Journal of Political Science*, 23, 3.

Norris, P. and Lovenduski, J. (1989) 'Women Candidates for Parliament: Transforming the Agenda?', *British Journal of Political Science*, 19, 1.

Norris, P., Lovenduski, J. and Campbell, R. (2004) *Gender and Political Participation* (London: Electoral Commission).

Norton, P. (1990) 'The Lady's Not for Turning', *Parliamentary Affairs*, 43, 1.

Norton, P. and Aughey, A. (1981) *Conservatives and Conservatism* (London: Temple Smith).

Nunn, H. (2002) *Thatcher, Fantasy and Politics* (London: Lawrence and Wishart).

Pattie, C., Johnston, R. and Stuart, M. (1998) 'Voting Without Party?', in P. Cowley (ed.) *Conscience and Parliament* (London: Frank Cass).

Perrigo, S. (1996) 'Women and Change in the Labour Party 1979–1995', in J. Lovenduski and P. Norris (eds) *Women in Politics* (Oxford: Oxford University Press).

Perrigo, S. (1995) 'Gender Struggles in the British Labour Party from 1979 to 1995', *Party Politics*, 1, 3.

Perrigo, S. (1986) 'Socialist-Feminism and the Labour Party: Some Experiences from Leeds', *Feminist Review*, 23, 1.

Phillips, A. (1995) *The Politics of Presence* (Oxford: Clarendon Press).

Phillips, A. (1993) *Democracy and Difference* (Cambridge: Polity).

Phillips, A. (1991) *Engendering Democracy* (Cambridge: Polity).

Pitkin, H. F. (1969) *Representation* (New York: Atherton Press).

Pitkin, H. F. (1967) *The Concept of Representation* (Berkeley, Los Angeles: University of California Press).

Poguntke, T. and Webb, P. (2005) *The Presidentialization of Politics* (Oxford: Oxford University Press).

Quinn, T. (2008) 'The Conservative Party and the "Centre Ground" of British Politics', *Journal of Elections, Public Opinion and Parties*, 18, 2.

Rehfeld, A. (2009) 'Representation Rethought', *APSR*, 103, 2.

Reingold, B. (2008a) *Legislative Women, Getting Elected, Getting Ahead* (Colorado: Reiner).

Reingold, B. (2008b) 'Women as Officeholders, Linking Descriptive and Substantive Representation', in C. Wolbrecht, K. Beckwith and L. Baldez (eds) *Political Women and American Democracy* (Cambridge: Cambridge University Press).

Reingold, B. (2000) *Representing Women* (Chapel Hill: University of North Carolina Press).

Rogers, R. and Walters, R. (2006) *How Parliament Works* (London: Longman).

Rose, R. (1964) 'Parties, Factions and Tendencies in Britain', *Political Studies*, 12, 1.

Ruiz Jiménez, A. M. (2003) 'Conservative Parties and Feminist Demands Viewed in an International Perspective: Making Sense of the Partido Popular in Spain', Estudio/Working Paper 2002/185.

Ruiz Jimenez, A. M. (2009) 'Women and Decision Making Participation within Rightist Parties in Portugal and Spain', *Analise Social*, 44, 191.

Russell, A. (2005) 'The Party System in 2004', *Parliamentary Affairs*, 58, 2.

Russell, M. (2009) 'House of Lords Reform: Are We Nearly There Yet?', *Political Quarterly*, 80(1).

Russell, M. (2005) *Building New Labour* (Basingstoke: Palgrave).

Saatchi, M. (2005) *If this is Conservatism, I am a Conservative* (London: Centre Policy Studies).

Sambonmatsu, K. (2008) 'Representation by Gender and Parties', in C. Wolbrecht, K. Beckwith and L. Baldez (eds) *Political Women and American Democracy* (Cambridge: Cambridge University Press).

Saward, M. (2006) 'The Representative Claim', *Contemporary Political Theory*, 5, 3.

Sawer, M., Tremblay, M. and Trimble, L. (2006) *Representing Women in Parliament: A Comparative Study* (New York: Routledge).

Schreiber, R. (2008) *Righting Feminism* (Oxford, NY: Oxford University Press).

Schreiber, R. (2009) 'Injecting a Woman's Voice', in A. G. Jonasdottir and K. B. Jones (eds) *The Political Interests of Gender Revisited* (Manchester: Manchester University Press).

Seawright, D. (2010) *The British Conservative Party and One Nation Politics* (London: Continuum).

Shephard, G. (2000) *Shephard's Watch* (London: Politicos).

Shepherd-Robinson, L. and Lovenduski, J. (2002) *Women and Candidate Selection* (London: Fawcett Society).

Snowden, P. (2010) *Back From the Brink* (London: HarperCollins).

Sones, B., Moran, M. and Lovenduski, J. (2005) *Women in Parliament, the New Suffragettes* (London: Politicos).

Speaker's Conference (2010) *Speaker's Conference on Parliamentary Representation* (London: TSO)

Squires, J. (2008) 'The Constitutive Representation of Gender', *Representation* 44, 2.

Squires, J. (2007) *The New Politics of Gender Equality* (Basingstoke: Palgrave).

Stacey, J. (1983) 'The New Conservative Feminism', *Feminist Studies*, 9, 3.

Swers, M. L. (2002) *The Difference Women Make: The Policy Impact of Women in Congress* (Chicago: University of Chicago Press).

Tamerius, K. L. (1995) 'Sex, Gender, and Leadership in the Representation of Women', in G. Duerst-Lahti and R. M. Kelly (eds) *Gender Power Leadership and Governance* (USA: The University of Michigan Press).

Taylor, I. (2003) 'The Conservatives, 1997–2001: A Party in Crisis?', in M. Garnett and P. Lynch (eds) *The Conservatives in Crisis* (Manchester: Manchester University Press).

Thomas, S. (2003) 'The Impact of Women in Political Leadership Positions', in S. J. Carroll (ed.) *Women and American Politics* (Oxford: Oxford University Press).

Thomas, S. (1998) 'Women and Elective Office', in S. Thomas and C. Wilcox (eds) *Women and Elective Office* (Oxford: Oxford University Press).

Thomas, S. (1994) *How Women Legislate* (Oxford: Oxford University Press).

Thomas, S. (1991) 'The Impact of Women on State Legislative Policies', *Journal of Politics*, 53, 4.

Thomas, S. and Welch, S. (1991) 'The Impact of Gender on Activities and Priorities of State Legislators', *Western Political Quarterly*, 44.

Tremblay, M. (1998) 'Do Female MPs Substantively Represent Women?', *Canadian Journal of Political Science*, XXXI, 3.

Trimble, L. and Arscott, J. (2003) *Still Counting: Women in Politics across Canada* (Canada: Broadview).

Vallance, E. (1979) *Women in the House* (London: The Athlone Press).

Vickers, J. (1997) 'Toward a Feminist Understanding of Representation', in J. Arscott and L. Trimble (eds) *In the Presence of Women* (Toronto: Harcourt Brace).

Waller, R. and Criddle, B. (2007) *The Almanac of British Politics* (London: Routledge).

Wangnerud, L. (2009) 'Women in Parliaments: Descriptive and Substantive Representation', *Annual Review of Political Science*, 12.

Waylen, G. (2004) 'Putting Governance into the Gendered Political Economy of Globalization', *International Feminist Journal of Politics*, 6, 4.

Webb, P. (2008) 'The Attitudinal Assimilation of Europe by the Conservative Parliamentary Party', *British Politics*, 3, Nov.

Webb, P. (2000) *The Modern British Party System* (London: Sage).

Webb, P. (1997) 'Attitudinally Clustering within British Parliamentary Elites', *West European Politics*, 20.

Webb, P. and Childs, S. (forthcoming) 'Wets and Dries Resurgent? Intra-party Alignments among Contemporary Conservative Party Members', *Parliamentary Affairs*.

Weldon, S. L. (2002) 'Beyond Bodies: Institutional Sources of Representation for Women in Democratic Policymaking', *The Journal of Politics*, 64, 4.

Whiteley, P. (2009) 'Where Have all the Members Gone', *Parliamentary Affairs*, 6, 2.

Whiteley, P., Seyd, P. and Richardson, J. (1994) *True Blues* (Oxford: Clarendon Press).

Wolbrecht, C., Beckwith, K. and Baldez, L. (2008) *Political Women and American Democracy* (Cambridge: Cambridge University of Press).

Yoder, J. (1991) 'Rethinking Tokenism: Looking Beyond Numbers' *Gender and Society*, 5, 2.

Young, L. (2003) 'Can Feminists Transform Party Politics', in M. Tremblay and L. Trimble (eds) *Women and Electoral Politics in Canada* (Oxford: Oxford University Press).

Young, L. (2000) *Feminists and Party Politics* (Ann Arbor: University of Michigan Press).

Young, L. and Cross, W. (2002) 'The Rise of Plebiscitary Democracy in Canadian Political Parties', *Party Politics*, 8, 6.

Index

CPI Antony Rowe
Eastbourne, UK
August 13, 2019